To Live in Freedom

George Henderson

To Live in Freedom

HUMAN RELATIONS
TODAY
AND TOMORROW

UNIVERSITY OF OKLAHOMA PRESS : NORMAN

By George Henderson

Foundations of American Education (with William
B. Ragan) (New York, 1970)
Teachers Should Care (with Robert F. Bibens) (New
York, 1970)
*America's Other Children: Public Schools Outside
Suburbia* (editor) (Norman, 1971)
*To Live in Freedom: Human Relations Today and
Tomorrow* (Norman, 1972)

Library of Congress Cataloging in Publication Data

Henderson, George 1932–
    To live in freedom.
    Includes bibliographies.
    1. U.S.—Social conditions—Study and teaching. 2. U.S.—Race ques-
tions—Study and teaching.
I. Title.
HN58.H38   309.1'73   72–857
ISBN 0–8061–1017–1

Copyright 1972 by the University of Oklahoma Press,
Publishing Division of the University. Composed and
printed at Norman, Oklahoma, U.S.A., by the University of Oklahoma Press. First edition.

To my mother—

the most humane person I know

Preface

Each year, growing numbers of colleges and universities are offering interdisciplinary studies which focus on aspects of human relations. Few textbooks, however, provide an interdisciplinary view of our society.

In order to use a broad literary brush to paint a portrait of America as it has been, as it is, and as I wish it would become, I have drawn heavily from my own experiences and colored them with materials from the social sciences, the humanities, education, and business administration.

Much of this book discusses black-white problems because they mirror other majority-minority-group problems. Indeed, the human rights which are sought by blacks, the largest minority group in America, are the same basic rights sought by all groups: to be granted equal opportunities in all areas of human interaction.

This book focuses on behavior that is tearing us apart as a nation, and behavior that may bring us together. It was not written to frighten or frustrate readers; rather, it was written to challenge them to build a more humane society. To a great extent this book is based on the dream of Martin Luther King, Jr.—that all people will someday live in freedom.

If this book is of value, it is because of the many excellent suggestions I received from Sarah Burns, Mary Ann Merz, and Virginia Bell. I am pleased to have received permission from Mary Hamra, Jacquelene Peters, Diane Roether, and Patricia Westbrook to include papers by them. Finally, I am grateful to the following authors and publishers who granted me permission to reprint their poems: Langston Hughes,

GEORGE HENDERSON

Norman, Oklahoma
January 15, 1972

Contents

A Self-Examination in Human Relations

Answer the following questions and ask some friends to answer them too. Compare your answers.

Below are some statements regarding American beliefs with which some people agree and others disagree. Record your opinions, that is, whether you strongly agree (A), agree (a), are uncertain (U), disagree (d), or strongly disagree (D).

1. Everyone in America should have an equal opportunity to get ahead.

   A_____ a_____ U_____ d_____ D_____

2. All people should be treated as equals in the eyes of the law.

   A_____ a_____ U_____ d_____ D_____

3. People should help each other in time of need.

   A_____ a_____ U_____ d_____ D_____

4. All children should have equal educational opportunities.

   A_____ a_____ U_____ d_____ D_____

5. People with similar qualifications should have equal right to hold public office.

   A_____ a_____ U_____ d_____ D_____

6. Each person should be judged according to his individual worth.

   A_____ a_____ U_____ d_____ D_____

7. I believe in the principle of brotherhood among men.

    A_____ a_____ U_____ d_____ D_____

8. Businesses offering accommodations should make their services equally available to everyone.

    A_____ a_____ U_____ d_____ D_____

9. Under our democratic system people should be allowed to live where they please if they can afford it.

    A_____ a_____ U_____ d_____ D_____

10. I believe that public recreational facilities should be equally available to all people.

    A_____ a_____ U_____ d_____ D_____

   Below are some statements regarding social issues with which some people agree and others disagree. What are your opinions?

11. Sometimes I feel all alone in the world.

    A_____ a_____ U_____ d_____ D_____

12. Some races of people are born inferior.

    A_____ a_____ U_____ d_____ D_____

13. Anyone who wants to work badly enough can find a job.

    A_____ a_____ U_____ d_____ D_____

14. The city in which I live is a friendly place.

    A_____ a_____ U_____ d_____ D_____

15. There is little chance for promotion on the job unless a man gets a break.

    A_____ a_____ U_____ d_____ D_____

16. There are few dependable ties between people anymore.

    A_____ a_____ U_____ d_____ D_____

17. People are just naturally friendly and helpful.

    A_____ a_____ U_____ d_____ D_____

18. I would be willing to have a family of another race as my next-door neighbor.

    A_____ a_____ U_____ d_____ D_____

19. I would not mind if my children attended schools in which most of the students were of another race.

    A_____ a_____ U_____ d_____ D_____

20. I would welcome a man of another race as my son-in-law.

    A_____ a_____ U_____ d_____ D_____

The following statements can be checked for validity. Answer each question true or false and check your answers as you read this book.

21. Group size does not affect the manner in which group members interact._____

22. Intragroup cooperation is superior to intragroup competition._____

23. Effective managers give their subordinates self-respect._____

24. All group-related problems can be solved in an encounter or training group._____

25. Our human relations problems are as old as our nation._____

26. Every baby is born free of prejudice._____

27. All men are of the same genus and species._____

28. Seldom do we desire to know other people because of altruistic reasons._____

29. Group membership is a primary source of both security and insecurity for the individual._____

30. All conflict is destructive._____

31. Some people do not need confirmation of their positive self-worth in order to have a healthy personality._____

32. Every individual is capable of solving most of his problems and learns to use his own resources._____

33. Whether a child can learn depends on his biological makeup; what he learns depends on his culture._____

34. The civil rights movement began in the twentieth century._____

35. While the Civil War may have settled the issue of physical slavery, it did not significantly alter the generally accepted white-supremacy attitudes in regard to race._____

36. Blacks invented the vacuum pan that revolutionized the sugar-refining industry and also the automatic traffic light._____

37. Large numbers of blacks have engaged in rioting and other aggressive actions directed at white Americans._____

38. Recent studies indicate that over one-third of the United States population is anti-Semitic._____

39. Few attitudes are learned from other people._____

40. Attitudes are frequently formed by logic._____

41. Attitudes are seldom formed by personal experience._____

42. Most communication studies conclude that change in attitude is a combined function of the individual's initial position, his attention to the message and to the communicator, his understanding of the message, and his acceptance of the message._____

43. Some adults are free of prejudice._____

44. Whether veterans or civilians, blacks currently have higher rates of unemployment than their white counterparts._____

45. To date, school-desegregation efforts have been characterized by the closing of predominantly white schools._____

46. Puerto Ricans are last in housing, education, employment, and income when compared with other minorities in New York City._____

47. Until the 1970 United States census, American Indians were not even listed as an identifiable ethnic group._____

48. Most Indian children are benefiting from bilingual language materials._____

49. Vine Deloria, Jr., a member of the Standing Rock Sioux tribe, became the first American Indian to win a Pulitzer Prize._____

50. Most Mexican-Americans are too drowsy and too docile to carry on a sustained fight against poverty and discrimination._____

51. Chinese-Americans are sometimes held up by white Americans as the "model American minority" primarily because they are the best educated of all groups and have achieved a high level of economic and social success without rebelling._____

52. Women lose more days from work each year than men do._____

53. Women drivers have fewer accidents than men do._____

54. Women college graduates earn three-fourths as much as male college graduates._____

55. In the Judeo-Christian culture male homosexuality is viewed more tolerantly than female homosexuality._____

56. The ability of group leaders to achieve and maintain objectivity is the key to the entire problem-solving activity._____

57. The more successful human relations programs focus on a single approach._____

58. Attitudinal and behavior change is more likely to occur when there is free expression within the group without fear of reprisal._____

59. Most people prefer to express their real feelings._____

60. Good human relations can be delegated to subordinates._____

61. Most Americans are very knowledgeable about violence. Public concern and public understanding is growing._____

62. Despite much breast-beating about democracy in work situations,

most employees assume that autocratic control is necessary to get the work done._____

63. Approximately 90 per cent of all scientific achievements have occurred in the twentieth century._____

64. One person in ten is affected by mental illness._____

65. Computers are destroying society, and there is little that man can do to stop the trend._____

66. In democratic social planning the person is not treated as an end. The major focus is on group consensus._____

67. The pure-science model is of great value to social scientists involved in social-action programs._____

68. The most insidious prejudices are the negative attitudes directed toward groups._____

To Live in Freedom

CHAPTER 1

Toward a Science of Human Relations

"Why read about human relations? I don't need to read about human relations; I live them every day." This attitude is common among persons beginning formal study in human relations. While it is true that every day of our lives we experience a series of human relationships, it is also true that formal studies in human relations are necessary. Only by becoming objectively aware of the ramifications of our behavior are we able to improve upon them systematically.

This chapter is designed to serve both as a summary of current studies and as an introduction to future studies of human relations. It is important to note at the outset that this book is only a beginning for those who want to become acquainted with the broad body of literature pertaining to the study of individual and group interactions and the application of appropriate behavior to resolve problems growing out of those interactions.

Small-Group Research

In the past quarter-century many books about human relations have appeared for professional and lay readers. Most of these books have been practical guides to better living or to philosophies of life. Few have presented objective data or validated conclusions. In most instances findings have been sparse and usually unrelated to one another. In addition, the quality of evaluative research has been very poor. Only within the last decade has there been a significant movement toward objectively validating human relations programs and procedures.

The earliest studies of human relations focused on "scientific" methods for allocating authority in business organizations. Human relations in business became a subject of precise analysis in the late nineteenth century, when Max Weber provided an astute description of bureaucratic organizations. At the same time, scholars of what was known as the "scientific management movement" prescribed a rigid set of administration principles that they believed were applicable to all organizations.

Using time and motion studies, the proponents of scientific management developed practices for improving the operation of many line jobs that required technical skills, including bricklaying. They stressed the improvement of organizational efficiency through increasing technical competencies of administrators and workers. The most common means to this goal was establishing clear patterns of authority. Gradually, as it became evident that some skills could not be routinized through time and motion study, the "universal" principles of organization gave way to more flexible, human-interaction guidelines.

In retrospect, the academic study of human relations grew out of management principles and practices during the late nineteenth and early twentieth century. Two men, Henri Fayol and Frederick Taylor, stood out above all others. Fayol, the father of *management*, was the first person to state and widely publicize principles of management; while Taylor, the father of *scientific management*, was the first person to use a precise analytical approach to the problems of productivity.

However, it was not until 1927 that a human relations emphasis emerged. Elton Mayo's Hawthorne researches (1927–32) led to his being labeled the father of the *human relations approach to management*. The final cornerstone of the human relations foundation was laid by Kurt Lewin in the late 1930's. Lewin, who developed the concept of field theory, was the father of modern *group dynamics*.

In the late 1920's the dominant role of legal authority and technical knowledge became secondary to other human factors. The now-classic study of Western Electric's Hawthorne plant made by Harvard University professors proved that production is more closely related to interpersonal norms than to management's concept of the balance between fatigue and monetary reward. Several years later George Homans made the insightful observation that when unrelated individuals are drawn together in a common activity group norms emerge out of individuals' likes and dislikes of each other. Furthermore, he concluded, the codes of any group are difficult for outsiders to comprehend.

From such studies it became clear that there are three ways to approach the study of human relations. One approach is through behavior attributed to uncontrolled, short-term changes in the social environment or in the individual. Since it is not intentionally produced, such behavior is of little interest to social practitioners. The second approach to human behavior takes into account uncontrolled long-term changes in the social environment or in the individual. Again, such behavior does not lie within the purview of social practitioners. The third approach, the study of social change that can be consciously induced, is the area of interest to human relations practitioners and researchers. In most instances the practitioner or leader in human relations techniques is not a researcher, though he uses the findings of research to help people solve their intergroup and intragroup problems.

Most of the definitive studies in human relations have resulted from small-group research. The *small group* is usually defined as one made up of two to thirty persons. In 1904, Lewis Terman conducted the first recorded studies of leadership in small groups.[1] It was not until the late 1940's, however, that Kurt Lewin and others began small-group research on a broad scale. Since then many studies have been conducted, focusing on group size, group composition, group-member reward systems, natural detrimental processes in group development, the effects of forced interaction, the effect of group discussion, the influence of objective feedback, and the processes of behavior change.[2]

Group Size

Several studies indicate that group size affects both quantitatively and qualitatively the manner in which group members interact. The smaller the group, the more opportunity each individual has to participate and, therefore, the less likely the members are to be frustrated by the interaction. In addition, as the group grows larger, problems of maintaining effective leadership and interaction increase. Smaller groups tend to be more efficient and productive than larger ones. Furthermore, the larger a group becomes, the more difficulty it will have in reaching a quick decision (of course, quick decisions are not necessarily the best decisions).

Composition

There appears to be significant correlation between the ability and adjustment of group members and their capacity to function together

[1] Lewis M. Terman, "A Preliminary Study of the Psychology and Pedagogy of Leadership," *Pedagogical Seminary*, Vol. 11 (December, 1904), 413–51.

[2] See John Mann, *Changing Human Behavior* (New York, Charles Scribner's Sons), 1965.

effectively. Individuals tend to follow or resist authority, to be intimate or to resist intimacy in group situations. Different personality types—laissez-faire, authoritarian, democratic—function differently in groups. Democratic leaders tend to have more influence and encourage more interaction than either the laissez-faire or the authoritarian leaders. There are, however, some settings in which group members expect and accept authoritarian leadership.

Reward Systems

Members of cooperative groups tend to be less resistant to change, to be more independent and friendly, to be more productive, and to have more influence on each other than those in competitive groups. Military, business, and industrial organizations have come to realize that intragroup cooperation is superior to and more productive than intragroup competition.

Natural Detrimental Processes in Group Development

Participation among group members tends to be unequal, with the result that a few individuals do most of the talking. There is also a tendency toward unequal distribution of group rewards. Jacob Moreno called this condition a "sociodynamic law."[3] Moreno's law states the obvious fact that in most groups social status differs from member to member. A third group process that inhibits individual behavior is the natural tendency for groups to establish norms and standards that express the will of the majority.

Forced Interaction

The amount of freedom with which individuals may participate in group decisions influences their emotional satisfaction. In short, their satisfaction is related to their opportunities to participate. Several studies have concluded that negative attitudes can be changed by forcing individuals to participate in role playing, a procedure requiring each individual to create spontaneously a role assigned to him. The degree of attitude and behavior change is directly proportional to the commitment to the group and to the degree of participation in the role-playing activity.

[3] Jacob L. Moreno, "Contributions of Sociometry to Research Methodology in Sociology," *American Sociological Review*, Vol. 12 (June, 1947), 287–92.

Group Discussion

Most studies conclude that group discussion is more effective in behavior change than the lecture method. There is little objective evidence, however, to support the popular belief that group discussion alone produces personality changes among the members. Group discussion is effective in bringing about behavior change only when group norms are changed to conform to a consensus that grows out of the discussion. Haphazard discussion, then, is not likely to change attitudes or behavior.

Objective Feedback

Feedback consists of the overt responses of a listener that may cause a speaker to shape or modify his subsequent communication. Objective feedback produces considerably more improvement in problem solving than do subjective evaluations. Specifically, objective feedback increases the accuracy of the information transmitted, as well as the sender's confidence that his message will be correctly decoded. Because many human relations problems are caused by faulty communication, techniques for improving communication are of special interest to human relations practitioners.

Processes of Behavior Change

Since 1951, when Dorwin Cartwright's study of behavior change appeared, little has been done to formulate comprehensive principles of behavior change in small groups. The following principles established by Cartwright still appear valid:

1. In order for the group to act as the medium of change, its members must have a strong sense of belonging.

2. When a process to bring about change is introduced, its success will to a great extent be in proportion to the relation it has to the members' reasons for joining the group.

3. Within the group itself, the greater the prestige of the individual, the more he can influence others.

4. If the proposed change will cause group members to deviate from group norms, they will resist the change.

5. Effective change in behavior can most easily be induced by creating a shared perception of the need for the new behavior, so that its desirability becomes a group norm.

6. To maximize the probability of successful and lasting change, it is

important that the planning and implementation of the change is a group activity.[4]

Many of the observations relevant to small groups have been expanded to include large-group interactions, especially business organizations.

Human Relations in Management

Most social analysts now agree with Abraham Maslow that values related to work are related not only to physiological needs (thirst, hunger, avoidance of injury, and so on) but also to psychological needs (affection, security, response, and so on). The purpose of social organizations is to allow people to accomplish in concert those goals which unrelated individuals cannot achieve.

Business organizations are excellent illustrations of systems created to satisfy physiological and higher-level individual psychological needs. Most managers and employees prefer maximum job security and a minimum of fatigue from their jobs. In any business there are prominent areas in which managers and employees tend to focus their values. William Guth and Renato Taguiri identified four areas:

1. *Striving for achievement.* This is valuing seeing the job done well.
2. *Striving for membership and affiliation.* This is valuing association with other people who are supportive of our activities.
3. *Striving for knowledge.* This is valuing knowledge achieved through scientific, critical, and rational process of analysis.
4. *Striving for power and status.* This is valuing authority over other people, seeking possession and control of large amounts of financial and physical resources.[5]

Effective supervisors no longer manage by tradition but, instead, by human relations expertise. Even when they administer rules, they do so with human relations finesse. As students of human behavior they seek involvement through *personal commitment, competence*, and *energy*.

Commitment to organizational goals and methods is the foundation of any organizational structure. Many supervisors have belatedly learned

4 Dorwin Cartwright, "Achieving Changes in People: Some Applications of Group Dynamics Theory," *Human Relations*, Vol. 4 (1951), 381–93.

5 William D. Guth and Renato Taguiri, "Personal Values and Corporate Strategy," *Harvard Business Review*, Vol. 43 (September–October, 1965), 125–26.

that commitment must be earned from employees who, as a group, find it easier to be noncommitted. On the other hand, commitment is not worth much without competence, which is needed in order to make a commitment operational. A loyal employee lacking necessary skills is akin to an athlete who is a good cheerleader but an ineffective player. It is necessary for managers to identify the skills of each of their subordinates and help those who are deficient to improve. Finally, energy is needed to stay with a job over a long pull. It is relatively easy to spark the enthusiasm of workers on new, interesting jobs, but they must also be encouraged to maintain a high-energy level when working on routine, long-term projects.

Robert Tannenbaum and Sheldon Davis observed that the traditional views of organizations as rigid bureaucratic structures are out of phase with contemporary realities. Managerial values, they concluded, are becoming increasingly more humanistic. They defined this transition in terms of the following shifts in organizational values:

1. Away from a view that man is essentially bad toward a view of him as basically good.

2. Away from avoidance or negative evaluation of individuals toward confirming them as human beings.

3. Away from a view of individuals as fixed, toward seeing them in process.

4. Away from resisting and fearing individual differences toward accepting and utilizing them.

5. Away from utilizing an individual primarily with references to his job description toward viewing him as a whole person.

6. Away from walling-off the expression of feelings toward making possible both appropriate expression and effective use.

7. Away from marksmanship and game playing toward authentic behavior.

8. Away from use of status for maintaining power and personal prestige toward use of status for organizationally relevant purposes.

9. Away from distrusting people toward trusting them.

10. Away from avoiding facing others with relevant data toward making appropriate confrontation.

11. Away from avoidance of risk-taking toward willingness to risk.

12. Away from a view of process work being unproductive effort toward seeing it as essential to effective task accomplishment.

13. Away from a primary emphasis on competition toward a much greater emphasis on collaboration.[6]

[6] Robert Tannenbaum and Sheldon A. Davis, "Values, Man and Organizations," *Industrial Management Review*, Vol. 10 (Winter, 1969), 67–83.

Douglas McGregor emphasized the changing concept of management's task in terms of "Theory Y," which is replacing "Theory X."[7] According to McGregor, "Theory X," the outdated conventional conception of management's roles is based on the following assumptions:

1. Management is responsible for organizing the elements of the productive enterprise—money, materials, equipment, people—in the interest of economic ends.

2. With respect to people, this process involves directing their efforts, motivating them, controlling their actions, and modifying their behavior to fit the needs of the organization.

3. Without the active intervention by management, people would be passive—even resistant—to organizational needs. They must, therefore, be persuaded, rewarded, punished, controlled—their activities must be directed. This is management's task: Getting things done through other people.

"Theory X" does not work, McGregor believed, because management cannot give a man self-respect, respect of his fellow workers, or self-actualization. Management can, however, create conditions that encourage and enable a man to achieve these ends. These results come about, McGregor concluded, when management accepts and acts upon the following assumptions in "Theory Y":

1. Management is responsible for organizing the elements of productive enterprise—money, materials, equipment, people—in the interest of economic ends.

2. People are not by nature passive or resistant to organizational needs. They have become so as a result of experience in organizations.

3. The motivation, the potential for development, the capacity for assuming responsibility, the readiness shown in direct behavior to achieve organizational goals are all present in people. Management does not put them there. It is a responsibility of management to make it possible for people to recognize and develop these characteristics for themselves.

4. The essential task of management is to arrange organizational conditions and methods of operation so that people can achieve their own goals by directing *their own* efforts toward organizational objectives.

There is a growing trend in business to analyze the effects of "Theory X" and "Theory Y" in terms of a *systems concept*. A *system* is a collection of interrelated parts working to achieve a common goal. A *social system* is an organized and complex set of subprocesses which form a unitary

---

[7] Douglas M. McGregor, "The Human Side of Enterprise," *Management Review*, Vol. 46 (November, 1957), 22–28, 88–92.

whole. Basically, managers must learn to function in two types of systems, closed and open. The closed system is isolated from its surrounding environment and contained within itself, while the open system, which is by far the most prevalent, interacts with and is influenced by the surrounding environment. Along with the changes in management concepts have come innovations in management-training programs.

Whether in large groups or in small ones, individuals responsible for training programs are becoming more professional and experimental in their approaches to training. Much of this change can be attributed to the emergence of training groups and therapy groups.

Human Relations Training

Over the years human relations focus has moved from lectures to conferences, from conferences to case studies, from case studies to role playing, and from role playing to sensitivity training and confrontation games. Each activity represents an effort to gain greater insight into the whole person. Recently several human relations approaches have emerged: training groups (T-groups), group dynamics, confrontation groups, encounter groups, awareness or experience groups, growth-experience laboratories, and sensitivity groups. All these programs have been designed to help the individual become sensitive to himself and others, using the group as the primary means of change. The various programs fall in two categories: training groups and encounter groups (see "Glossary of Human Relations Terms" at the end of this book).

Training Groups

T-groups began in 1946, in New Britain, Connecticut.[8] In that year the Connecticut Inter-Racial Commission, the Connecticut Department of Education, and the Research Center for Group Dynamics sponsored a workshop to solve the state's interracial problems. The leaders of the workshop, Leland Bradford, Kenneth Benne, and Ronald Lippitt, drawing on the writings of Kurt Lewin, adopted group discussion, supplemented by role playing, as the major learning-teaching method. The major goal of the workshop was to discover all (or most) of the participants' problems, as well as to design and implement problem-solving techniques.

In 1947 the National Training Laboratories (NTL) were established at Bethel, Maine. This was the beginning of the group dynamics movement. Group dynamics grew out of small-group research. Though designed to integrate training and research functions, the group dynamics movement has actually separated them. From its beginning the T-group program was committed to gaining an objective understanding of the manner in which small groups function and utilizing this understanding to facilitate individual and group change:

> The T-group consists of normal persons who meet for a number of sessions under the guidance and leadership of a professionally trained scientist who, during the meetings, will educate them in the processes that characterize small-group functioning. The T-group is unusual from several points of view. First, it has no assigned task. If the members had one, they would be too busy fulfilling it to observe their own actions and those of others. Second, the members are encouraged to analyze their reactions to themselves and to each other. Third, the trainer refuses to provide positive group leadership by telling the members what to do. Rather, he tends to interpret to them the reason that things are happening as they are. It is generally assumed by most trainers that enhanced understanding of small-group processes will not only increase the diagnostic skills of the group members, but may

8 Leland P. Bradford, Jack R. Gibb, and Kenneth D. Benne (eds.), *T-Group Theory and Laboratory Method* (New York, John Wiley & Sons, Inc., 1964).

also lead to new forms of behaviors as members become aware of how others are reacting to them.[9]

With the entry of clinical psychologists in 1950, the T-group became a combined process of group dynamics and individual therapy. Today in the category of T-groups are such innovations as sensitivity groups, human relations laboratories, human dynamics groups, and confrontation groups. The purpose of the T-group is to allow members to learn interpersonal and intrapersonal skills so that they can function more effectively "back home." With the exception of NTL, which has stringent requirements for its trainers, or group leaders, there are no requirements for group leaders. Some of the earlier rules are still in force: the training group does not have an agenda, and the leader remains nondirective in his approach. However, all T-groups are based on trust developing between group members. All such groups employ feedback so that participants can gain insight into their own behavior and that of others:

> In the successful laboratory training the optimum tension level of the group is constantly raised so that members can more authentically confront each other about themselves and the group.
> Proper exercise of . . . feedback . . . constitutes a way of life, a culture, if you will, by which people can constructively confront each other and continue to grow as individuals and professionals. . . . Where enough people begin to develop the skills and practice the courage for more authentic self and other confrontations, a new culture is being seeded.
> Personal feedback helps a member to consider changing his behavior . . . but does not mean that if someone is given accurate feedback, which he accepts, that he has to change in the direction implied by the observation or impression. What he wants to do with that information remains entirely within his prerogative.[10]

Personal feedback leads to individual growth when it is (1) descriptive rather than evaluative, (2) specific rather than general, (3) mutual rather than one-way, (4) functional or practical rather than dysfunctional, (5) solicited rather than imposed, (6) well timed rather than random, and (7) checked rather than assumed to be understood.

[9] Mann, *Changing Human Behavior*, 95.
[10] Howard W. Polsky, "Notes on Personal Feedback in Sensitivity Training," *Sociological Inquiry*, Vol. 41 (1971), 180.

Encounter Groups

Encounter, or therapy, groups are also an outgrowth of NTL. Their process has been described by Carl Rogers as "therapy for normals."[11] These groups have many other titles—awareness-of-experience groups, growth-experience laboratories, and human-potential laboratories. The encounter group gained national prominence in 1962 at the Esalen Institute in Big Sur, California. Michael Murphy and Richard Price, founders of the Esalen Institute, based the new technique on Western humanistic psychology and Eastern concepts of body awareness.

Combining verbal, nonverbal, and physical experiences, along with gestalt psychology, the encounter group differs from the T-group in several important respects. The purpose of the encounter group is to relieve the "distress" (overt or covert) of individual group members by helping them to modify attitudes and behavior which are believed to contribute to their distress. Though the encounter group sets no basic requirements for leadership, psychologists, psychiatric social workers, and psychiatrists usually conduct the sessions. Unlike the T-group leader, the leader of an encounter group assumes a role of directional leadership to help group members define their areas of stress. Trust tends to form more slowly in the encounter group than in the training group. Finally, in the encounter group the point of focus is on the individual, whereas in the training group the focus is on the group as a whole.

Leaders of both kinds of groups caution the public against programs run by inadequately trained or irresponsible leaders. It is also important to note that not all group-related problems can be solved in an encounter or training group:

> Sensitivity training appears to have been so effectively oversold to an unaware public, clamoring for psychiatric and psychological insights, that it is not uncommon for teachers, business representatives, high government officials, and others to be required, as a function of their jobs, to participate in these sessions. As a consequence, these participants involuntarily and unknowingly may be subjected to personal onslaught in a pseudo-psychotherapeutic situation characterized by inappropriate transferences and unrelenting group social pressures to "reveal themselves," while unprotected by the ethical safeguards which are inherent in a professional therapeutic encounter. . . . It is a disservice to the unaware consumer who

11 Carl Rogers, "The Group Comes of Age," *Psychology Today*, Vol. 3 (December, 1969), 27.

enrolls hoping to deal with cognitive and affective factors relating to problem-solving of real-life situations but finds himself limited to a morass of emotional content via the T-group methodology.[12]

The following suggestions by Thomas Wiggins on sensitivity training merits the attention of those involved in both training and encounter groups:[13]

1. The term sensitivity training should be eliminated and replaced by the expanded concept of human relations training.

2. Human relations training should be used only when clearly defined goals and behaviorally defined objectives are established.

3. Research should be conducted to provide empirical evidence as guideposts to direct application of human relations training.

4. Standards of professional performance on the part of trainers should be developed and enforced to ensure quality control.

5. Evaluation models to assess the results of training programs should be developed.

Accuracy in predicting how a person or a group will think and behave is not merely a good measure of the effectiveness of a human relations program but is, in fact, *the* measure. Therefore, practitioners must constantly refine their program designs. A scientifically-sound program evaluation will employ valid criteria for measuring success in achieving the goals of training and set up an experimental design which clearly isolates the various factors affecting the results of the training. Few human relations program designs use evaluative measures on experimental and control groups *before* and *after* training sessions. Most programs use evaluative measures only after training has ended and without a control group.

The Human Relations Practitioner	Broadly speaking, human relations encompass all the many ways in which people interact with each other to form social units. This fact alone does not distinguish the study of human relations from psychology, sociology, social psychology, or the other social sciences, but there are differences in the disciplines.

12 Joseph T. English, "Sensitivity Training: Promise and Performance," *American Journal of Psychiatry*, Vol. 126 (1969), 143.

13 Thomas W. Wiggins, "Sensitivity Training: Salvation or Conspiracy?" *Educational Leadership*, Vol. 28 (December, 1970), 58–61.

Unlike social scientists, who are interested primarily in describing *what is*, students of human relations are also concerned with determining *what may be done* to foster positive group interactions.

George Herbert Mead has stated: "There is no reason why social institutions should be oppressive or rigidly conservative, or why they should not rather be, as many are, flexible and progressive, fostering individuality rather than discouraging it."[14] Accepting Mead's premise, human relations specialists attempt to understand both the *objective* and the *subjective* aspects of interpersonal behaviors and, if necessary, recommend changes.

Since very little human behavior reflects conscious motivation, the study of human relations necessarily involves delving into the subconscious or unconscious motivations of people. For example, many parents say to their children: "I am older and have more experience than you. Therefore, I will tell you what to do, and check up on you, encourage you, discipline you, and otherwise control you. By so doing, I will prevent you from making all the mistakes that I have made. Look at what I do for you because I love you." Objectively, parents are older than their children. They have had more experience than their children. And, of course, many parents are able to counsel their children to avoid making disastrous mistakes. Subjectively, however, some parents may be less concerned with what is good for their children and more concerned with reliving their lives through their children. Other parents may not even like their children and as a result may behave in a rigid, authoritarian manner to punish their children for having been born and requiring care and feeding.

We do not get to know the whole of another individual simply by hearing his words and observing his deeds. Through observation we merely get to know *what* an individual does. We must also understand *why* he behaves as he does. To paint a realistic portrait of group interaction, we must know all that we can about each individual, including his subjective values. A chief concern in human relations, then, is to understand the visible and hidden selves of people.

We tend to judge as unacceptable behavior that deviates or appears to deviate from our own adopted norms. The conflicts growing out of such human relationships take many forms: adolescent rebellion, generation gap, racism, and sex rivalry. Examples of such conflicts are seen when parents ridicule adolescents, conservative adults reject liberal youth, blacks

14 George Herbert Mead, "Mind, Self, and Society," in Alfred R. Linesmith and Anselm L. Strauss (eds.), *Readings in Social Psychology* (New York, Holt, Rinehart & Winston, Inc., 1969), 10.

challenge whites, and men discriminate against women. To see conflict is one thing; to resolve it is another. It is important to remember that the final resolution of conflict rests with the individuals caught up in the interaction.

No matter which technique he uses, the human relations practitioner tries to induce constructive behavior change in individuals or groups. There are many models of behavior change. In 1938, Saul Rosenzweig observed that behavior-change techniques can be divided into two broad categories: (1) processes which through a slow, gradual process increase frustration tolerance in individuals and (2) processes which provide an immediate temporary relief of specific problems.[15] Twenty years later Ronald Lippitt, Jeanne Watson, and Bruce Westley created a conceptual scheme that is applicable to different practitioners (*change agents*) and different forms of behavior change.[16] They concluded that all change agents work through certain "channels" and utilize certain "procedures." That is, when trying to alter the internal structure of a group, the practitioner will attempt to reorganize the distribution of power by finding new sources of power or by making the existing source of power more representative of the structure as a whole.

A second task of the practitioner, according to Lippitt and his associates, is to increase the efficiency with which group energy is used. This goal is achieved by abandoning inefficient techniques and substituting new patterns of task distribution that increase the efficiency of group-member performance. Increased efficiency is more likely assured when the channels of communication are kept open and free of distortion.

Finally, the human relations practitioner acts as an educator teaching problem-solving skills to trainees. By doing so, he hopes to provide the trainees with necessary skills so that they can solve their own problems without becoming dependent on him. He must also be able to distinguish between *cognitive* (intellectual), *affective* (emotional), and *behavioral* (action) components of group interactions. Admittedly, this is easier said than done. But it is not impossible:

> A possible interpretation is that a change agent is likely to be effective to the extent that the following conditions hold: (1) he is personally secure and nondefensive in the change situation; (2)

[15] Saul Rosenzweig, "A Dynamic Interaction of Psychotherapy Oriented Towards Research," *Psychiatry*, Vol. 1 (November, 1938), 521–26.

[16] Ronald Lippitt, Jeanne Watson, and Bruce Westley, *The Dynamics of Planned Change: A Comparative Study of Principles and Techniques* (New York, Harcourt, Brace & World, Inc., 1958).

he is in touch with the concerns and feelings of his clients; (3) he is congruent, in the sense that what he says is consistent with what he is actually thinking and feeling; and (4) he possesses a "cognitive map"—a theory, a set of concepts, a set of effective heuristics, as it were—which makes reasonable sense of the change situation and suggests strategies for behavior which are appropriate to his own personality. . . . This also implies that the change agent who has been indoctrinated in a theory of change which is incompatible with his own personal style can never be maximally effective because he is unable to feel comfortable and secure in what he is doing.[17]

Many of the human relations professionals employed in private, state, and federal agencies are members of the National Association of Human Rights Workers (NAHRW). The headquarters of NAHRW is New Haven, Connecticut, and its publication, the *Journal of Intergroup Relations*, offers practical guides to individuals seeking to become more effective change agents.

In academe many individuals concerned with humanistic education are members of the Association for Humanistic Psychology (AHP), in San Francisco. AHP's commitment to the valuing of the dignity and worth of man and interest in the development of the potential inherent in every person is the theme of many articles in AHP's publication, the *Journal of Humanistic Psychology*.

The future of human relations in our own country, as well as the future of relations among nations, depends on human relations practitioners and social scientists who will join forces to assist in creating humane approaches to problem solving. We are still waiting for the Einstein or Newton of human relations.

[17] Lee Bolen, "Some Effects of Trainers on Their T-Groups," *Journal of Applied Behavioral Science*, Vol. 7 (1971), 324.

Suggested Reading

Argyris, Chris. *Intervention Theory and Method: A Behavioral Science View*. Reading, Mass., Addison-Wesley Publishing Co., Inc., 1970.

Bales, Robert F. *Interaction Process Analysis: A Method for the Study of Small Groups*. Reading, Mass., Addison-Wesley Publishing Co., Inc., 1969.

Barnard, Chester I. *The Functions of the Executive*. Cambridge, Mass., Harvard University Press, 1938.

Beckhard, Richard. *Organization Development: Strategies and Models*. Reading, Mass., Addison-Wesley Publishing Co., Inc., 1969.

Benne, Kenneth D., and Robert Chin. *The Planning of Change*. 2d ed. New York, Holt, Rinehart & Winston, Inc., 1969.

Bennis, Warren G. *Organization Development: Its Nature, Origins, and Prospects*. Reading, Mass., Addison-Wesley Publishing Co., Inc., 1969.

————, ed. *Interpersonal Dynamics: Essays and Readings on Human Interaction*. Homewood, Ill., Dorsey Press, 1968.

Berne, Eric. *Games People Play*. New York, Grove Press, Inc., 1958.

Blake, Robert R., and Jane S. Mouton. *Corporation Excellence Through Grid Organization Development: A Systems Approach*. Reading, Mass., Addison-Wesley Publishing Co., Inc., 1969.

Bonner, Hubert. *Group Dynamics: Principles and Applications*. New York, The Ronald Press Company, 1959.

Bradford, Leland P., et al., eds. *T-Group Theory and Laboratory Method: Innovation in Re-Education*. New York, John Wiley & Sons, Inc., 1964.

Burton, Arthur, ed. *Encounter: Theory and Practice of Encounter Groups*. San Francisco, Jossey-Bass, Inc., 1969.

Cartwright, Dorwin, and Alvin Zander, eds. *Group Dynamics: Research and Theory*. Evanston, Row, Peterson, 1960.

Chapman, A. H. *Put-offs and Come-ons*. New York, G. P. Putnam's Sons, 1968.

Cooley, Charles H. *Social Organization*. New York, Scribner, 1927.

Culbert, Samuel A. *The Interpersonal Process of Self-Disclosure: It Takes Two to See One*. Washington, D.C., National Education Association, 1968.

Davis, Keith, ed. *Human Relations and Organizational Behavior: Readings and Comments*. New York, McGraw-Hill Book Company, 1969.

————, and W. G. Scott, eds. *Readings in Human Relations: A Focus in Executive Training*. New York, McGraw-Hill Book Company, 1969.

Fast, Julius. *Body Language*. New York, M. Evans & Co., Inc., 1970.

Festinger, Leon A. *A Theory of Cognitive Dissonance*. California, Stanford University Press, 1957.

Suggested Reading (continued)

Golembiewski, Robert T., and A. Blumberg. *Sensitivity Training and the Laboratory Approach: Readings About Concepts and Applications.* Itasca, Ill., F. E. Peacock Publishers, Inc., 1970.

Guest, Robert H. *Organization Change: The Effect of Successful Leadership.* Homewood, Ill., Dorsey Press, 1962.

Gunther, Bernard. *Sense Relaxation: Blow Your Mind.* New York, Collier Books, 1968.

Hall, Edward T. *The Silent Language.* Greenwich, Conn., Fawcett Publications, Inc., 1959.

Hare, Alfred P., et al. *Small Groups: Studies in Social Interaction.* New York, Alfred A. Knopf, Inc., 1955.

Harris, Thomas A. *I'm OK: You're OK: A Practical Guide to Transactional Analysis.* New York, Harper & Row, 1967.

Homans, George C. *The Human Group.* New York, Harcourt, Brace & World, Inc., 1950.

Hovland, Carl L., et al. *Experiments on Mass Communications.* New Jersey, Princeton University Press, 1949.

Howard, Jane. *Please Touch: A Guided Tour of the Human Potential Movement.* New York, McGraw-Hill Book Company, 1970.

Johnson, James A. *Group Therapy: A Practical Approach.* New York, McGraw-Hill Book Company, 1963.

Katz, Daniel, and Robert Kahn. *The Social Psychology of Organizations.* New York, John Wiley & Sons, Inc., 1966.

Lawrence, Paul A., and Joy W. Lorsch. *Developing Organizations: Diagnosis and Action.* Reading, Mass., Addison-Wesley Publishing Co., Inc., 1969.

Levy, Ronald. *Human Relations: A Conceptual Approach.* Scranton, International Textbook Company, 1969.

Lewin, Kurt. *Field Theory in Social Science.* New York, Harper & Row, 1951.

———. *Principles of Topological Psychology.* New York, McGraw-Hill Book Company, 1936.

Lifton, Walter M. *Working with Groups: Group Process and Individual Growth.* New York, John Wiley & Sons, Inc., 1962.

Likert, Rensis. *The Human Organization.* New York, McGraw-Hill Book Company, 1961.

———. *New Patterns of Management.* New York, McGraw-Hill Book Company, 1961.

Lippitt, Ronald, et al. *The Dynamics of Planned Change: A Comparative Study of Principles and Techniques.* New York, Harcourt, Brace & World, Inc., 1958.

Luft, Joseph. *Group Processes: An Introduction to Group Dynamics*. Palo Alto, National Press Books, 1970.

McGregor, Douglas. *The Human Side of Enterprise*. New York, McGraw-Hill Book Company, 1960.

————. *Leadership and Motivation*. Cambridge, Mass., Massachusetts Institute of Technology Press, 1969.

Mann, John. *Changing Human Behavior*. New York, Charles Scribner's Sons, 1965.

————. *Encounter: A Weekend with Intimate Strangers*. New York, Grossman Publishers, Inc., 1970.

March, James G., ed. *Handbook of Organizations*. Chicago, Rand McNally & Co., 1965.

Roby, Thornton B. *Small Group Performance*. Chicago, Rand McNally & Co., 1968.

Roethlisberger, Fritz, and William J. Dickson. *Management and the Worker*. Cambridge, Mass., Harvard University Press, 1939.

Rogers, Carl. *Carl Rogers on Encounter Groups*. New York, Harper & Row, 1970.

Schein, Edgar H. *Process Consultation: Its Role in Organization Development*. Reading, Mass., Addison-Wesley Publishing Co., Inc., 1969.

————, and Warren G. Bennis. *Personal and Organization Change Through Group Methods*. New York, John Wiley and Sons, Inc., 1965.

Schutz, William C. *Joy: Expanding Human Awareness*. New York, Grove Press, Inc., 1967.

Shepard, Martin, and Marjorie Lee. *Games Analysts Play*. New York, G. P. Putnam's Sons, 1970.

————, and ————. *Marathon 16*. New York, G. P. Putnam's Sons, 1970.

Walton, Richard E. *Interpersonal Peacemaking: Confrontations and Third Party Consultation*. Reading, Mass., Addison-Wesley Publishing Co., Inc., 1970.

Warren, Roland C. *Truth, Love, and Social Change*. Chicago, Rand McNally & Co., 1971.

Weber, Max. *The Theory of Social and Economic Organization*. Trans. by A. M. Henderson and T. Parsons. New York, Oxford University Press, 1947.

Whyte, William F. *The Organization Man*. New York, Simon and Schuster, 1956.

CHAPTER 2

One Nation

In 1968 the National Advisory Commission on Civil Disorders reported:

> Our nation is moving toward two societies, one black, one white—separate and unequal. . . . Discrimination and segregation have long permeated much of American life; they now threaten the future of every American. The deepening racial division is not inevitable. The movement apart can be reversed. . . . To pursue our present course will involve the continuing polarization of the American community and, ultimately, the destruction of basic democratic values. The alternative is not blind repression or capitulation to lawlessness. It is the realization of common opportunity for all within a single society. This alternative will require a commitment to national action—compassionate, massive, and sustained, backed by the resources of the most powerful and the richest nation on this earth. From every American it will require new attitudes, new understanding, and, above all, new will.[1]

America continues to be a troubled nation. Public rallies, mass marches, picket lines, and impassioned speeches are the milder forms of protest. The more violent forms include riots and assassinations. Many citizens are beginning to ask whether we are not in fact a violent nation. Other citizens are less concerned with labels and are more concerned with trying to make this nation live up to the democratic

[1] *National Advisory Commission on Civil Disorders* (New York, Bantam Books, 1968), 1–2.

principles that form its philosophical bases. In many ways we have advanced little since our Republic was founded.

In
The
Beginning

On June 21, 1608, the Reverend Robert Hunt held the first Protestant service in America. Those historic rites were performed in Jamestown, Virginia, under a part of a ship's sail hung between trees, with a pulpit made of a bar of wood and worshipers seated on unhewed logs. In 1634, led by Lord Baltimore, the first Catholics to settle in the original thirteen colonies came to Maryland. In 1654, Jacob Barsimson, the first Jew known to settle in America, arrived on these shores. Ironically, along with these settlers in search of religious freedom came indentured servitude and slavery. Thus began the contradictory conditions of the New World—religious freedom and human bondage. Indeed, our human relations problems are as old as our nation.

Although most of the early settlers came to America in search of religious and political freedoms, most of them also immediately tried to deny similar freedoms to those of other persuasions. Historians point out that at one time or another during the colonial period, the religious rights of every group—Anglicans, Baptists, Catholics, Jews, Lutherans, Moravians, Presbyterians, Quakers, deists, atheists—were taken away. So it was that the pattern was set in which Americans would seek freedom *from* people instead of freedom *to be with* people.

Soon it became clear, as Benjamin Franklin so aptly stated, that the early Americans had to hang together to keep from hanging separately. Only after other influential leaders warned that religious and political freedoms were being threatened, however, did the precarious state of America's human relationships come into sharper public focus. Belatedly acknowledging their inhumanity, the colonists made a landmark decision in human relations. For the first time in history a nation dedicated itself to living an Old Testament message (later inscribed on the Liberty Bell): "Proclaim liberty throughout all the land unto all the inhabitants thereof." America became the first nation in history to commit itself to the principles of democracy on a national scale. Though tried on a small scale in several other countries of the world, only America dared to adopt nationally the axiom that "all men are created equal." To be sure, the not-too-silent majority within the colonies was already behaving as though some men were more equal than others.

From the beginning, then, it was evident that individual and group differences would plague the spirit—if not the letter—of the principles of the American Constitution. Not only were Indians and slaves denied the political democracy later made explicit in the Bill of Rights, but conflicts between religious and nationality groups continued as a way of life. Church buildings were burned, individuals were beaten and sometimes killed, and groups were ostracized because they were "different." This was the beginning of America's recurring social nightmare, complete with verbal and physical violence.

There were many instances when older immigrant groups discriminated against new immigrants. In 1846, for example, riots broke out against the Irish in Boston, New York, and Philadelphia. Most of the citizens participating in these riots failed to realize that their forefathers were also immigrants. Only the Indians had a legitimate complaint about foreigners invading their land. The early settlers seemed unable to learn from history. They continued to segregate and abuse "foreigners." Worse yet, they continued to segregate themselves socially. But the great tragedy was not that they failed to learn from history but that they failed to unlearn inhumane behavior even after becoming familiar with past injustices.

Behavior That Separates Us

The newborn baby has been called the best representative of democracy that any nation has been able to produce.[2] Every baby is born free of prejudice and in that sense is "democratic." Unfortunately, this condition is only temporary, for every baby quickly learns the prejudices that are a part of his environment. Though every individual comes into the world prejudice-free, most are socialized by extremely prejudiced people.

Many of our personal preferences are prejudgments—decisions made on the basis of inadequate information. However, being against someone or something is not necessarily a *prejudice*. When based on facts, an attitude opposing someone or something is a *bias* which does not violate democratic principles. For example, an individual is not behaving prejudicially if he concludes after interacting with others that he doesn't like them. But few people collect enough facts to allow them to make objective judgments.

It is also important to note that not all prejudices are harmful or negative. Some, such as clothing preferences, are both harmless and a

2 Mary E. Goodman, *Race Awareness in Young Children* (Cambridge, Mass., Addison-Wesley Publishing Co., Inc., 1952).

source of amusement to others. Prejudicial behavior can support a group rather than oppose it. Black, Brown, and Red Power advocates, for instance, state that they are for their people and not against other groups.

The most insidious prejudices are those negative attitudes directed toward groups, especially religious and racial groups.[3] They take the form of assumptions or generalizations about all or most members of a particular group ("You know how *those* people are!"). Such *in-group* versus *out-group* hostility threatens the very existence of our nation. We are employed, housed, married, and buried with one major criterion in mind: our group affiliation. The behavior, customs, and habits of out-group people are labeled "strange" and "inferior." Every aspect of growing up and becoming a member of a group adds to the probability of interpersonal rivalry. In most instances, social groups reinforce individual prejudices. Whites learn to dislike blacks, blacks learn to dislike whites, and Indians learn to dislike both whites and blacks.

It is both amazing and frightening to observe people rejecting others without knowing whom or what they are rejecting. When such rejection occurs, people are hating on the blind faith that they are right and that others are wrong. *Ignorance*, therefore, is one of the primary causes of prejudice. Without knowing the aims, values, and purposes of other people, we cannot know what they have in common with us. It stands to reason that without knowing others we cannot fully appreciate their cultural backgrounds and contributions. The most negative aspect of ignorance is that people afflicted with this social disease are also socially blind. Indifference is at one end of the continuum growing out of this kind of information gap; hostility is at the other end.

During the early years of our country, a rigid "cultural curtain" kept religious and racial groups apart. The twentieth-century ecumenical movement has done much to remove prejudices in the area of religion, but the cultural curtain still blocks our racial vision, causing us to cling to outmoded, unscientific definitions of race. This is not to suggest that anti-Semitism, anti-Catholicism, and anti-Protestantism are no longer problems. Racial minority groups are discriminated against on both counts, racial and religious. Foreign visitors to this country are appalled that many patriotic Americans dedicated to preserving democracy outside the United States hate fellow citizens of another color whom they do not know even casually.

Ignorance leads members of a racial group to assume that theirs is

[3] Gordon W. Allport, *The Nature of Prejudice* (Cambridge, Mass., Addison-Wesley Publishing Co., Inc., 1952).

superior to all others and is characterized by high intelligence, while members of other groups are of generally low intelligence. Persons engaging in such assumptions have not learned that (1) all men are of the same genus and species, (2) there are more differences within racial groups than among them, and (3) apparent group differences are largely due to environmental conditions and training.

But ignorance is not the only cause of prejudice. Universities and colleges have their share of well-educated but extremely prejudiced persons. Their prejudices, especially religious and racial prejudices, are deeply rooted in emotions. Scientific studies have concluded that prejudice is based on fear and that fear is based on insecurity. For example, many whites who are prejudiced against blacks are fearful that if blacks ever reach positions of power they will imitate racist whites and become hostile and repressive. Thus *hostility* growing out of frustration and insecurity is a second cause of prejudice. The irrational hatred of intellectuals makes it evident that, although scientific studies are necessary, they are not enough to prevent prejudices from forming.

Group prejudices are expressed in terms of *stereotypes*—false images of out-groups. Stereotypes are given verbal expression: "Jews are pushy," "Blacks are lazy," "Japs are sneaky," "Poor whites are trashy." Clearly these images are false, but they trigger the premature social and psychological deaths of the people so labeled. In most instances such images can be destroyed only after the prejudiced person has had a positive experience with a member of the stereotyped group. But it is also likely that a positive experience will only cause the prejudiced person to discount its significance by saying, "He is different, exceptional, not like the others of the group."

Daily we witness the negative aspects of racial prejudice. It creates inequalities, rejections, and exclusions which prevent people from being allowed to move into the mainstream of American life and denials which warp the personality of millions of Americans. When measured in terms of social effects, racial prejudice is more to be feared than cancer, tuberculosis, and heart disease. Prejudice engulfs the entire body and mind, defying the skills of social surgeons.

Cultural Pluralism   Since its birth as a nation, America has been plagued by the social disease of racial prejudice. Each year millions of parents pass this disease on to their children. Racial prejudice affects more people than any physical disease that man has ever known. Frustrations, fears, suspicions, and discrimination have caused too many Americans to become social zombies, the walking dead in social competition. The problem lies not in group differences but in our inhumane reactions to those differences. It is a gross understatement to note that our survival as a nation depends on our human relationships.

Perhaps it is inherent in the nature of dynamic societies that people and groups compete with their counterparts in order to emerge as the number-one player in the game of survival. Out of this competition have come negative attitudes, sometimes referred to as racism and intolerance. Often people ask, "Why should we expect more of Americans than of other people?" and "What is wrong with segregation?" Racism and segregation are wrong in America, because we are the only nation claiming to be the melting pot of *all* people. Despite this basic principle of our nation, separatism is increasing rather than decreasing in the United States.

The people of America have not fused together for some fairly obvious reasons. First, Indians, blacks, and other nonwhites have seldom been allowed to climb into the melting pot, and, second, whites who have come here from other countries have brought their own cultures with them and have been reluctant to lose their cultural identities through the process of assimilation. Imitating the dominant groups, minority groups are beginning to cling jealously to their respective heritages.

A new goal, *cultural pluralism*, is replacing the melting-pot concept. According to advocates of cultural pluralism, each group has distinctive values to add to our way of life. On the premise that no one culture has a monopoly on the favorable qualities of life, proponents of cultural pluralism further assert that America will be better if the best that each group has is shared and conserved. Diversity, rather than uniformity, would then become the dominant theme in the American dream. From this perspective, our survival as a nation is dependent on preservation of cultural differences.

Principles of Good Human Relations

The ultimate goal of human relations education is to foster understanding and acceptance among the many people of our nation. If this ever happens, democracy will become a reality and not remain the dream that men like Martin Luther King, Jr., Clyde Warrior, John Kennedy, Robert Kennedy, and Whitney Young, Jr., take with them to their graves. *Human relations involve people, not abstractions.* Human life necessitates human relations, good or bad. The goal then becomes to minimize "bad" relations and to maximize "good" relations. But what is good for one man may be viewed as bad for another. When it comes to human relations, Americans tend to feel more strongly and know less about it than any other subject. How strange it is that we understand killing, hating, and segregation but have much difficulty understanding what constitutes good human relations. In fact, most "experts" in human relations live in racially segregated neighborhoods and attend racially segregated religious services.

Three cornerstones—religion, democracy, and science—can provide a solid foundation for human relationships. Sadly enough, they have not yet done so.

Religion

We are a nation founded on the religious teaching of Judaism and Christianity, which affirms the supreme worth of each human being. While they differ on many points of theology, Protestants, Catholics, and Jews agree on the Brotherhood of Man under the Fatherhood of God. From this idea comes the basis for the common bond of all people. The words are right; the corresponding deeds are wrong. Few people live by the tenets of their religion. It is equally depressing to note that racist mobs are often made up of self-professedly religious people. An old slave prayer was dedicated to such people: "Lord, protect me from my friends, I know my enemies." Too many "religious" people believe that they are their brothers' keepers. People should free people, not keep them. The quest for freedom has caused several minority-group leaders to cry, "Free me or exterminate me!" Black Americans and Puerto Ricans have been kept too long in their slums and urban ghettos. Mexican-Americans have been kept too long in migrant workers' camps. American Indians have been kept too long on reservations. And rural poor whites have been kept too long on welfare.

Democracy

The foundation of our government is the "American creed," which reaffirms the words of the Declaration of Independence that "all men are created equal." Unfortunately, like the early colonists, many who adhere to this principle add the divisive clause that some men are created more equal than others. Yet the dream of equality and their inability to achieve it haunts the innermost thoughts of disadvantaged Americans. At its best this dream becomes the impetus for constructive change. At its worst it becomes a nightmare driving men to riot and to kill. The democratic creed includes respect for each individual. But, like our religious principles of brotherhood, there is a wide gap between creed and deed. Some patriots are hypocrites of the lowest order. They wave the American flag as they verbally and physically try to kill off dissenting minorities. Out of this insanity has come such slogans as: "Kill a Communist for Christ."

Science

During the twentieth century a growing number of Americans have turned to the social sciences for guidance. The physical and natural sciences have allowed us to master matter and space. Now we look to the social sciences in hopes of learning how to master ourselves. We appear to be winning the battles of space and disease but losing the war of human survival. More often than not, Americans "listen" to what social scientists say but fail to "hear" the implications of their findings. Sociologists tell us that cooperation, not conflict, is the basis of national survival. Historians tell us that our civilization is the product of many cultural influences. Psychologists tell us that prejudices lead to faulty reasoning and destructive behavior. Anthropologists tell us that there is no pure race. Social psychologists tell us that race riots are symptoms of group frustrations growing out of minority-group status. From the social sciences have come additional concepts of human relations:

1. *Every individual is entitled to equal rights and dignities.* We cannot "grant" rights and dignities to others. They are entitled to them by the virtue of being human. This principle is embodied in the Golden Rule: "Do unto others as you would have others do unto you." Indeed, in the Judeo-Christian tradition one is to love his neighbor as himself. Little dignity accrues to people whom we call niggers, dagos, honkies, freaks, queers, wops, Christ killers, red savages, and so forth. Nor is it likely that recipients of such epithets will receive equal rights.

2. *The right to be free implies the right to be different.* The American Revolution was fought to free us from the tyranny of the British Empire, which limited our political thoughts and actions. A basic point of contention was the right to be different. Reminiscent of the English tyranny that led to the Revolution are the restrictive acts of the superpatriots who would silence individuals desiring to exercise *their* right to be different. Bumper stickers saying, "America—Love It or Leave It" are rightly countered by stickers saying, "America—Change It or Lose It."

3. *We should try to understand cultures different from our own.* The beginning of good human relations is learning about cultures different from our own. From knowledge comes understanding. Much of our inability to get along with other people reflects our fears of the unknown. Instead of ridiculing, blaming, or even physically attacking people who are different, we must seek to understand them. While books and films are fine secondary sources, understanding comes best from primary sources— associations with members of different cultural groups. Often fear of the unknown is fear of ourselves—fear that we will discover that we have wasted valuable time and energy hating people who though culturally different are similar to us in many ways.

4. *All groups share certain common needs.* There is remarkable similarity in the needs of culturally different peoples. All people seek the same basic social needs, such as good health, adequate employment, and protection from the elements. Above all else, everyone shares the need for a positive self-image. Young militants say that it is better to die a brave man than to live as a degraded slave. But why must men die in order to be free? In the 1940's the National Resources Planning Board drew up the following "Bill of Rights" for all Americans:

1. The right to work, usefully and creatively, through the productive years.

2. The right to fair pay, adequate for the necessities and amenities of life . . . in exchange for their services.

3. The right to adequate food, clothing, shelter, and medical care.

4. The right to security, with freedom from fear of old age, want, dependency, sickness, and the like.

5. The right to live in a system of free enterprise.

6. The right to come and go, to speak or be silent, free from the spying of secret political police.

7. The right to equality before the law, with equal access to justice in fact.

8. The right to education for work, for citizenship, for personal growth and happiness.

9. The right to rest, to recreation and adventure, to the enjoyment of life and an advancing culture.[4]

In summary, the board reiterated the need that all people have to be an integral part of their society.

5. *Each individual should be evaluated on his own merit.* Because it requires less time, we tend to categorize people or lump them together instead of evaluating individuals on their own merits. This tendency leads to stereotyped thinking about groups and, therefore, individuals, as witness conversations about "*the* Baptists," "*the* Lutherans," "*the* Methodists," "*the* Presbyterians," "*the* Catholics." Stereotyping can lead to negative and even destructive human relations.

6. *America is a culture of all groups.* The contributions of Europeans, Asians, and Africans in building America have been well documented. We are now turning our efforts to an understanding of the cultural contributions of other groups. Courses in and conferences about minority groups—American Indians, Afro-Americans, Puerto Ricans, and Mexican-Americans—are ways to gain this understanding.

7. *Democracy cannot work for some unless it works for all.* "One nation, under God, indivisible, with liberty and justice for all" is but one

4 To compare the similarities in "rights" demanded after 1940, see Henry Steele Commager, *The Struggle for Racial Equality* (New York, Harper & Row, 1967).

way of saying that until all citizens are free none are free. We form a human chain that is only as free or as enslaved as the individuals who make up its links. Despite Abraham Lincoln's warning that this country cannot continue to exist "half slave and half free," we seem determined to prove otherwise. Racial discrimination is pulling us apart as a nation, and economic discrimination is keeping us apart as groups. We must accelerate our efforts to come together as a nation. In the jargon of the young, "We've got to get ourselves together."

The term *democracy* encompasses the whole interrelated set of ideals which emphasize public policy determination by the majority rather than the minority, but not to the extent that minorities are deprived of their equality, freedom, respect, and dignity. Democracy has as its central value the potential of developing the distinctive human qualities—imagination, sensitivity, and rationality—in all people, rather than in a few.

It is ironic that, while we are predominantly a nation of immigrants, a nation of many religions and colors built to preserve individual freedom and equality, we are also a nation with little practical experience in implementing democracy. Our human relations efforts to date leave much to be desired.

The Question of Survival

Americans of all ages are hooked on separatism, and unless we can kick the habit, we will die socially and psychologically from an overdose of hate, prejudice, and racial discrimination. As if under a witch's spell, social practitioners run aimlessly from one social problem to another without adequately resolving any of them. It is not a witch's spell, however, but social conditioning that has produced inhumane Americans. Of course, there are humane Americans, but they seem to be outnumbered by the advocates of separatism and racism.

As a nation we seem to lack the will and the tenacity to abate the conditions creating racial discrimination, poverty, crime, and student unrest. Critics abroad point out that Americans can successfully send men to the moon but have yet to integrate most of their neighborhoods and public schools. Indeed, in this period of riots, protests, and backlash, it is difficult to distinguish clearly the good guys from the bad guys. Unlikely allies have started and perpetuated riots—the radical left who want to tear down "the system" and the conservative right who want an excuse to move in and "beat the heads of the liberals." We live in what is in many ways a perverse society, as witness the fact that some Americans believe that violence is the best way to break up nonviolent protests.

Our vision is greatly distorted when we focus exclusively on the problems of blacks versus whites, ignoring American Indians, Mexican-Americans (Chicanos), Puerto Ricans, Jews, Japanese-Americans, Chinese-Americans, and Filipinos. We seem continually to be plagued with tunnel vision, unable to see the broad picture of human relations. Equally disturbing are the large numbers of misguided radicals who are determined to save minority groups even if they have to enslave them. It is also ironic that many vigilantes guarding against the advance of communism in the Far East and Central Europe do not hesitate to use tactics which right-wingers associate with communism to curb the influence of Marxism and Maoism in America. And, frequently, those who would deny academic freedom and equality of opportunity in our universities and cities will use whatever force is necessary to ensure those rights in foreign countries. It is this kind of priority setting that angers minority groups.

The problem of survival is global, not local. The odds against the world surviving are reduced each year by such threats as the following:

1. *The population bomb.* Our individual spaces of free movement are restricted by the growing number of people. We can run but not hide from people. Some fanatics believe that their chances of survival will be enhanced by implementing programs that reduce the number of "undesirable" people—usually members of a racial minority group.

2. *Nuclear threat.* Our capacity for destruction may soon outstrip our capacity for control. It seems idiotic to boast about how many times we can overkill the enemy. One moment of uncontrolled anger by a national leader, and most of the world would become extinct.

3. *Environmental pollution.* Air and water are rapidly becoming detrimental to our health. The air in many cities has been polluted to the point where breathing it for twenty-four hours has the same effect as smoking two packs of cigarettes. Our rivers and lakes are becoming sewers and fetid cesspools. More than four-fifths of our original forests have been destroyed, and much of the wildlife has been exterminated. The land is being ruined by overgrazing, overfarming, overlogging, and overmining, and each day approximately three thousand acres are displaced by blacktop and concrete. The problems of air pollution, water pollution, land pollution, noise pollution, and thermal pollution are increasing at such

rates that many writers now speculate that self-destruction is more likely than nuclear disaster.

4. *The empathy gap.* We are faced not so much with a generation gap as with an empathy gap. Cultural insensitivities seem to be growing at a geometric rate. We have eyes but frequently do not "see" culturally different people. We have ears but frequently do not "hear" the cries of the disadvantaged. Majority and minority groups do not understand each other, men and women do not understand each other, and government officials and their constituents do not understand each other. How can we be so much alike and yet so far apart?

5. *Mechanization, urbanization, and cybernation.* The world of work is being altered so drastically that we must now rethink our concepts of jobs, pay, and styles of living. We live in an instant-reaction, now-you-see-it world where the rich seem to get richer and the poor get poorer, and all of us are destined for an early retirement.

Technology is man-created and man-controlled; it has been used and abused. While the issue of survival is international, few people are able to discuss and resolve an aspect of human relations on a large scale. Most of us are better able to come to grips with the human relations problems in our homes, our neighborhoods, and our states. The effort begins with our children. There are several steps that adults can take to prepare children for survival in a humane world.

Adults can teach children to *hate* not each other but the generalizations, clichés, and slogans which separate people. If children must hate, let them hate the words and deeds which tear us apart as a nation.

Adults can teach children to *accept* members of different groups and also to accept themselves, so that they will not want to strike out at people who are religiously, socially, and physically different.

Adults can teach children to *understand* that all people are entitled to respect and dignity because we are all of the same genus and species, belonging to one race—the human race.

Before adults can teach these lessons to children, they not only must themselves believe in the worth and dignity of all people but also must be willing to work in their homes and communities to exemplify this belief. There are too many haters wearing masks of brotherhood, too many people who do not realize that we are all extensions of each other—humane and inhumane, affluent and poor, white and nonwhite, liberal and conservative.

We cannot continue to kill a portion of ourselves socially, psychologically, or physically and maintain that we are as well and as healthy as ever. America, the most powerful and creative nation in history, is slowly committing cultural suicide. A crucial question is: Who or what will survive? Equally important: How can we change in order to survive?

The original swinging society

Apes have a very low crime rate. They pay no taxes, never go to war, never go into debt. They have no population explosion nor any threatened food shortage. No one has to spend big ad dollars to tell them, "Never put bananas in the refrigerator." They don't need a beautification program because they don't spoil their surroundings. They don't pollute their air; don't waste their water. Their government is a model of efficiency and simplicity. True, they don't have Scotch whisky, cellophane, jet planes, ice cubes or pro football, but they *have* established a balanced equilibrium with their natural environment. A hundred million years ago, an ape-like creature came swinging out of the trees and said, "I'm going to stand on two feet, call myself Man, and build a *better* world." *Isn't it time we got started?*

This message is from **Newsweek**

COPYRIGHT © 1968 BY NEWSWEEK, INC.

5 "The Original Swinging Society," *Newsweek*

Suggested Reading

Adelstein, Michael E., and Jean G. Pival, eds. *Ecocide and Population*. New York, St. Martin's Press, Inc., 1972.

Allport, Gordon W. *The Nature of Prejudice*. Cambridge, Mass., Addison-Wesley Publishing Co., Inc., 1952.

Andrews, Lewis M., and Marvin Karlins. *Requiem for Democracy?* New York, Holt, Rinehart & Winston, Inc., 1971.

Baldwin, James M. *Social and Ethical Interpretations*. New York, The Macmillan Company, 1897.

Barth, Alan. *Heritage of Liberty*. New York, McGraw-Hill Book Company, 1965.

Bell, Daniel, ed. *The Radical Right*. New York, Doubleday & Company, Inc., 1963.

Berger, Bennett M. *Looking for America*. Englewood Cliffs, N.J., Prentice-Hall, Inc., 1971.

Bloom, Benjamin S. *Stability and Change in Human Characteristics*. New York, John Wiley & Sons, Inc., 1959.

Bonner, Herbert. *On Being Mindful of Man*. Boston, Houghton Mifflin Company, 1965.

Brant, Irving. *The Bill of Rights: Its Origins and Meaning*. Indianapolis, The Bobbs-Merrill Co., Inc., 1965.

Broyles, J. Allen. *The John Birch Society: Anatomy of a Protestant*. Boston, Beacon Press, 1964.

Buber, Martin. *Between Man and Mind*. Boston, Beacon Press, 1961.

Bugental, J. *The Search for Authenticity*. New York, Holt, Rinehart & Winston, Inc., 1965.

Cartwright, Dorwin. *Studies in Social Power*. Ann Arbor, University of Michigan Press, 1959.

Combs, Arthur W. *Perceiving, Behaving, Becoming*. Washington, D.C., National Education Association, 1961.

DeBell, Garrett. *The Environmental Handbook*. New York, Ballantine Books, Inc., 1970.

DeHuszar, G. B. *Practical Applications of Democracy*. New York, Harper & Brothers, 1945.

Douglas, Jack D. *Freedom and Tyranny: Social Problems in a Technological Society*. New York, Alfred A. Knopf, Inc., 1970.

Ebenstein, William. *Today's Isms*. Englewood Cliffs, N.J., Prentice-Hall, Inc., 1964.

English, Oliver, and G. Pearson. *Emotional Problems of Living*. New York, W. W. Norton & Company, Inc., 1955.

Erikson, Erik H. *Childhood and Society*. New York, W. W. Norton & Company, Inc., 1950.

Fadiman, James. *The Proper Study of Man*. New York, The Macmillan Company, 1971.

Suggested Reading (continued)

Farb, Peter. *Man's Rise to Civilization as Shown by the Indians of North America, from Primeval Times to the Coming of the Industrial State*. New York, E. P. Dutton & Co., Inc., 1968.

Friedman, M. *The Knowledge of Man*. New York, Harper & Row, 1964.

Fromm, Erich. *The Art of Loving*. New York, Harper & Row, 1956.

————. *Escape from Freedom*. New York, Holt, Rinehart & Winston, Inc., 1941.

————. *Man for Himself: An Inquiry into the Psychology of Ethics*. Greenwich, Conn., Fawcett Publications, Inc., 1947.

Ginzberg, Eli. *The Development of Human Resources*. New York, McGraw-Hill Book Company, 1966.

Goffman, Erving. *Interaction Ritual*. New York, Doubleday & Company, Inc., 1967.

————. *The Presentation of Self in Everyday Life*. New York, Doubleday & Company, Inc., 1959.

Goodman, Mary E. *Race Awareness in Young Children*. Cambridge, Mass., Addison-Wesley Publishing Co., Inc., 1952.

Hegel, George W. F. *The Philosophy of Right*. Trans. by S. W. Dyde. London, George Bell and Sons, 1896.

Heschel, Abraham J. *Who Is Man?* Stanford, Stanford University Press, 1965.

Hoffer, Eric. *The True Believer*. New York, Harper & Row, 1951.

Homans, George C. *Human Groups*. New York, Harcourt, Brace & World, Inc., 1950.

————. *Social Behavior*. New York, Harcourt, Brace & World, Inc., 1961.

Hunter, Floyd. *Community Power Structure: A Study of Decision Makers*. New York, Doubleday & Company, Inc., 1963.

Huxley, Julian. *Man in the Modern World*. New York, The New American Library, Inc., 1944.

Jourard, Sidney M. *The Transparent Self*. Princeton, D. Van Nostrand, 1964.

Kaplan, Louis. *Foundations of Human Behavior*. New York, Harper & Row, 1965.

Kerner, Otto. *Report of the National Advisory Commission on Civil Disorders*. New York, Grosset & Dunlap, Inc., 1968.

Kielsen, R. B. *Politics and Paranoia*. San Francisco, Braden and Sons, Inc., 1965.

Klein, J. *Study of Groups.* New York, Humanities Press, Inc., 1961.

Linton, Ralph. *The Study of Man: An Introduction.* New York, Appleton-Century-Crofts, 1936.

————, ed. *The Science of Man in the World Crisis.* New York, Columbia University Press, 1945.

Maslow, Abraham H. *New Knowledge in Human Values.* New York, Harper & Row, 1954.

May, Rollo. *Man's Search for Himself.* New York, W. W. Norton & Company, Inc., 1953.

Mayo, Elton. *The Human Problems of an Industrial Civilization.* New York, The Viking Press, Inc., 1960.

Mead, Margaret. *Cultural Patterns and Technical Change.* New York, The New American Library, Inc., 1955.

Mills, C. Wright. *Images of Man.* New York, George Braziller, Inc., 1960.

————. *Power, Politics, and People.* New York, Oxford University Press, 1963.

Morris, Desmond. *The Human Zoo.* New York, McGraw-Hill Book Company, 1969.

Murphy, Gardner. *Human Potentialities.* New York, Basic Books, Inc., 1958.

Pareto, Vilfredo. *The Mind and Society.* Trans. by A. Bongiorno and A. Livingston. New York, Harcourt, Brace & World, 1935.

Rokeach, Milton. *The Open and Closed Mind.* New York, Basic Books, Inc., 1960.

Rossiter, Clinton. *Conservatism in America.* New York, Alfred A. Knopf, Inc., 1962.

Shostrom, Everett L. *Man, the Manipulator.* Nashville, Abingdon Press, 1967.

Southard, Samuel. *People Need People.* Philadelphia, The Westminister Press, 1970.

Steinfield, Melvin. *Cracks in the Melting Pot: Racism and Discrimination in American History.* Beverly Hills, Calif., Glencoe Press, 1970.

Stuber, Stanley I. *Human Rights and Fundamental Freedoms in Your Community.* New York, Association Press, 1968.

Tapp, June L., and Fred Krinsky. *Ambivalent America.* Beverly Hills, Calif., Glencoe Press, 1971.

Taylor, William. *Hanging Together: Equality in an Urban Nation.* New York, Simon & Schuster, Inc., 1971.

Tiger, Lionel. *Men in Groups.* New York, Random House, Inc., 1969.

Tillich, Paul. *The Courage to Be.* New Haven, Yale University Press, 1952.

Toynbee, Arnold. *A Study of History*. Ed. by D. C. Somerell. New York, Oxford University Press, 1946.

Van Dyke, Vernon. *Human Rights, the United States, and World Community*. New York, Oxford University Press, 1970.

Wheelis, Allen. *The Quest for Identity*. New York, W. W. Norton & Company, Inc., 1958.

White, Ralph K., and Ronald Lippit. *Autocracy and Democracy*. New York, Harper & Row, 1960.

Williams, Robin M. *American Society*. New York, Alfred A. Knopf, Inc., 1951.

SALLY BANANAS

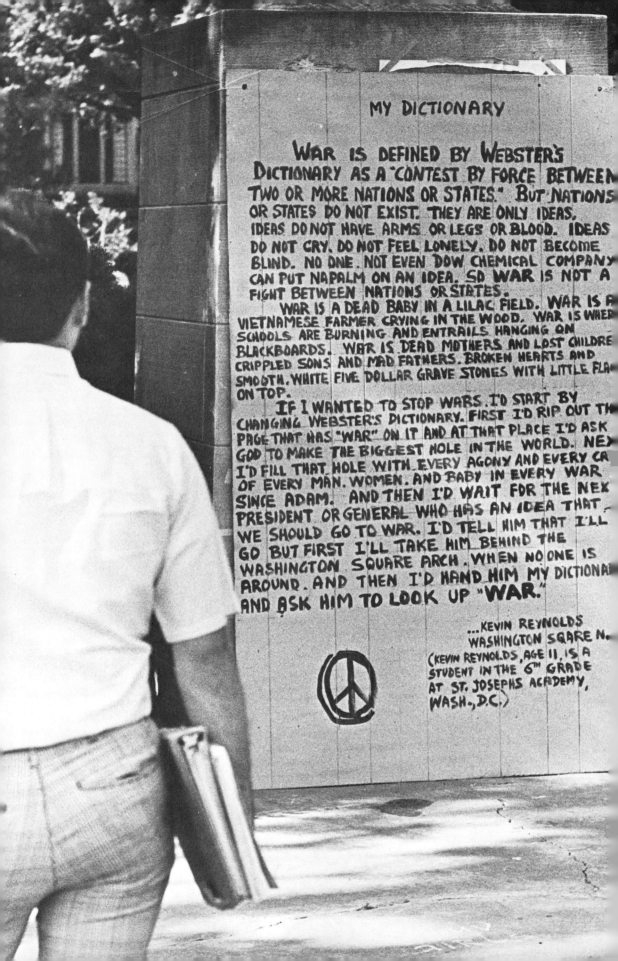

MY DICTIONARY

WAR IS DEFINED BY WEBSTER'S
DICTIONARY AS A "CONTEST BY FORCE BETWEEN
TWO OR MORE NATIONS OR STATES." BUT NATIONS
OR STATES DO NOT EXIST. THEY ARE ONLY IDEAS.
IDEAS DO NOT HAVE ARMS OR LEGS OR BLOOD. IDEAS
DO NOT CRY. DO NOT FEEL LONELY. DO NOT BECOME
BLIND. NO ONE. NOT EVEN DOW CHEMICAL COMPANY
CAN PUT NAPALM ON AN IDEA. SO WAR IS NOT A
FIGHT BETWEEN NATIONS OR STATES.

WAR IS A DEAD BABY IN A LILAC FIELD. WAR IS A
VIETNAMESE FARMER CRYING IN THE WOOD. WAR IS WHERE
SCHOOLS ARE BURNING AND ENTRAILS HANGING ON
BLACKBOARDS. WAR IS DEAD MOTHERS AND LOST CHILDRE
CRIPPLED SONS AND MAD FATHERS. BROKEN HEARTS AND
SMOOTH. WHITE FIVE DOLLAR GRAVE STONES WITH LITTLE FLA
ON TOP.

IF I WANTED TO STOP WARS. I'D START BY
CHANGING WEBSTER'S DICTIONARY. FIRST I'D RIP OUT TH
PAGE THAT HAS "WAR" ON IT AND AT THAT PLACE I'D ASK
GOD TO MAKE THE BIGGEST HOLE IN THE WORLD. NEX
I'D FILL THAT HOLE WITH EVERY AGONY AND EVERY CR
OF EVERY MAN. WOMEN. AND BABY IN EVERY WAR
SINCE ADAM. AND THEN I'D WAIT FOR THE NEX
PRESIDENT OR GENERAL WHO HAS AN IDEA THAT
WE SHOULD GO TO WAR. I'D TELL HIM THAT I'LL
GO BUT FIRST I'LL TAKE HIM BEHIND THE
WASHINGTON SQUARE ARCH. WHEN NO ONE IS
AROUND. AND THEN I'D HAND HIM MY DICTIONA
AND ASK HIM TO LOOK UP "WAR."

...KEVIN REYNOLDS
WASHINGTON SQARE N.
(KEVIN REYNOLDS, AGE 11, IS A
STUDENT IN THE 6TH GRADE
AT ST. JOSEPHS ACADEMY,
WASH., D.C.)

CHAPTER 3

Human Relations Today

America is a preserver of cultural differences. Specifically, it is a nation dedicated to preserving the many cultural heritages that make us a unique collection of people. At our best we are a nation of great humanness and social vision. At our worst we are like the characters in the following story.

Once upon a Time[1]

This is a literary comment on what I consider to be the heart of all problems in the field of human relations. It was written to express my feelings about the single most important factor contributing to the deterioration of human relations. The analogy and the characters exemplify the cycle as I perceive it, and this piece is a product of an overview I have obtained from my classes, readings, and personal observations.

Just to get the amenities over with, my name is Humpty, though many of my friends refer to me as Dumpty. Generally, I'm in good humor, but I'll have to warn you that you've caught me on a bad day. So, if you don't want to stick around, then you might as well split.

Not discouraged? Well, all right, but I won't apologize for my mood: you had the option to leave, don't forget. However, since you're here, I'll have to admit that it *is* kind of nice having someone to talk with. Seem to have

[1] Paper by Mary Hamra, graduate student, University of Oklahoma. Used with permission.

a lot to get off my chest lately. Strange . . . that never used to be the case. I can remember when contentment was the rule, not the exception. It's been a long time ago, but there *was* a time when I didn't face all these adversities and my existence wasn't threatened so. When? Oh, many years ago. Things have been getting progressively worse. Still, all in all, things have never looked as dismal as they do right now.

Specifically? Oh, it's hard to be specific and I'm not sure I can pinpoint it for you; but . . . if you're of a mind to listen, I suppose I *could* clarify things a bit. First of all, I don't mind sayin' (and this is not for repeatin') that my position in relation to this wall is shaky at best. What do you mean, "How's that"? I should think it would be obvious. Didn't you see that couple on your way up? Down there, the ones right down there. They've been axing away at this wall with their picks and shovels for centuries. Generally, progress has been slow, but they're getting better at it now.

Why? Well, now that's beyond *me*. All the psychiatrists relate everything to background and experiences. Maybe they haven't had such good experiences. All I know for a fact, though, is their names and what I've observed from watching 'em all these years. The big one? Yeah, he's a giant of a fella, isn't he—swings a *mean* ax, too. Guess you've noticed by now that he's the one doin' the most damage. What? Oh, his name is Fear; at least, that's what I've been told. Sure, his size worries me, but the real problem is that he's so all-fired determined. Now the little one next to him (the girl) doesn't scare me as much right now, but Fear keeps eggin' her on and helpin' her out. They call her Concept, Self-Concept I think it is. I'll be damned if she's not the *weakest* thing I've ever seen. Yeah, I know, she's determined, but not like Fear. That's the one to be careful of.

Where? Over there? Oh, great! Now they're back. Yep, they're kids all right. Belong to the couple we were talkin' about. Prejudice, Loneliness, and Hate, they're called—meanest brats around. They're constantly making trouble and gettin' under foot. They have made life absolutely miserable for me and my friends.

Now, here we've come to the crux of the matter—those *blasted* kids! Until they came along, Fear and Self-Concept weren't makin' much progress. I'll have to give those two credit for one thing: they're *sure* devoted to those kids. They'll do anything to keep those brats happy. That, in fact, is where *all* my problems started. Can't decide why those kids took a dislike to me. I don't know if it's inherited or environmental (probably both). Anyway, now *all five* of them want me off this wall; and if they keep weakenin' this spot I'm sittin' on, they'll *succeed!*

The worst part of it is, though, that if I fall it won't be a simple

matter of a broken arm. We're talkin' about my precious body shat-
terin' to pieces. Who? The king's horses and the king's men? I know,
I know! That crowd is under the impression they can put me back
together again if I should meet with misfortune, but they're *sadly*
mistaken. You see this little hole in my arm and this big one here in
my stomach? Well, the whole story is too painful to relate, but some
unfortunate circumstances inflicted these wounds. We tried for years
to make the pieces fit again, but never with any success. So, as you can
see, it's left me *permanently scarred*; and, by the same token, if I fall
off this wall, I'll be *permanently shattered*.

What do you mean, "What happens then?" You aren't much on
brains, are you? Even a moron can understand that if I'm gone Fear
and his family will take over my position. That's not bad enough. Oh,
no! The real disaster is those kids. When Hate, Loneliness, and Prejudice grow up and have kids of their own, *those* brats will be the
spittin' image of their grandparents, only stronger and more determined! Now, *there* we have the beginning of a vicious cycle. It's a sad
state of affairs as I see things!

Oh, sure, sure I understand—everyone's busy. Well, nice to
make your acquaintance and I appreciate your listening. Could you
do me one small favor on your way down? See if you can stall Fear
and Self-Concept for a little while. Thanks. By now.

That evening on the news:

Anchorman: Good evening. Sociologists and other experts report
a tragedy in the field of human relations today. Our
correspondent at the wall reports.

Announcer: Humpty Dumpty sat on a wall
Humpty Dumpty had a great fall
All the king's horses and all the king's men
Couldn't put Humpty together again.

This is the epic of what has happened here today. In
the wake of this tragic coup, the revolutionary Fear
and his followers have become the new leaders. Now
back to the studio.

Anchorman: Humpty, our informers tell us, was a mysterious
creature, difficult to know, yet an invaluable part of
our world. His friends called him Dumpty, but those
who knew him really well claim that this is an alias.
With this report our researchers went into the field and
found that Humpty Dumpty was, in fact, living under

an assumed name. We mourn the death not of
Humpty Dumpty but of an obscure being named
Trust.

Good night.

Understanding Our Humanness

Far too often we take our humanness for granted. W.
Paul Torrance offered the following thought-provok-
ing description of the characteristics and processes of
becoming human:

1. *"Wanting to Know."* We see it in the curios-
sity of the preschool child, always asking questions, becoming completely
absorbed in the search for the truth, trying to make sense out of his world,
making guesses and testing them, trying to discover his limits and the
limits of his situation. . . .

2. *"Digging Deeper."* The genuinely human person is not satisfied
with quick, easy, superficial answers. . . .

3. *"Looking Twice and Listening for Smells."* We can be satisfied at
first by a look from a distance or just by seeing. Then we want to look from
different angles, to take a closer look, and to experience with all our
senses. . . .

4. *"Listening to a Cat."* Many adults can neither talk to nor listen to
a cat with understanding. Much human communication is nonverbal.
Words are insufficient for the communication of the deepest and most
authentic emotions of love and the genuine concern of one person for
another. . . .

5. *"Crossing Out Mistakes."* The person who strives honestly to
achieve his potentialities inevitably makes mistakes. . . . We lose in humanness whenever we shrink from doing difficult and worthwhile things because we are afraid we will make a mistake and be punished for it. . . .

6. *"Getting into and out of Deep Water."* It means testing the limits
of one's skills and abilities, the situation, and one's resources. It means
taking calculated risks. It means asking questions for which no ready
answers exist. . . .

7. *"Having a Ball."* To become human, one must be able to laugh,
play, fantasy, and loaf. . . .

8. *"Cutting a Hole to See Through."* It requires a tolerance for complexity. . . . Out of complexity, incompleteness, and imperfection come the breakthroughs, genuine innovations in contrast to marginal improvements. . . .

9. *"Building Sand Castles."* It means seeing things not only as they are but as they might be with imaginative, constructive, courageous action.

10. *"Singing in Your Own Key."* Thoreau stated this idea very powerfully, as follows: "If a man does not keep pace with his companions, perhaps it is because he hears a different drummer. Let him step to the music that he hears, however measured or far away. It is not important that he matures as an apple tree or an oak. Shall he turn his spring into summer . . . ?"

11. *"Plugging in the Sun."* This can be interpreted both as working hard or as maintaining a connection with resources outside oneself—the support and stimulation of a group, a wide store of knowledge and experience, spiritual resources, and the like. . . .

12. *"Shaking Hands with the Future."* Finally, becoming human means . . . helping children become human.[2]

The essence of humanness revolves around social relations that exist whenever people behave in patterned ways determined by their joint awareness of one another. We have only to look at our immediate environment to realize that social relations are almost infinite in both number and character.

Seldom do we desire to know other people because of altruistic reasons. Rather, we tend to be concerned about others for very selfish reasons: What can they do for me? What can they do for us? Only on rare occasions do we ask, "What are they really like?" We are preoccupied with seeing people in order to get something from them. People who satisfy our needs are called "good," "warm," and "sensitive." We like people whose behavior indicates that they like us. On the other hand, we dislike people who thwart our needs. To them we attach the labels "bad," "cold," and "insensitive."

To learn about other people, we must be sensitive to them. That is, we must be *open to new experiences* and be willing to accept new ideas about

2 E. Paul Torrance, "What It Means to Become Human," in Mary-Margaret Scobey and Grace Graham (eds.), *To Nurture Humanness: Commitment for the '70's* (Washington, D.C., Association for Supervision and Curriculum Development, National Education Association, 1970), 1–10.

them and ourselves. In order to do so, *motivation* is essential. We learn only what we want to learn. After acquiring openness to new experiences and motivation we must become *actively involved in the learning process*. This involvement includes approaching people, asking questions, and exchanging feelings in an honest, nondefensive way. Finally, *feedback* is necessary either to substantiate or to refute our judgments of others. Thus sensitivity includes the ability to predict what an individual will feel, say, or do. We are insensitive to most of the people around us.

Social Roles

A *social role* is a pattern of expected behavior associated with a certain position in a society. The degree of social awareness and the actions which develop from it are dependent upon each individual's *definition of situations*—the meanings which he attaches to situations and their consequences. If two people define each other as friends, for instance, they will behave differently toward each other than if they define themselves as enemies. In other words, our humanness reflects a highly organized system of social roles. The adult male in the United States, for example, has a pattern of culturally defined behaviors ascribed to him merely because of his adultness and maleness. Only recently have members of women's liberation organizations begun trying to alter traditional male-female roles.

Social life is made up of a network of role expectations. Some expectations are complex; for example, when a man and a woman marry, they set in motion a chain of expected responses of whose nature and complexity they are only vaguely aware. The consequences of complex role expectations cause us to say, "If I'd known what I know now, I'd have done things differently." In most cases, our hindsight is infinitely more profound than our foresight.

The shared expectations of a group center on and are maintained through social interaction. The most important single characteristic of social interaction is its mutual or reciprocal nature. Each individual is made aware not only of his own expected behaviors but also of the expected behaviors of others. It is this factor that distinguishes social action from physical action. A man, for example, may react violently when he hits his finger with a hammer, but this physical action is not predetermined by an expected reaction on the part of the hammer. Action on the social level, however, always carries with it an expectation of appropriate responses from other persons involved. We would not expect another person to hit our finger with a hammer, but if he did, he should expect our reactions to be directed toward him.

Group Norms

A *social group* may be defined as any system of social relationships in which the members, united by a sense of emotional solidarity and of common purpose, have a culture which defines the roles and standards by which members are differentiated from nonmembers. It is not uncommon for members of groups to exhibit *ethnocentrism*—the belief that their group is the best and that all others are inferior to it. Since human groups differ in various ways from one another, it is dangerous to use one group to serve as an illustration for all others. It is meaningful, however, to recognize the various forms of social interaction within and between groups.

As norms emerge from group interactions, they define what is "right" and "wrong," what should and should not be. In short, social expectations can take on moral overtones. It is this normative aspect of behavior that constitutes a major difference between human and animal behavior. Assigning meaning to verbal and nonverbal behavior, man is the only animal to set up norms by which he judges his own behavior and that of others.

We do not voluntarily join all the groups in which we have membership. We are born into some, such as our family or ethnic group, and we are placed in others (for example, in "culturally disadvantaged groups") by people who have more power than we do. Once we are in a group, by whatever the selection process, however, our lives are affected.

Group membership is a primary source of both security and insecurity for the individual. In many ways it seems as if we cannot live with people and we cannot live without them. As a result, our emotional adjustment is deeply and continuously affected by the groups to which we belong. These groups serve as the foremost determiners of our self-esteem, or feelings of worth. Moreover, our personal feelings of worth depend upon the social status of the groups to which we belong. Self-hatred and feelings of worthlessness tend to characterize people who believe that they are members of underprivileged or low-status groups.

There is ample documentation that membership in a group provides both satisfaction and frustration of individual needs. A person's level of aspiration and, relatedly, his experience of success and failure are greatly influenced by the groups to which he belongs. This condition is complicated by the fact that group goals are sometimes inconsistent with individual goals, increasing the probability of individual frustrations. A common source of frustration is a group rule that does not allow for individual initiative or innovation. Frustrations also arise in organizations that permit their members little freedom to pursue personal goals, such as the freedom to wear certain hair styles.

Philip Selznick noted five kinds of individual behavior (derived imperatives) which lead to conflict between individual aspirations and organizational goals: (1) behavior affecting the organization's external environment and security, (2) behavior which affects the stability of lines of authority within the organization, (3) behavior which threatens the stability of informal power relations within the organization, (4) behavior endangering the consensus with respect to the meaning and role of the organization, and (5) behavior which challenges the legitimacy of the organizations operating procedures.[3]

In most instances individuals behaving in ways which threaten organizational stability and integrity become the objects of reprisals. The effects of organizational pressure upon deviant individuals are not uniform; under pressure some innovators buckle and conform, but others continue to lobby for changes.

Every group demands of its members some degree of conformity in behavior, attitudes, beliefs, and values. And because we are all simultaneously members of more than one group, we are constantly trying to adjust to conflicting group expectations and demands. Many sociological studies have been conducted in an attempt to discover more precisely the effects of group memberships on personal goals and satisfactions. Some studies have concluded that we have no real identity apart from various group identities.

Forms of Social Interaction

The major forms of social interaction are competition, cooperation, conflict, accommodation, and assimilation. *Competition* is the process through which the distributive and ecological order of society is created and maintained. Competition determines the distribution of goods, services, and status. It is the most impersonal of the social processes. If social systems were fair systems, competition would take place between equals. But they are seldom fair in the struggle for scarce goods. American children learn competitive goals in the process of becoming "good" citizens. Few people would deny that

[3] Philip Selznick, "Foundations of the Theory of Organization," *American Sociological Review*, Vol. 13 (February, 1948), 25–35.

competition is an important factor in American life and that it is both the cause and the effect of social change.

Cooperation is a form of social interaction in which two or more individuals or groups work together toward a common end. Competition and cooperation may be distinguished in terms of means and ends. Both processes are forms of social interaction between two or more individuals or groups directed toward the same end. Through competition the end sought can be achieved by some but not by all of the participants, whereas through cooperation the end can be achieved by all the individuals involved. As described in the language of games theory, competition is a *zero-sum-game* (some people must win and others must lose); and cooperation is a *non-zero-sum-game* (all participants win or all participants lose). Our society tends to encourage competition and to discourage cooperation, as illustrated in education, sports, and economic activities. American parents tend to ask their children: "What grade did you get?" "Who won the game?" "How much money did you earn?" And their children respond by saying: "*I* got...," "*I* won...," "*I* earned...." Yet in national and international relations impending disasters suggest that cooperation is necessary if nations are to survive. We must learn to play non-zero-sum games of life.

Conflict is the rivalrous interaction which emphasizes the differences between people and minimizes their similarities. Both competition and conflict are marked by an attempt of two or more persons to reach certain goals. In competition the emphasis is primarily upon the acquisition of scarce goods, and individuals are of secondary importance. In conflict the emphasis is primarily on individuals who may be trying to handicap, injure, or even destroy each other. While competition tends to be continuous and impersonal, conflict is intermittent and personal. Even though every dynamic society contains many factors that lead to conflict, efficient social functioning requires that conflict be controlled. If left unchecked, it can destroy the stability and eventually the very existence of a society. This fact is vividly illustrated in the area of race relations. It is important to note, however, that not all conflict is destructive.

Accommodation refers to either a permanent or a temporary termination of conflict which permits the rivalrous parties to function together without open hostility. Forms of accommodation include the truce, the compromise, subordination-superordination arrangements, arbitration, and toleration. American children are conditioned to accept accommodation through such phrases as: "Live and let live," "Don't win the battles and lose the war," "It doesn't matter who wins as long as it's a good, fair game." While commendable in principle, critics conclude, few people are rewarded for being losers. Few nationalists realize that some form of accommodation is necessary in a pluralistic nation. But accommodation is not synonymous with assimilation.

Assimilation is the gradual process by which cultural differences disappear. Because the ability to communicate is the most important requisite for successful assimilation, a common language is necessary. College students, as an illustration, are not likely to become sociologists until they learn to speak what sometimes is called the jargon of sociologists. Of course, speaking a special language but failing to master its academic subtleties will render the student relatively ineffective as a sociologist.

Assimilation occurs readily when the contacts are intimate, personal, and face-to-face and occurs more slowly when contacts are impersonal, casual, and indirect. Thus racial separatism makes it extremely easy for nationalistic groups to resist assimilation. Besides, they ask, why should any group want to lose its cultural identity and heritage? Cries for black, red, white, yellow, and brown nationalism impede efforts to achieve racial assimilation. Societies such as ours, with many different subcultures, create special problems for individuals committed to assimilation. Most of us belong to different groups and are expected to conform to different and often contradictory norms. When these norms contradict one another or when they conflict, we are forced to make a choice between them. What will a black separatist do when he is offered a supervisory position in a white organization? Or what will a white separatist do when offered a promotion in a unit headed by a black supervisor? Conformity to one set of norms is frequently tantamount to violation of another.

Many conflict situations are the results of social change. Some social scientists believe that conflicting norms are mainly responsible for the high incidence of mental disease in our society. *It is not that there are too many norms to which the individual is expected to conform but that there are too many contradictory norms.* Religious norms differ from business norms, family norms differ from college norms, and so on. We should be wary of accepting generalizations, such as, "All conflict is bad, and all cooperation is good."

Theories and concepts have value only as means for deriving solutions to problems. Rigid rules and laws seldom fit the needs of marginal cases. And certainly no amount of theories or concepts is an adequate substitute for getting to know people on a personal basis. It is imperative, therefore, that we understand the need for friendly, cooperative, and relaxed human relations. Only thus can we move from human experiences to humane conditions. To those who doubt our common needs, or even our common existence, Sarah Burns offers the following sobering thoughts:

> Each human being shares with all other human beings certain needs which he must fill in order to ensure his continuing existence. Certainly we can discuss the possibility—and even allow for it—that we, in our present state, actually do not exist; however, discussion of our nonexistence seldom leads men to cease filling the vital needs, whether these needs and their fulfillment are illusions or reality. Therefore, we can postulate that, since all men seem to exhibit common needs in existence and similar ways of filling those needs, we can show the commonality in our existence.[4]

Our common needs are met through the many groups to which we belong. Every employee, for example, seeks certain satisfactions from his job. Yet even here an old adage is true that one man's meat is another man's poison. Or, stated more positively, any activity is capable of satisfying someone. For some employees the challenge inherent in work per se is adequate satisfaction. For others a salary is their incentive. Still others enjoy the companionship of their fellow workers.

Group Ecological Factors

The emotional state of group members is greatly dependent upon certain properties of the group, such as the style of leadership, the ease of communication among members, the forms of internal stratification of members, and the clarity of definition of individual functions.[5] In most instances the emotional behavior of an individual will not be stable until he becomes a truly integral member of a group. The emotional tone of any group is affected by what may be termed *group ecological factors*, which include such things as the availability of facilities required for group activities, the physical and spatial characteristics of the group's environment, and the physical, economic, and legal limitations of the group. Without a doubt the mental attitude of members of groups is affected by the physical restraints on their movements.

Some groups display characteristics that foster positive human relations, while others display characteristics that impede such relations.

---

[4] Sarah Burns, "On Being Human" (unpublished paper, Norman, University of Oklahoma, 1970), 1.

[5] Bernard Barber, *Social Stratification: A Comparative Analysis of Structure and Process* (New York, Harcourt, Brace & World, Inc., 1957), 52.

Chronic breakdown in communication, inability to reach group decisions, failure to follow through with group actions, excessive expenditure of energy, and reaction to symptoms rather than attacks on causes of problems are examples of impeded group interactions. In line with this conception is the need for well-coordinated and well-trained group members. It is a well-known fact that groups become more effective as their members become better adjusted emotionally.

For a group to endure, its members must remain together. Stability, in turn, rests on interstimulation and communication among the members. The preferential feeling which members of a group have for each other is a cohesive factor of group life. As noted earlier, there is a general tendency to regard one's own associates as the "best." The more consensus group members have about the advantages of their group and the disadvantages of others, the higher the degree of *social integration*. Lack of social integration is measured in terms of remarks in which "I" is used rather than "we" when individual members describe their group activities.

An organization also tends to be more highly integrated if its norms are consistent; for when they are not, the members work at cross-purposes. From the military we learn that discipline within the ranks integrates a group and makes it resistant to disruption. Harsh discipline, however, creates a morale problem. Ultimately, the degree to which an individual will adhere to group norms is dependent on the ability of the group to meet his basic human needs.

Basic Human Needs

Ros: He said we can go. Cross my heart.

Guil: I like to know where I am. Even if I don't know where I am, I like to know *that*. If we go, there's no knowing.

Ros: No knowing what?

Guil: If we'll ever come back.

Ros: We don't want to come back.

Guil: That may very well be true, but do we want to go?

Ros: We'll be free.

Guil: I don't know. It's the same sky.

Ros: We've come this far. (He moves toward exit. Guildenstern follows him.) And besides, anything could happen yet. (They go.)[6]

---

[6] Tom Stoppard, *Rosencrantz and Guildenstern Are Dead* (New York, Grove Press, Inc., 1969), 95.

   We are, like Rosencrantz and Guildenstern, frequently torn between
the desire on the one hand to stay with the familiar and on the other hand
to venture forth into new activities. *New experience* occurs when the individual encounters something which, in part or in whole, he has never faced
before. Too, a new experience may be an old situation to which a new
variable has been introduced—for example, minority groups who suddenly
must adjust to newly achieved equal employment opportunities. The need
for new experience is the antithesis of the wish for maintaining the status

quo. New experience describes actions which disturb the status quo, such as the behavior of a man who takes a vacation, quits his job, or laughs at his girl friend's new dress. Experiences which are too radical are usually disturbing rather than stimulating. To be commercially successful, for example, a new piece of music, a novel, or a clothing style must ordinarily be the familiar done over in a slightly different manner.

The need for *security* can be seen in all actions which contribute to keeping things as they are. Efforts to keep a job or retain one's youth are examples of wishes or motives for security. Most people tend to resist revolutionary changes. Most of the social history of the later Middle Ages is a chronicle of the efforts of a majority to prevent a minority from introducing novel inventions and methods. The history of early science is characterized by the struggle against conservatism. Even today we cling tenaciously to old cultural norms, however willing we profess to be for change. To illustrate, most industries still have double promotion standards for men and women, with women generally receiving fewer opportunities for supervisory positions. Much of human conservatism is traceable to the fact that, once a reasonably effective pattern of behavior is learned, any change which makes that pattern less effective is psychologically or socially distressing.

We also have a need for *recognition*, the need to be acknowledged for an accomplishment. To fail to be recognized by people important to us is one of the most dreaded forms of punishment. For instance, a civic group may decide to recognize a minority-group leader. They schedule a banquet in his honor and invite many people, including representatives of the press. No matter how elaborate the preparation of food and decorations and certificates of honor, if the invited guests do not attend the banquet, the minority-group leader has not received recognition. In highly competitive societies a great amount of human action has no other objective than that of individuals trying to assert their superiority over their associates. Members of competitive societies are, by conditioning, egoists, each trying to rise above the others.

Closely related to recognition is our need for *response* from members of our groups. Because we derive our definition of self from others, we need feedback from them to help us shape our behavior. The social self arises in interaction with other persons as we look at ourselves through their eyes. We feel happy or sad as we evoke praise or blame from those with whom we identify. Mead described this process as follows:

> The individual . . . enters his own experiences as a self or indi-

vidual . . . only insofar as he first becomes an object to himself just as other individuals are objects to him in his experience; and he becomes an object to himself only by taking the attitudes of other individuals toward himself within a social environment . . . in which both he and they are involved.[7]

All individuals have the need to receive *affection*, which provides confirmation of their positive self-worth. This kind of reinforcement is the basis of healthy personalities. It is a simple but significant fact that all of us need affection from other people in order to develop and maintain healthy personalities. Yes, people do need people.

Every social organization may be viewed as a miniature society, having its own norms which affect the attitude and behavior of its members in various ways. Members of an organization are controlled by three kinds of influence: (1) the formal structure of the organization, (2) the informal structure and norms of the subgroups within the organization, and (3) the surrounding community.

It is an established fact that we learn values, attitudes, and behavior from our social environment. Whether these experiences are planned or just happen, they form our basis for accepting or rejecting other people. For this reason attention must be paid to the quality of interactions within and outside a group, since the quality of interactions significantly affects the ease with which each member will function.

For those who want to prevent or abate problems growing out of the group relationships, it is necessary to focus on the past, the present, and the future. The major emphasis, however, should be on immediate reality —what is occurring today, not what happened yesterday. Those who dwell exclusively on historical grievances, such as race or sex discrimination, are likely to become hardened, bitter people who see little hope in the present or the future. Those who spend most of their time dreaming of the future are likely to lose touch with reality. Ultimately, leaders of organizations must be able to design human relations activities that are relevant for today and tomorrow.

The foremost goal of any human relations program should be to aid each individual in realizing his optimum individual and social growth. This goal necessarily includes freedom for individuals to express themselves, as long as they do not infringe on the constitutional rights of others.

[7] George Herbert Mead, "Mind, Self, and Society," in Alfred R. Linesmith and Anselm L. Strauss (eds.), *Readings in Social Psychology* (New York, Holt, Rinehart & Winston, Inc., 1969), 10.

Specifically, a human relations program should teach individuals that cultural and racial differences are not valid reasons for rejecting others. They must become willing to live with and accept cultural differences.

Because we learn what we live, the major emphasis in human relations training should be on living good human relations. Reading books about other people is not enough; we must become able to live with them. Interaction is the best way to find out about people. For example, well-read white and nonwhite employees who segregate themselves on the job are not likely to learn all they can about each other. Their knowledge of each other will probably remain grossly inadequate.

On the premise that good human relations is not only good business but also desirable business, many industries are implementing training programs designed to improve human relations. The following concepts form the foundation for understanding and working with other people:

1. Every individual is the sum total of all his experiences (objective interactions and subjective feelings), and he behaves in terms of these experiences.

2. Every individual is endowed with psychological drives toward health, growth, and adjustment.

3. Every individual perceives and behaves in terms of his own needs for security, acceptance, achievement, and independence.

4. Every individual is capable of solving most of his problems if he understands the problems and learns to use his own resources.

Suggested Reading

Allen, Francis R. *Socio-Cultural Dynamics*. New York, The Macmillan Company, 1971.

Bendix, Reinhard, and Seymour M. Lipset, eds. *Class, Status and Power: A Reader in Social Stratification*. Glencoe, Ill., The Free Press, 1953.

Benedict, Ruth. *Patterns of Culture*. Boston, Houghton Mifflin Company, 1935.

Bennis, Warren G., ed. *Interpersonal Dynamics: Essays and Readings on Human Interaction*. Homewood, Ill., Dorsey Press, 1968.

Blake, Robert R., and Jane S. Mouton. *Building a Dynamic Corporation Through Grid Organization Development*. Reading, Mass., Addison-Wesley Publishing Co., Inc., 1969.

Blau, Peter, and R. Schoenherr. *The Structure of Formal Organizations*. New York, Basic Books, Inc., 1971.

Burns, Tom, and G. M. Stalker. *Management of Innovation*. Chicago, Quadrangle Books, Inc., 1962.

Cohen, Albert K. *Deviance and Control*. Englewood Cliffs, N.J., Prentice-Hall, Inc., 1966.

Cooley, Charles H. *Human Nature and Social Order*. New York, Scribner's, 1909.

Coser, Lewis A. *The Functions of Social Conflict*. Glencoe, Ill., The Free Press, 1956.

Dahrendorf, Ralph. *Class and Class Conflict in Industrial Society*. Stanford, Stanford University Press, 1959.

Davis, Kingsley, *Human Society*. New York. The Macmillan Company, 1949.

Eisenstadt, Samuel N. *From Generation to Generation: Age Groups and Social Structure*. Glencoe, Ill., The Free Press, 1956.

Etzioni, Amitai, and Eva Etzioni, eds. *Social Change*. New York, Basic Books, Inc., 1964.

Festinger, Leon. *A Theory of Cognitive Dissonance*. Stanford, Stanford University Press, 1957.

Gerth, Hans, and C. Wright Mills. *Character and Social Structure*. New York, Harcourt, Brace & World, Inc., 1964.

Homans, George C. *The Human Group*. New York, Harcourt, Brace & World, Inc., 1950.

Lawrence, Paul R., and Jay W. Lorsch. *Developing Organizations: Diagnosis and Action*. Reading, Mass., Addison-Wesley Publishing Co., Inc., 1969.

Lewin, Kurt. *Field Theory in Social Science*. New York, Harper & Row, 1951.

Luft, Joseph. *Of Human Interaction*. Palo Alto, Calif., National Press Books, 1969.

Marini, Frank, ed. *Toward a New Public Administration: The Minnowbrook Perspective*. San Francisco, Chandler Publishing Co., 1971.

Mead, George H. *Mind, Self, and Society: From the Standpoint of a Social Behaviorist*. Ed. by C. W. Morris. Chicago, University of Chicago Press, 1934.

Merton, Robert K. *Social Theory and Social Structure*. Rev. ed. Glencoe, Ill., The Free Press, 1952.

Mills, Theodore M. *Group Transformation*. Englewood Cliffs, N.J., Prentice-Hall, Inc., 1965.

————. *The Sociology of Small Groups*. Englewood Cliffs, N.J., Prentice-Hall, Inc., 1967.

Moment, David, and Abraham Zaleznik. *Role Development*

Suggested Reading (continued)

and Inter-Personal Competence. Cambridge, Mass., Harvard University Press, 1963.

Monane, Joseph H. *A Sociology of Human Systems.* New York, Appleton-Century-Crofts, 1967.

Montagu, Ashley. *The Direction of Human Development.* New York, Hawthorne Books, 1970.

Murdock, George P. *Social Structure.* New York, The Macmillan Company, 1949.

Orleans, Peter, ed. *Social Structure and Social Process: An Introductory Reader.* Boston, Allyn and Bacon, Inc., 1969.

Oswalt, Wendell. *Understanding Our Culture: An Anthropological View.* New York, Holt, Rinehart & Winston, Inc., 1970.

Phillips, Bernard S. *Sociology: Social Structure and Change.* New York, The Macmillan Company, 1969.

Rommetveit, Ragnar. *Social Norms and Roles*, Minneapolis, University of Minnesota Press, 1955.

Sayle, Leonard, and George Strauss. *Human Behavior in Organizations.* Englewood Cliffs, N.J., Prentice-Hall, Inc., 1966.

Scobey, Mary-Margaret, and Grace Graham, eds. *To Nurture Humanness: Commitment for the '70's.* Washington, D.C., Association for Supervision and Curriculum Development, National Education Association, 1970.

Shepherd, Clovis R. *Small Groups: Some Sociological Perspectives.* Scranton, Chandler Publishing Co., 1964.

Sherif, Muzafer, and Carolyn Sherif. *Reference Groups.* New York, Harper & Row, 1964.

Simmel, Georg. *Conflict and the Web of Group Affiliations.* Trans. by K. A. Wolff. Glencoe, Ill., The Free Press, 1955.

Sorokin, Pitirim. *Social and Cultural Mobility.* Glencoe, Ill., The Free Press, 1957.

Sumner, William G. *Folkways: A Study of the Sociological Importance of Usages, Manners, Customs, Mores, and Morals.* New York, Simon and Schuster, 1956.

Taylor, Howard F. *Balance in Small Groups.* New York, Van Nostrand Reinhold Company, 1970.

*"Obviously a case of mistaken identity.
Whoever oppressed you for four hundred years would
have to be a lot older than I am."*

Independence
Freedom
Peace
Justice
FOR ALL BLACK
PEOPLE
CHARLES

CHAPTER 4

With Liberty and Justice for All

A major determinant of our human relationships is the kind and the quality of information we have about our universe. The formal inquiry into our universe and the knowledge we have about it has preoccupied philosophers from at least the time of the ancient Greeks and probably long before then. Because our sense organs permit us to experience a narrow range of light waves, sound frequencies, and a few other physical conditions, each individual gets to know only a limited aspect of the world. The degree to which we are dependent on our senses is vividly illustrated in cases of individuals who suddenly become blind or deaf. The tenuous quality of our perceptions is further restricted by the language and thought structures our cultures impose on us. Above all else, it is culture that both defines and restricts our human relationships.

The Importance of Culture

Culture, the material and nonmaterial products of a society, is transmitted not through the germ plasm but through learning.[1] While the genes have a great deal to do with genius, the chromosomes have nothing to do with culture. Look, for example, at a nursery of squalling and squirming newborn babies. They come in various sizes, shapes, and colors. There is no physical examination that can tell us which of them will become a Protestant or which will speak Spanish. If, however, we know the family in which the infant will be reared, we are better able to make such predictions.

[1] Warren R. Baller (ed.), *Readings in the Psychology of Human Growth and Development* (New York, Holt, Rinehart & Winston, Inc., 1962), part III.

A man without a culture is in a real sense a feral man—a wild man, more like an animal than a human being. The human infant, sometimes fondly referred to as an alimentary canal with a lot of noise at one end and utter irresponsibility at the other, has to be "domesticated" through interaction with other people. It is a truism that we must learn to behave as human beings. *Whether* a child can learn depends upon his biological makeup; *what* he learns depends upon his culture.

If culture must be learned, even though most of the learning is unconscious imitation, so too must it be taught. In fact, most teaching is unconscious instruction. Parents seldom decide what they will teach their children. Most children infer the lessons by observing parental behavior. Whenever a generation fails to transmit a part of its culture to the next generation, that aspect of the culture will disappear, and, if it is to be adopted again, it must be reinvented or rediscovered. People of previous generations knew how to do many things that have been lost to our generation. For instance, no one today can duplicate the art of violinmaking mastered by Antonio Stradivari in the eighteenth century. While we have learned to do many things unknown to earlier peoples, we have forgotten some things known to them.

Culture may be viewed as a stream flowing down from one generation to another. When viewed in this manner, culture becomes synonymous with *social heritage*. Each generation contributes something to this stream, but in each generation something is washed ashore and left behind. The archives of libraries contain many artifacts that are no longer an essential part of our culture. This is not to suggest that all cultural items should be passed on to future generations. Rather, it highlights the fact that the cultures of any given time, with their attendant human relations, have both historical and unique characteristics.

It is culture that distinguishes us from other animals; and even though animals of some species have remarkable learning ability, the fact that they do not learn language prevents them from communicating what they learn to the next generation. *Language is the most important part of culture*, for without language culture could not accumulate. Imagine what would happen to each generation if we did not have language.

Because of language, the same "physical" objects often assume quite different "cultural" meanings. For example, a piece of cloth of the same color, texture, and composition may be used as a shirt in one society, a diaper in another, and a flag in still another. Similarly, paper of the same grade and quality may become a calendar, a diploma, or a bill of indictment in a court of law. Culture does indeed determine what we learn about our world.

Before real learning can begin to occur, a response of sorts must be made.[2] Assuming that a response is made, however it happens, learning does not occur unless the individual receives a *reward* or *punishment*. Reward means pleasant consequences; it satisfies the individual. As a result, the response that is rewarded tends to become a habit. Without reward, especially if replaced by punishment, the act tends to disappear. We also learn *not* to respond in a given manner. The preceding points can be illustrated by examining the historical rewards and punishments which conditioned Africans to become slaves, then coloreds, then Negroes, then Afro-Americans, and now blacks.

The Black Heritage

From the beginning, the social and psychological conditions in America created what may be referred to as a "Negro mood of unfulfillment." Black Americans have been and still are treated as second-class citizens. This status has been reflected in our songs, stories, plays, and poems. Within black communities

[2] Neal Miller and John Dollard, *Social Learning and Imitation* (New Haven, Yale University Press), 1941.

this inequality became a part of black speech: "This is the white man's world," "We can go only as far as the Man will let us." Yet out of this deprivation have emerged tenacious and surprisingly loyal black Americans. This cultural conditioning can be found in objective and subjective interpretations in the works of black writers.[3]

Slavery

The civil rights movement, the quest for full citizenship, did not begin in the twentieth century. It began when the first slaves were brought to America in the early seventeenth century. The black quest for equality was perpetuated by the slave revolts on southern plantations. Some of the revolts were integrated, involving black slaves and white indentured servants. These and other incidents refuted the "happy darky" tales found in early literature.

For those who want to be precise about the advent of black culture in America, most historians cite the year 1619, when twenty indentured black servants were brought to the New World (black explorers came to the New World much earlier than 1619, however). Within a few years the slave trade was at its peak. The slave trade ushered in the period of slavery, the ultimate in man's inhumanity to his fellow man. Slaves were brought to this country under conditions that could be compared with those used in shipping cattle. They were examined for defects, branded with hot irons on the chest, and chained by their ankles before being herded onto ships. Some were chained by the neck and legs to shelves no more than eighteen inches high. All were stowed at the bottoms of the ships, where inadequate air, space, and food caused the deaths of nearly two-thirds of each cargo.

The brutality of the slaves' lives on the plantations is a matter of record. They were whipped, and their family life was disrupted—children were separated from their parents, and husbands and wives were separated from each other. Black men and women were encouraged to breed like animals, in and out of wedlock, so that slaveholders could acquire more slaves. Today some outraged white citizens talk about the weakened structure of the black family. It was not weakened during the era of slavery; it was broken. The slavery period produced the first of the black generations that would cook, garden, and care for other peoples' children and thereby be denied an opportunity to care for their own.

The destruction of the black family structure was not without its effect

---

[3] For a comprehensive overview of black history, see John Hope Franklin, *From Slavery to Freedom: A History of American Negroes*, 3d ed. (New York, Alfred A. Knopf, Inc., 1967).

on the white family. The once-rigid physical distinctions between Negroes and Caucasians became permanently blurred through miscegenation. The multicolored black Americans of today are living proof of after-dark integration between white men and black women in the days of slavery. A poem by Langston Hughes captures something of the early black-white interactions:

Cross

My old man's a white old man
And my old mother's black.
If ever I cursed my white old man
I take my curses back.

If ever I cursed my black old mother
And wished she were in hell,
I'm sorry for that evil wish
And now I wish her well.

My old man died in a fine big house.
My ma died in a shack.
I wonder where I'm gonna die,
Being neither white nor black?

Approximately 100,000 slaves escaped the South before the Civil War by way of the Underground Railroad, an organization of white sympathizers and escaped or freed slaves who smuggled blacks to the North and to Canada. But it became painfully clear that the "free" North was not much freer than the enslaved South. In 1787 blacks tried unsuccessfully to persuade the Massachusetts State Legislature to provide them with equal educational facilities. In 1830 the National Negro Convention met in Philadelphia to assert the proposition that "all men are born free and equal." Similar meetings were held later in Illinois, Ohio, California, Louisiana, and Texas. In 1834 the first school paid for and run by blacks was opened in Cincinnati. Black Americans were eager to become an integral, wanted part of America, as another poem by Langston Hughes illustrates:

I, Too

I, too, sing America.
I am the darker brother.
They send me to eat in the kitchen
When company comes,
But I laugh,
And eat well,
And grow strong.

Tomorrow,
I'll be at the table
When company comes.
Nobody'll dare
Say to me,
"Eat in the kitchen,"
Then.

Besides,
They'll see how beautiful I am
And be ashamed—
I, too, am America.

Emancipation and the Rise of the Black Movement

While the Civil War may have emphatically settled the issue of physical slavery, it did not significantly alter the generally accepted white-supremacy attitudes in regard to race. Even the Thirteenth, Fourteenth, and Fifteenth Amendments to the Constitution failed to close the social, economic, and political gaps between black and white citizens. Much of this early lag can be attributed to the Reconstruction period, described by historians as a period of military rule, disfranchisement of the southern whites, Negro enfranchisement, and social upheaval. In 1896, nineteen years after the Reconstruction period, the United States Supreme Court, in *Plessy* v. *Ferguson*, formally subscribed to the doctrine that "legislation is powerless to eradicate racial instincts." Separate but equal became the legal way of life, accepted by both whites and blacks.

The modern history of the Negro or black protest began in 1905, when W. E. B. DuBois organized a group of fellow black intellectuals in a

Negro movement, founded at the Niagara Conference. The purpose of the conference was to protest segregation and to encourage blacks throughout America to seek the equality promised in the Emancipation Proclamation of 1863. In 1910 the National Association for the Advancement of Colored People (NAACP) was created, followed by the organization of the Urban League in 1912.

World War I took many black GI's to Europe, where they received better treatment than they had in America. Many of them returned home unwilling to accept their prewar second-class citizenship. In the summer of 1919 a series of racial incidents erupted. The bloodletting caused some writers to call it the "Red Summer"—more blacks were killed than during the riots of the 1960's. Later, in 1921, an entire black community was burned out in Tulsa, Oklahoma.

Disillusioned by the slow-paced tactics of the NAACP and the Urban League, some blacks began to espouse separatist philosophies. Marcus Garvey's back-to-Africa movement of the 1920's was the forerunner to present-day black separatist ideologies. Turning once more to Langston Hughes, we can see the frustration of black Americans in a portion of his poem "Harlem":

> *What happens to a dream deferred?*
> *Does it dry up*
> *Like a raisin in the sun?*
> *Or fester like a sore—*
> *And then run?*
> *Does it stink like rotten meat?*
> *Or crust and sugar over—*
> *Like a syrupy sweet?*
> *Maybe it just sags*
> *Like a heavy load.*
> *Or does it explode?*

Nonviolence

The depression of the 1930's and the onset of World War II exploded the dream of equality. During this period blacks lost ground socially and economically when compared with their white counterparts. Few people have realized that the nonviolent direct-action activities grew out of this period. A. Phillip Randolph's March on Washington of 1940 was the first mass black-American protest officially endorsing the principle of non-violent direct action. On June 16, 1942, blacks turned out their lights in Harlem to protest racial discrimination. Later that year the Congress of Racial Equality (CORE) was founded in Chicago. CORE took over many of the principles laid down by Randolph and began to work in the area of public accommodations, especially restaurants.

Contrary to popular opinion, the twentieth-century civil rights movement was not the beginning of a revolution to secure "new" citizenship rights. It reflected black Americans' attempts to secure "old" rights guaranteed by the Constitution. In education the most promising development came in 1954 in the United States Supreme Court's decision in *Brown* v. *Board of Education.* The court ruled: "We conclude that in the field of public education the doctrine of 'separate but equal' has no place. Separate educational facilities are inherently unequal."

On December 1, 1955, in Montgomery, Alabama, Mrs. Rosa Parks, a black seamstress, refused to move to the back of a bus. When she sat down, thousands of blacks began to stand up. The resulting successful bus boycott led to the rise to national prominence of the Reverend Martin Luther King, Jr., and the Southern Christian Leadership Conference (SCLC). The late 1950's and early 1960's were characterized by sit-ins, kneel-ins, and sleep-ins. The first formal sit-in took place in Oklahoma City on August 19, 1958, when the NAACP Youth Council, led by fourteen-year-old Barbara Ann Posey, sat at public lunch counters. Throughout this period, less innovative but equally determined hostile whites responded with traditional tactics, ranging from setting dogs on blacks to burning churches and killing civil rights workers.

In April, 1960, the Student Nonviolent Coordinating Committee (SNCC) was organized in Raleigh, North Carolina. At this point, the civil rights campaign took on a collegiate, interstate character, with black and white college students testing the integration of interstate transportation. Later they focused on voting rights. Such slogans as "Black and White Together" echoed the integrated nature of the activities.

Black Identity

By 1963 a few Negro leaders had begun to emphasize the need for black identity. Despite economic gains it was evident that most blacks harbored negative self-concepts. Waring Cuney expressed it in a poem:

No Images

She does not know
Her beauty
She thinks her brown body
Has no glory
If she could dance
Naked,
Under palm trees
And see her image in the river
She would know.
But there are no palm trees
On the street,
And dishwater gives back no images.

Most Americans either consciously or subconsciously identified black as the symbolic antonym of white. More often than not white was associated with everything that was good—Christ and the angels, cleanliness and virtue. On the other hand, black was associated with all that was bad. A review of literature reveals that at various times black has stood for dirt, sin, and the devil.

The metaphorical use of black as evil and white as good are abundant throughout the Bible; they are ingrained into the writings of ancient and contemporary literature; and, indeed, they are woven into almost every fabric of the symbolism in which our history is clothed. One can find the contrasts in dictionaries, ranging from "white hope" to "whitewash," from "blackball" to "blackmail."

The Bible's central theme of good (light) and evil (darkness) remains a chief source of reference for racial bigots, as illustrated by the Imperial Instructions of the Ku Klux Klan: "Every Klansman should read [the Bible] the first thing every morning and endeavor to live by it during the day."[4] Shakespeare adopted similar imagery. For example, in *Love's Labour's Lost* the King of Navarre says: "O' paradox! Black is the badge of hell, / The hue of dungeons and the scowl of night." In yet another scornful tone Shakespeare had Macbeth cry out to a servant: "The devil damn thee black . . . !" Both utterances illustrate the symbolic joining of evil and blackness. The examples in both theology and literature are endless.

4 Document No. 11, Series A.D. 1966.

The elevation of white and the debasement of black have been marked deep in the minds of all Americans, and most whites have more or less unconsciously taken it as a nourishment for their own self-esteem. Like the English child in one of Blake's poems, white Americans are already the color of angels, while blacks can only yearn after whiteness, whether of character, soul, or skin, and hope that by becoming "like" the white man they will be loved. James Baldwin described the tragic poignance of such hopes:

> At home one's hair was always being attacked with hard brushes and combs and Vaseline; it was shameful to have "nappy" hair. . . . One was always being mercilessly scrubbed and polished as though in hope that a stain could thus be washed away. . . . The women were forever straightening and curling their hair, and using bleaching creams. And yet, it was clear that none of this would release one from the stigma of being a Negro; this effort merely increased the shame and rage. There was not, no matter where one turned, any acceptable image of oneself, no proof of one's existence. One had the choice, either, of "acting just like a nigger" or of not acting just like a nigger and only those who have tried it know how impossible it is to tell the difference.[5]

Baldwin was writing of black Americans of the years before the 1960's. Most blacks of that period spent a major portion of their waking hours yearning and trying to become white. They were exposed to the brainwashing reassurances of their inferiority. The educated, the illiterate, the strong, and the weak were constantly reminded of their inferiority. Black Americans learned the lesson well, too well. They believed that black was ugly—something to be ashamed of. Only a few proud black people responded by saying, "The blacker the berry, the sweeter the juice." A childhood poem captured their self-degradation :

> *If you're white, you're right.*
> *If you're brown, stick around.*
> *If you're yellow, you're mellow.*
> *If you're black, get back.*

Though attitudes have begun to change, and blacks (and some whites) have begun struggling to counter these images, under the present socioeconomic conditions, black Americans still begin life with the odds

[5] James Baldwin, *Nobody Knows My Name* (New York, The Dial Press, Inc., 1961), 73.

against them. Whitney Young, Jr., described those odds in *To Be Equal*.[6] The black is more likely to die in infancy than the white. The chances that his mother will die in childbirth are relatively high—the mortality rate for black mothers is four times as high as that of white mothers. Eighty per cent of black babies are born to families living in urban slums. They are crowded into dilapidated housing—quarters structurally unsound or inadequate to keep out the cold, wind, rain, snow, rats, or insects. With larger families, blacks must exist on a median family income that is lower than the median white family income. Finally, most blacks still attend schools with inferior facilities and equipment and inadequately trained personnel.

Black Power

In 1966, Stokely Carmichael ushered in a new phase of the civil rights movement: Black Power and Black Pride.[7] The two concepts are interrelated. White Americans could understand Black Pride, but they found it virtually impossible to understand Black Power. In bewilderment many whites asked: "Can these be our musical, lazy, happy-go-lucky Negroes, these people talking about Black Power? It must be a Communist plot." The critics responded as though Carmichael created Black Power. He did not. He was merely born black. And he did not create power.

In fairness to white Americans, it should be noted that Black Power also scared many black people. In 1966 and 1967 most black leaders admitted that, while they could understand Money Power, White Power, and other kinds of power, they could not grasp the significance of Black Power. By 1970, however, black and nonblack leaders had come to realize that the essential features of institutionalized power center on group consensus about who shall exercise it, how it will be used, and to what purpose. To grasp the significance of Black Power, we need only to examine the scope and magnitude of White Power:

White Power is the boards of directors of the largest corporations and businesses, which influence the rate of national economic growth, the rise and fall of the stock market, and the number and kinds of jobs available.

White Power is professional associations, which through their publications, seminars, and advertisements influence public opinion.

[6] Whitney M. Young, Jr., *To Be Equal* (New York, McGraw-Hill Book Company, 1964), 67–68.

[7] Stokely Carmichael and Charles V. Hamilton, *Black Power: The Politics of Liberation* (New York, Random House, Inc., 1967).

White Power is boards of trustees of colleges and universities, which establish the policies of higher education and hire and fire administrators, faculty, and staff.

White Power is boards of education of public and private schools, which determine the quality of elementary and secondary education, as well as desegregation programs (often involving busing blacks to white schools and closing black schools).

White Power is the military complex, which implements the policies established by the National Security Council and the Defense Department. Such activities include recruiting and training blacks to defend other peoples' freedom throughout the world and fight urban rioters seeking freedom at home.

White Power is the executive branch of the federal government, which often takes the initiative in matters of legislation and federal spending.

White Power is local governments, which continue to be insensitive to the needs of the poor.

White Power is the technological fraternity, which can build nuclear weapons that can exterminate all forms of life but lacks the will to eradicate institutional racism.

Finally, White Power is the ability to write an analysis of urban riots, conclude that America is a white racist society, and tell black Americans to "Cool it—don't be so hostile."

Power is neither good nor bad. Power is neutral. The people who wield the power are good and bad. To say this is to acknowledge that there are both good and bad white Americans in positions of power. There are concerned, sensitive white people in power positions. Unfortunately, they are too few in number.

Black Pride

Black Pride is black people redefining themselves, and only they can do it. It is discovering and reclaiming their history in order to create a sense of black community and togetherness. For many, this process begins with accepting the term *black* and rejecting the term *Negro* because the latter term was given to them by white Americans. Not all Negroes find terminology particularly important, but there is almost total consensus on the need to learn black history. Through black history they find that

We are Estevanico, an African with the Spanish explorers, who explored the Arizona and New Mexico territories in 1538.

We are Phillis Wheatley, slave, who in the 1760's began writing poetry that was read throughout the world.

We are Jean Point du Sable, a Negro trader who founded Chicago.

We are Peter Salem, distinguished soldier of the battles of Lexington, Concord, and Bunker Hill.

We are five thousand slaves and free blacks who served in the Continental Army and Navy between 1776 and 1781.

We are the Philadelphia blacks, forced out of the white church in 1787 and told to form our own church.

We are black abolitionists Frederick Douglass and Sojourner Truth, and rebel slaves Denmark Vessey, Gabriel Prosser, and Nat Turner.

We are the black scout George W. Bush, who led white settlers into the Oregon Territory in 1844.

We are Norbert Rillieux, who in 1846 invented the vacuum pan, which revolutionized the sugar-refining industry.

We are Lewis Temple of Massachusetts who invented the toggle harpon in 1848.

We are James Beckwourth, born a slave, who discovered an important pass through the Sierra Nevada in 1850.

We are John M. Langston of Ohio, in 1855 the first black elected to a political office in America.

We are thirteen of the fourteen jockeys to ride in the first Kentucky Derby in 1875.

We are Jan Matzeliger who in 1883 invented the first machine that manufactured an entire shoe.

We are Dr. Daniel Hale Williams, who in 1893 was the first to perform a successful open-heart operation.

We are Matthew Henson, who accompanied Commander Robert E. Peary on his North Pole expedition in 1909.

We are Garrett A. Morgan, who in 1923 invented the automatic traffic light.

We are Marian Anderson, who, when denied a Washington auditorium in 1939, sang before seventy-five thousand people at the Lincoln Memorial.

We are Dr. Charles Drew, who in 1941 developed the blood transfusion process—and who died because a white hospital refused to give him a transfusion.

We are Dorie Miller, first American hero of World War II, who shot down four Japanese planes at Pearl Harbor in 1941.

We are Martin Luther King, Jr., Malcolm X, Whitney Young, Jr., and many others. Yes, we are beautiful people. How tragic it is that, after more than four hundred years, few whites know us.

President Nixon's 1972 visit to Communist China has brought about ironic changes in America's reading habits. It is likely that within the next few years most Americans will be better acquainted with the culture of the people of Communist China than with the culture of black Americans.

Black Power is what Stokely Carmichael referred to as "political modernization." This process includes (1) questioning old values and institutions of black society, (2) searching for new forms of political structure to solve political and economic problems, and (3) broadening the base of political participation to include more black people in the decision-making processes.

In 1972 there were 2,200 black elected officials in America, compared with 1,860 in 1971. However, the increase merely resulted in blacks comprising 0.3 per cent of all elected officials in America. The percentage of blacks holding positions of power in other formal situations was also small. It is powerlessness, not power, that characterizes blacks.

In an attempt to increase their political unity and power, 4,200 black delegates, alternates, and observers convened for the first national black political convention at Gary, Indiana, on March 10, 1972. Blacks of various political affiliations—Democratic, Republican, and independent—met for three days under the leadership of the mayor of Gary, Richard G. Hatcher; United States Representative Charles C. Diggs, Jr., of Detroit; and poet Imamu Amiri Baraka (LeRoi Jones). Many writers compare this convention to the historic Niagara Movement in 1909, out of which grew the NAACP.

For some blacks, Black Power is rejection of the goal of assimilation into white middle-class America because the values of that class are believed to be antiblack. They believe that white middle-class citizens tend to want good government for themselves and segregated schools for their children. According to the black separatists, these whites are the same salaried workers who steal into black communities early in the morning and rush out in the evening, taking the money out of black communities into the white suburbs. They are the pawnbrokers of racism. When they are not exploiting black people in the ghetto, they are fighting off the handful of affluent blacks who want to move into the suburbs.

To most blacks, Black Power means helping the black masses solve their problems. Helping individual blacks solve their problems does little to alleviate the problems of the masses. America has a long history of a few token blacks who have "made it" out of their deprivations. The ultimate goal of Black Power is the full participation of blacks in decisions affecting their lives. This does not mean simply putting blacks in office. Black visibility is not ipso facto equated with Black Power. Rather, Black Power becomes a reality when *responsible* black people are placed in positions of authority. To accomplish this end, some blacks believe that they must become militant and even violent. Black Africans had to fight white Africans to gain their *uhuru* ("freedom"). Most black Americans want to gain their uhuru without fighting white Americans, but each day that the masses of blacks are denied equality of opportunity, the potential for violence grows.

To date only small numbers of blacks have engaged in rioting and other aggressive actions directed at white Americans. Their restraint has puzzled many social scientists. The amazing fact, they conclude, is that there have been so few acts of black aggression. Perhaps the black quest for freedom has been basically nonviolent because blacks have learned to be more humane than whites. Or perhaps blacks realize that whites could exterminate them if a war broke out between the two groups. It should be clear from the review of black history that blacks, too, are Americans, and they should have the opportunity to share in all activities described as being American.

The black is not alone in his dilemma. Similar analogies can be drawn for other minority groups.

Who Will Free Us Now?

Who will be the modern abolitionists? Who will free the blacks, Indians, Mexican-Americans, Puerto Ricans, and members of other minorities? An abolitionist is one who favors destroying certain laws, customs, or institutions. To most Americans, an abolitionist is one who favors the elimination of slavery or the remnants of slavery's influence. Seventeenth-, eighteenth-, and nineteenth-century abolitionists generally considered themselves humble men called by God to accomplish social good by freeing the slaves. The slaveholders called them "agitators" because they wanted to destroy what most people considered a natural order.

The work of abolitionists consists chiefly of talk; their primary function is not to make laws or determine policy but to influence public opinion in order to bring about social change. Although the abolition movement was most active in Britain, the United States, and western Europe in the eighteenth and nineteenth centuries, there was considerable abolition sentiment and activity as early as the seventeenth century. It is disheartening to realize that abolitionists have been active for more than three hundred years but that some Americans still are not free.

Out of a sense of moral urgency most early American abolitionists denounced the established laws upholding slavery. They also condemned as bulwarks of evil those institutions which refused to turn their authority against slavery. To some, abolitionists appeared to be wild enthusiasts, agitators, and radicals. To others they were morally correct, sympathetic reformers. But by whatever standard used, these men and women were indeed a minority group: they were opposed by many local governments, newspapers, mobs, and churches.

Showing fantastic inner strength, most abolitionists did not fear institutional reprisals because they believed that their values were set not by institutions but by God. William Ellery Channing, the "Apostle of Unitarianism" and noted social reformer, said of the abolitionists: "They were sufferers for the liberty of thought, speech, and the press; and in maintaining this liberty amidst insult and violence they deserve a place among its most honored defenders. . . . Of such men I do not hesitate to say, that they have rendered to freedom a more essential service, than any body of men among us."[8]

The abolitionists contributed much to the strategies for social change. Some taught *agitation*, others emphasized *pacifism*, and most used tactics of *nonresistance*. Through their prodding they produced a national feeling of guilt about racial oppression. The guilt-stricken conscience continues to be the most powerful weapon against slavery. In another passage Channing said: "There is a tendency in the laying bare of deep-rooted abuse to throw a community into a storm, . . . [but] the progress of society depends on nothing more, than on the exposure of time-sanctioned abuses."[9]

Only when the abolitionists succeeded in winning over large numbers of northerners to the view that slavery was a sin did the Civil War become a moral war. The defeat of the South meant the end of legalized slavery. But the equally important issue, the moral commitment to the rights for the Negro as a human being, suffered a cruel defeat. The Emancipation Proclamation did not put the abolitionists out of work. Black bodies were freed, but their minds remained enslaved.

The modern era of abolitionism has been led by several black Americans, including Martin Luther King, Jr., Bayard Rustin, Ralph Abernathy, Frederick L. Shuttlesworth, Roy Wilkins, Whitney Young, Jr., Jesse Jack-

[8] Quoted in Betty Fladeland, "Who Were the Abolitionists?" *Journal of Negro History*, Vol. 49 (April, 1964), 114.
[9] *Ibid.*, 115.

son, Floyd McKissick, Elijah Muhammed, Malcolm X, Stokely Carmichael, Dick Gregory, and James Meredith. The modern abolitionist
goals were described by Martin Luther King, Jr. with three words: *"all,
now, here."* The primary goals of the new abolitionist movement are equal
education, employment, and housing opportunities. The abolitionists of
early and modern times share the same basic attitudes, desires, determination, and tactics. Both groups are genuine revolutionaries, intent on realizing the goals of racial equality and social justice. Both have tried to coun-
teract the forces of prejudice and to ensure the inherent rights of all men—
life, liberty, and the pursuit of happiness.

The early abolition movement was limited in its approach, relying
mainly on rhetoric and the concept of gradualism. Neither rhetoric nor
gradualism did much to convince slaveholders that it was their duty to free
their slaves. In the 1950's and early 1960's the modern abolition movement
also used a limited approach, relying primarily on the social welfare activities of the National Urban League and the legal tactics of the NAACP.

The revolutionary philosophy of William Lloyd Garrison of the years
before and during the Civil War, and the direct-action approach of SCLC,
CORE, and SNCC in the late 1960's, gave their respective movements
viable alternatives for action. Leaders in both periods had to learn that
nonviolence is never an effective weapon if violence is not an alternative.
When it became clear that blacks would not only peacefully negotiate but
also burn buildings to gain attention, government officials realized the
necessity for resolving conflicts before violence erupted.

Another similarity of the two movements is the active participation
and leadership of ministers. The Reverend Amos Phelps, in an 1834 address to clergymen, said, "Ministers are in an eminent degree, the *hinges*
of public sentiment in respect to all prevailing sins."[10] Many religious
leaders have taken up the challenge to free enslaved people, and a few of
them have sparked local and national changes, inspiring their followers to
move courageously to victory. Through their messages from the pulpit the
public sentiments of communities have been revolutionized. The Kings,
Abernathys, Shuttlesworths, and Jacksons, along with many white members of the clergy, have offset some of the inhumaneness of organized
Christianity.

In 1967, Dr. King summed up what must be done: "We are now faced
with the fact that tomorrow is today. We are confronted with the fierce
urgency of *now.* . . . We still have a choice today: nonviolent coexistence

[10] Harvey Swados, "Freedom Now," *Commentary*, Vol. 36 (November, 1963), 407.

or violent coannihilation. This may well be mankind's last chance to choose between chaos and community."[11] His words, and the urgency of which he wrote, remain true today. In a similar message Milton R. Konvitz wrote:

> The American people—through Congress, through the Supreme Court, through states' civil rights and fair employment practices acts, through executive action affecting the military and civilian population, and through a Civil War that was the bloodiest and costliest war in American history—have rejected the slavery arguments for the inherent inferiority of the Negro race. With the ending of slavery, a hundred years ago, there should have come an end to the incidents and badges of slavery, concretized in racial segregation enforced by state law and custom. For these badges and incidents of slavery are based on an immoral opinion of what human nature is. Now Americans must still teach one another what it means to be a human being. The choice is not between law as a means and education as a means; for the law is itself a teaching device and education is itself an enforcing device. The disagreements are over the ends—the inclusion of the Negro race in the community of citizens and in the communion of human beings. . . .
>
> As the Negro struggles for freedom from dishonor and freedom from indignity, he struggles, too, to free America from dishonor and from indignity. The demand that the Negro makes today is as reasonable as that which Diogenes made of Alexander: "Stand out of my sunshine!"[12]

The work that remains for the modern abolitionist is to teach people to live with and accept their differences. It is imperative that we do not let our fears, rivalries, and conflicting loyalties cause us to lose sight of the common humanity characterizing all people. Human brotherhood underlies the oldest of moralities—the concern of a man for his brothers. Humanitarianism needs no apology. Unless we internalize this concern and act out brotherly acceptance of all men without exception, we will lose our humanity, the chief redeeming force in human history.

The job of the abolitionists in the coming years will continue to be to create a world where all men can live in freedom. Action speaks louder than words, especially if the action is directed toward the welfare, liberty, and freedom for all. The achievement of these goals necessitates a knowl-

[11] Martin Luther King, Jr., *Where Do We Go from Here: Chaos or Community?* (New York, Bantam Books, Inc., 1968).

[12] Milton R. Konvitz, *A Century of Civil Rights* (New York, Columbia University Press, 1961), 271–72.

edge of the injustices that still exist and a willingness to spare no effort to free the "slaves" living in our towns, country, and world. When Malcolm X, Martin Luther King, Jr., Whitney Young, Jr., and other leaders died, minorities throughout America cried, "Who will free us now?"

The answer: We must free ourselves.

Suggested Reading

Abrahamson, Julia. *A Neighborhood Finds Itself.* New York, Harper & Row, 1959.

Aptheker, Herbert. *American Negro Slave Revolts.* New York, International Publishers Co., Inc., 1963.

Baldwin, James. *Nobody Knows My Name.* New York, The Dial Press, Inc., 1961.

Bell, Inge P. *CORE and the Strategy of Nonviolence.* New York, Random House, Inc., 1968.

Bennett, Lerone, Jr. *Before the* Mayflower: *A History of the Negro in America, 1619–1964.* Rev. ed. Baltimore, Penguin Books, Inc., 1966.

Berger, Morroe. *Equality by Statute: The Revolution in Civil Rights.* Rev. ed. Garden City, N.Y., Doubleday & Company, Inc., 1967.

Blalock, Hubert M. *Toward a Theory of Minority-Group Relations.* New York, John Wiley & Sons, Inc., 1967.

Breitman, George. *The Last Year of Malcolm X: The Evolution of a Revolutionary.* New York, Merit, 1967.

Brim, Orville G., and Stanton Wheeler. *Socialization After Childhood: Two Essays.* New York, John Wiley & Sons, Inc., 1966.

Brown, Claude. *Manchild in the Promised Land.* New York, The Macmillan Company, 1965.

Brown, H. Rap. *Die Nigger Die.* New York, The Dial Press, 1969.

Carmichael, Stokely, and Charles V. Hamilton. *Black Power: The Politics of Liberation.* New York, Random House, Inc., 1967.

Chapman, Abraham H. *Black Voices: An Anthology of Afro-American Literature.* New York, The New American Library, Inc., 1968.

Clark, Kenneth B. *Dark Ghetto: Dilemmas of Social Power.* New York, Harper & Row, 1968.

Coombs, O., ed. *We Speak as Liberators: Young Black Poets.* New York, Dodd, Mead, Inc., 1966.

Drake, Thomas E. *Quakers and Slavery in America.* New Haven, Yale University Press, 1950.

Dumond, Dwight L. *Antislavery: The Crusade for Freedom in America*. New York, W. W. Norton & Company, Inc., 1961.

Epps, Archie. *The Speeches of Malcolm X at Harvard*. New York, William Morrow & Co., Inc., 1968.

Essien-Udom, E. U. *Black Nationalism: A Search for an Identity in America*. New York, Dell Publishing Co., Inc., 1967.

Fishel, L. H., and Benjamin Quarles. *The Negro American: A Documentary Story*. Glenview, Ill., Scott, Foresman and Company, 1967.

Grier, William H., and Price M. Cobbs. *Black Rage*. New York, Basic Books, Inc., 1968.

Guthrie, Robert V. *Being Black*. San Francisco, Canfield Press, 1970.

Isaacs, Harold R. *The New World of Negro Americans*. New York, Viking Press, Inc., 1963.

King, Martin Luther, Jr. *Where Do We Go from Here: Chaos or Community?* New York, Bantam Books, Inc., 1968.

Konvitz, Milton R., and Theodore Leskes. *A Century of Civil Rights*. New York, Columbia University Press, 1961.

Lester, Julius. *Look Out, Whitey—Black Power's Gon' Get Your Mama!* New York, Grove Press, Inc., 1968.

Malcolm X. *The Autobiography of Malcolm X*. New York, Grove Press, Inc., 1964.

Miller, Neal E., and John Dollard. *Social Learning and Imitation*. New Haven, Yale University Press, 1941.

Muse, Benjamin. *The American Negro Revolution: From Nonviolence to Black Power*. Bloomington, Indiana University Press, 1967.

Osofsky, Gilbert. *The Burden of Race: A Documentary History of Negro-White Relations in America*. New York, Harper & Row, 1967.

Pease, William, and Jane Pease. *The Anti-Slavery Argument*. New York, The Bobbs-Merrill Co., Inc., 1965.

Quarles, Benjamin. *The Negro in the Making of America*. New York, The Macmillan Company, 1964.

Redding, J. Saunders. *They Came in Chains*. New York, J. B. Lippincott Co., 1950.

St. James, Warren D. *The National Association for the Advancement of Colored People*. Jericho, N.Y., Exposition Press, Inc., 1958.

Schuchter, Arnold. *White Power, Black Freedom: Planning the Future of Urban America*. Boston, Beacon Press, 1968.

Suggested Reading (continued)

Sterling, Dorothy. *Forever Free: The Story of the Emancipation Proclamation.* New York, Doubleday & Company, Inc., 1963.

Ten Broek, Jacobus. *Equal Under Law.* Enl. ed. New York, Collier Books, 1965.

Thomas, John L. *Slavery Attacked: The Abolitionist Crusade.* Englewood Cliffs, N.J., Prentice-Hall, Inc., 1965.

Tuesday Magazine. *Black Heroes in World History: Biographies from Tuesday Magazine.* New York, Grosset & Dunlap, Inc., 1968.

Weinstein, Allen, and Frank O. Gatell, eds. *American Negro Slavery: A Modern Reader.* New York, Oxford University Press, 1968.

Wish, Harvey, ed. *The Negro Since Emancipation.* Englewood Cliffs, N.J., Prentice-Hall, Inc., 1964.

Woodward, C. Vann. *The Strange Career of Jim Crow.* New York, Oxford University Press, 1957.

Young, Whitney M., Jr. *To Be Equal.* New York, McGraw-Hill Book Company, 1964.

CHAPTER 5

An Interview with a Black Teacher

Not long ago a black teacher, a professor at a south-western university, was interviewed by a staff member of a student magazine. Portions of that interview are reproduced below to illustrate how prejudiced attitudes may be formed and changed. Some of the comments are dated now. The riots have diminished, and the Vietnam War is "winding down." Even so, the basic ideas discussed are still relevant to an understanding of black-white relations in America.

Childhood Background

Question: For openers, how did you get to be where you are now?

Answer: My background is not unlike that of many Negroes who are employed in a profession. I grew up in East Chicago, Indiana, in perhaps the largest middle-sized slum in the United States. The only city plan the city fathers had for my neighborhood was to tear it down and rebuild it. As a child, I remember playing in the alleys. I have never again seen rats as big as those in our alleys. In some of our baseball games, we belatedly realized that the guy playing first base wasn't a kid—that's how big the rats were.

Most of my friends and I were juvenile delinquents. I spent as much time in trouble as out, and I certainly wasn't a high achiever in school. Rather, I was a very successful school failure and an equally successful juvenile delinquent. In my peer group the norm for school behavior was failure. It wasn't until I realized that a few teachers really cared about me that I made any serious attempts to become a scholar. I will never forget the English teacher who, after trying to persuade me to study and adjust to an academic environment, began to cry. Only then did I decide that if she cared that much about an ornery kid like me I should at least care enough about her to try being a scholar.

But it was my mother who exerted the greatest influence on me. There is a considerable amount of talk about the Negro matriarchy. What most people don't realize is that a strong mother can be just as effective, I believe, as both a mother and a father. Certainly as a child I needed adult males in order to learn male roles, but it was my mother's brainwashing—that is the only way I can describe it—that gave me the idea that I was going to attend college. Her ideal college was the Tuskegee Institute in Alabama.

In elementary school, I wasn't as big as the others, and my mouth would always say things that would get the rest of my body in trouble. So I had to run to survive. I became the fastest sprinter in my elementary and secondary schools, and because my high school track coach was a graduate of Michigan State University, he persuaded me to accept a combined scholastic and athletic scholarship to Michigan State. I don't think my mother has ever forgiven me for going to Michigan State. Tuskegee, she said, should have been my school.

Question: Did either of your parents go to college?

Answer: Most of the parents in my neighborhood were grade school dropouts. In fact, even today most black communities have only a second generation of middle-class parents who are high school graduates. My mother went as far as the fourth grade; my father was a bit better educated —he completed the sixth grade.

Question: What was your father's occupation?

Answer: He worked at a variety of semiskilled jobs. In his last job he was a molder in a brickyard. It was backbreaking, lung-destroying work.

Role Models

Question: You were the exception in your environment. What does this mean to the Negroes who couldn't make it out of the ghetto?

Answer: Many white Americans who see a few successful Negroes conclude that they are ample proof that America is a land of equal opportunity. They point to a Ralph Bunche, a Jackie Robinson, or some other prominent black and say, "Look, here's an illustration of the fact that times have changed and things are better." I can't speak for the others, but my personal view has always been that a black usually does not succeed *because of* a greatly expanding opportunity structure but *in spite of* a very constricting opportunity structure. Most of the kids I grew up with are in jail, unemployed, or working in a semiskilled or unskilled occupation. I would guess that, of the one hundred blacks who entered junior high school with me, only fifteen went to college and ten of those graduated from college.

Question: If your parents had only a grade school education, where did your mother get the idea that you were going to college?

Answer: As a child she lived not far from Tuskegee and observed the college students there. Although my mother did not attend college, she vowed that, if she had children, they would attend college. She had no idea what was involved in going to college, but she believed that higher education was one of the best ways out of poverty, especially for Negroes.

Bigotry

Question: How has your college education changed your attitudes, as compared to those of your friends still in the ghetto?

Answer: My post–high school educational experiences have been a major factor in changing my attitudes toward white people. I grew up in a black community. We were very bigoted; we were taught to hate the "honkies" who lived across the tracks. Today when I encounter a black separatist he doesn't shock or puzzle me. I remember identifying vicariously with Joe Lewis, especially when he beat the whites. After the fights we would rush out into the streets and talk about how Joe wiped out the white fighters. My favorite pastime was to go across the tracks and beat up on white kids (of course, they also came across the tracks and beat us up). I grew up believing that there was nothing wrong with hating white people. In addition, I developed a superiority complex. I believed that blacks were not only as good as whites but better. Some of us proved it in athletic competition. When I got to high school, I also proved my superiority in the classroom: I was a member of the National Honor Society. My achievements in sports and in the classroom contributed to my white hate and black pride. Yes, I was a black bigot.

When I went to Michigan State, I was randomly assigned a white roommate. George lived in Dearborn, Michigan. There were no Negroes

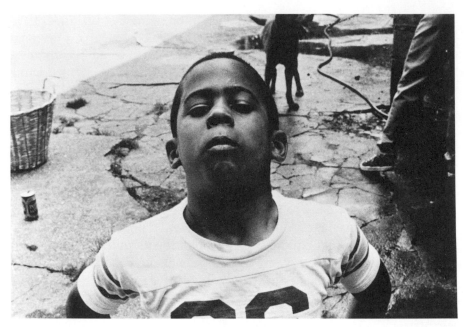

in Dearborn. George and I were excellent counterparts: he wanted to avoid contact with blacks, and I wanted to avoid contact with whites. There we were, a black bigot and a white bigot, rooming together. We spent the first two weeks sleeping in the lounge or the bathroom, trying to avoid each other. Finally we both realized that our behavior was ridiculous—paying for a room and not sleeping in it. So we decided to try living together. When we started rooming together and talking, I learned more about human relations and race relations than I learned in any college course I've ever taken. We had bull sessions that lasted for hours, sometimes from eleven at night until three or four o'clock in the morning. Other guys, black and white, would join us, throwing out questions which probably sounded very ignorant to the students enrolled in anthropology and sociology courses. For example, George asked me, "Do Negroes eat the same foods that whites eat? Is it true that you people are sexually more potent than white people?" We raised many questions and exploded many myths. In essence, we learned that people in other racial groups are human and that all groups are more alike than they are different. As a result of those bull sessions my attitude toward whites changed. In fact, George ultimately became my son's godfather.

   He never told his parents that I was his roommate. He couldn't: he didn't know how to tell them that he was rooming with a Negro. One day his parents made a surprise visit. His father walked into the room, and I was making my bed. "Say, boy," his father said (I guess he thought I was being paid to clean the room), "is this George's room?" I said, "Yes, sir, it is." "Would you tell him that his father is here?" he asked, as he flipped me a quarter. When I returned with George and was introduced as his room-mate, his father stood there petrified. It was beautiful! However, his parents did not change their basic attitude toward Negroes; they merely refenced their prejudices to *exclude me*—I was a "good" Negro. Obviously I was good. Their son was living with me.

Black Nationalism

Question: In considering the feelings of many of the people still in East Chicago—black nationalists, rioters, people who are very unhappy and frustrated— can you tell us what you know of their feelings? What they're based upon? And whether or not you agree with them?

Answer: To understand black nationalism, one has to understand thwarted aspirations. The black child is confronted with some very incon-sistent life situations. He is told that this is the land of the free, where there is equal opportunity for all citizens; but all around him he sees cases of chronic unemployment and underemployment. Democracy—or at least the American dream—appears to be a big lie for most blacks, something not really meant for them. As a result of broken dreams, hostility is gen-erated against "the Man." Adjusting to severely limited opportunity struc-tures, some blacks have decided that there is no reason to compete for the kinds of success symbols the dominant whites have. "Let's set up a new op-portunity structure where we will have only black role models to emulate," disgruntled blacks say. And it seems to make sense. If, for example, I take away white competitors, the probability of my success is much greater.

I understand this kind of black anger. I remember my years of frus-tration. I also understand how psychologically emasculated males feel when they are not allowed to role-play as masculine males in front of females. Many black males are embarrassed by white police officers, white social workers, and other representatives of the "system," and they become very bitter. In 1967, I saw emasculated black males in Detroit participate in an activity in which they could feel good about doing something: they were rioting. Some rioters said that they felt like men for the first time. They were able to show people watching them that they could break win-dows and steal as well as any other male. Before the rioting, most of these men had begged for a chance to prove their manhood through well-paying jobs.

For many Negroes black nationalism does indeed offer a way out. Contrary to popular view, there are positive aspects of black nationalism that do not involve physical aggression. The black-pride aspect has the same effect as psychotherapy. Black nationalism changes a black individual's conception of himself: Black is beautiful. It also changes an individual's perception of his relation to other people who are not like him: Black is better! These psychological changes have done much to improve the self-image of low-income blacks in particular. Black Muslims, for example, have been able to stop addicts from taking drugs, alcoholics from taking another drink, and men from deserting their wives and children.

Of course, there are negative aspects of nationalistic organizations. Black separatists want their own communities completely apart from white communities. I reject this idea because I believe that the pluralistic society is the best kind of society to live in. But, then, I am the product of public school indoctrination that held up racial cooperation as the most desirable goal. Perhaps I continue to feel this way in order to justify my move to the Southwest.

Question: You mentioned white social workers and police officers. Does their attitude offend you?

Answer: Not all of them are inhumane, but too many agency workers offer benevolent help which borders on the form of care once given to slaves on plantations. Historically, social workers have doled out favors to the poor. If we visited most welfare offices, we would see the ingratiating behavior poor people (both nonwhites and whites) engage in to receive assistance. First, there is usually a long period of waiting just to talk to someone to see whether he or she will let you fill out an application for assistance. During the interview there are many embarrassing questions to answer. Some of these questions are very personal. Women are often asked when they last slept with a man and whether they are sure they don't have any boyfriends. A large percentage of the caseworkers behave as though they are taking the money out of their own pockets to give to the applicants and that the applicants should be grateful to them. I firmly believe that some social workers have God complexes; they capriciously control the lives of *their* creatures, welfare recipients. The so-called War on Poverty was begun to change the ways social workers interact with their clients. To date there has been much rhetoric but few changes. The police departments have their share of inhumane people, too. But what agency doesn't? Even the church.

Question: Have recent administration attempts to improve the lot of the Negro been of significant help?

Answer: Initially the War on Poverty raised the aspirations of the poor without providing corresponding opportunities for achievement. Such frustration is psychologically devastating. Indeed, this kind of short-sightedness triggers community unrest. The War on Poverty has been more successful in employing previously underemployed middle-class Negroes than in finding jobs for the unemployed black masses. In fact, none of our governmental programs have done an adequate job of combating poverty.

The Views of Others

Question: What is the reaction of your friends when you visit your old neighborhood in East Chicago?

Answer: There is always a testing period. Because I walk around in the trappings of the white middle class, some of my friends wonder if I am a black Anglo-Saxon. With the exception of color, I look like, sound like, and smell like my white peers.

Question: Is your success held against you by your black friends?

Answer: No, most of my friends realize that my success—if that is what it can be called—has come from years of struggle. I wasn't always middle-income. I have worked at a number of menial jobs as well as a number of professional jobs. I have also participated in several civil rights activities. So my friends know that, even though I have the outward trappings of the white establishment, in many ways I am still the angry young black man they knew in East Chicago. I still "tell it like it is" and have not forgotten the people who have not made it out of the slums. I will always feel for them. I emphasize *feel for* because I can't *feel like* them anymore. I don't wake up in the morning wondering what, if anything, I am going to have to eat. So I no longer have that kind of gut-level identification with them; but I do remember what it was like, and I try to help others to succeed. On the other hand, I don't delude myself into thinking that I am a leader in the black community. I don't have my fingers on the pulse of the black community—not the angry black community, at least. We middle-class blacks have become fat cats. We are too concerned about a second car, a new suit, the menu at our favorite restaurant. Thus, even though I try to identify closely with the black masses, I know I have lost touch with a great amount of suffering in black communities.

Question: What about people like Jackie Robinson, Bill Cosby, Sammy Davis, Jr., the people who've made it big?

Answer: Jackie Robinson and the others are really the exceptionally talented people, and to expect to make it like them is not even the dream of many white youths. Few teachers realize the resentment they generate in young black minds when they use the Jackie Robinson types as role models. There is another aspect of the Jackie Robinson story. How long did it take him to make it? He had to prove that he was a super black in both ability and temperament before he was promoted to the major leagues. His success highlights the fact that most blacks have to be exceptional to make it in the white man's world and that the common, ordinary black person will have a difficult time merely surviving in the little leagues of life.

Black History

Question: If there is resentment against the Negro who has made it big in the white man's world, who are the Negroes respected by the lower classes?

Answer: There are certain characteristics of successful Negroes with which the black masses identify. For example, they identify with Jackie Robinson's baseball ability; they would like to have Wilt Chamberlain's money. But most blacks realize that they do not have Jackie's or Wilt's talents. Who, then, can they imitate? The list of heroes includes people who come back into the community and live. I caution my white students at the university not to minimize the effectiveness of a Stokely Carmichael or an Eldridge Cleaver. Nor should they minimize the effectiveness of any black demagogue, because these are the people spending time in the black communities talking about the concerns of black people.

Most middle-class blacks are spending very little time in black communities. They are spending most of their time in white communities, working for whites. Poor people in the black communities would like to have many of the luxuries enjoyed by middle-class people, but they do not expect to achieve them. For this reason the poor are more likely to identify with the demagogues and the hustlers. Low-income youths, for example, look around and see the hustlers—the pimps, the prostitutes, the numbers men—and they say, "I can make it like these people."

Question: One often thinks that there is more to Negro history than we know about, and there have been accusations of slanted histories in the schools. What's the word?

Answer: Until recently, the major textbook publishers had two sets of texts—one set for the more liberal northern schools and another set for the conservative southern schools. Both sets of books had sins of omission; both sets of texts tended to omit the positive contributions blacks and other minorities have made to this country. Students could always read about George Washington Carver and Booker T. Washington, but missing was mention of other Negroes who participated in some of the earlier battles for freedom or the famous black inventors or the black statesmen. We simply were not given an opportunity as a nation to learn about the achievements of Negroes. A black child could not develop a positive image of himself from his school texts.

Question: Doesn't the Black Muslim movement stress Negro history?

Answer: The Black Muslims are better acquainted with black history than any other group I know. They offer courses which stress the achievements of blacks in America and Africa. Well-educated Black Muslims can cite historical facts that will cause black children to feel proud of their heritage. As I said earlier, until recently most black children were not given this kind of history.

Priorities and Commitment

Question: What do you think is going to happen? The riots are getting worse. White people are getting worried and a little scared, and the combination isn't a good one.

Answer: I don't have a very positive prognosis for our cities in the next few years. I see more violence, more polarization of black-white attitudes. I hope that I am wrong in my prognosis. This is our moment of truth as a nation. Either whites are going to live with us as equal citizens, or they're going to exterminate us. We must be free. All people should be free.

Question: The war in Vietnam is consuming a great deal of our budget now. If this money were spent domestically, would it be possible to offer a concentrated program of Negro education, Negro opportunity, expanded employment that might solve our racial problems, or is there a more basic white and black problem that would hinder such an effort?

Answer: When I think about the war in Vietnam, I see more than dollars being wasted; I see wasted lives. Furthermore, I see a disproportionate number of black lives being wasted. To me, this is a far greater tragedy than the money being spent. We can print new money, but we can't bring back the dead. It seems a paradox that black GI's are considered equal in times of national emergency, especially in the opportunity to die, but are not equal when the emergency ends. If the war ended, you ask, could the money be diverted to provide more opportunities for equal rights? Yes! I also say this: We should not wait until the war ends to do something about the plight of minorities. I don't want to gamble on war funds, because after earlier wars government officials did not divert war funds to finding solutions to domestic problems. I would rather redirect the money being spent on foreign aid, supporting puppet governments. Minorities in America have the same needs as people receiving foreign aid. Who will feed our starving children or rebuild our dilapidated buildings or teach our illiterate children? After each war our enemies are forgiven, and they are allowed to move into neighborhoods, jobs, and schools which deny admission to blacks.

Question: If we had that money, what would be the best way to spend it? Education would probably top the list, but what about such situations as housing?

Answer: Yes, education would be at the top of my list of priorities. In addition, I would do something about expanding the job market and job retraining for poor people. During World War II, for instance, we took hundreds of thousands of illiterates and taught them to read and write so that they would be better soldiers. We were able to teach them to kill and to make machines that kill, and we won the war. A nation with this kind of ingenuity and initiative can also have a nationally coordinated program to abate its domestic problems.

As far as open occupancy in housing is concerned, some people say that this is taking rights away from the white majority and giving them to the nonwhite minorities. I only have one response to this complaint: Most nonwhites have been denied an opportunity to live where they desire in this country. But there is another side of the coin, too. Segregated housing means that a substantial number of whites are involuntarily denied the opportunity to live with nonwhites. Open occupancy doesn't mean that we will automatically eradicate prejudice. After living near blacks, for example, some whites will become positive that they do not like them. It is to be hoped that, after living in the same neighborhood, most people—as I did at Michigan State—will discover that racial groups are more alike than different.

Question: You've talked about the Negro who is willing to give up his position, even his life, for the cause. You are in the best of both worlds. Would you be willing to give up what you have attained to further the movement toward Negro rights?

Answer: I am willing to sacrifice my life for freedom. Even so, I have recurring questions. Am I most effective here at this university? Or should I be teaching in a black university? A major reason that I am not in a black university is because I believe that America has a *white* problem. Blacks are in a minority and cannot abate white racism (nor can the whites abate black racism). Neighborhoods, churches, schools, and jobs will not become integrated until the white society decides to straighten up and fly right. Therefore, I justify being at this university in this manner: I am able to teach white students who someday will shape the policies of industries, pass community ordinances, and take other actions that I hope will improve the living conditions of all minority groups. Even if I gave up my position here, there still would be a need for blacks to join this faculty and try to teach compassion and equality to whites. At times this becomes an extremely heavy social cross to carry.

Suggested Reading

Baldwin, James. *Nobody Knows My Name*. New York, The Dial Press, Inc., 1961.

Brooks, Gwendolyn. *Bronzeville Boys and Girls*. New York, Harper & Bros., 1956.

Brown, Claude. *Manchild in the Promised Land*. New York, The Macmillan Company, 1965.

Brown, H. Rap. *Die Nigger Die*. New York, The Dial Press, 1969.

Carmichael, Stokely, and Charles V. Hamilton. *Black Power: The Politics of Liberation*. New York, Random House, Inc., 1967.

Cleaver, Eldridge. *Soul on Ice*. New York, McGraw-Hill Book Company, 1968.

Cruse, Harold. *The Crisis of the Negro Intellectual*. New York, William Morrow and Company, Inc., 1967.

Suggested Reading (continued)

Cullen, Countee. *On These I Stand: An Anthology of the Best Poems of Countee Cullen.* New York, Harper & Row, 1947.

Du Bois, W. E. B. *Dusk of Dawn: An Essay Toward an Autobiography of a Race.* New York, Harcourt, Brace & World, 1940.

Ellison, Ralph. *Invisible Man.* New York, Random House, Inc., 1952.

Frazier, E. Franklin. *Black Bourgeoisie.* Glencoe, Ill., The Free Press, 1957.

Gregory, Dick. *Nigger.* New York, Pocket Books, Inc., 1965.

Grier, William H., and Price M. Cobbs. *Black Rage.* New York, Basic Books, Inc., 1968.

Hansberry, Lorraine. *A Raisin in the Sun.* New York, New American Library of World Literature, Inc., 1966.

Hare, Nathan. *The Black Anglo-Saxons.* New York, Collier, 1970.

Hughes, Langston. *The Best of Simple.* New York, Hill and Wang, Inc., 1961.

Joseph, Stephen M., ed. *The Me Nobody Knows: Children's Voices from the Ghetto.* New York, Avon Books, 1969.

Jones, Leroi. *Home: Social Essays.* New York, William Morrow and Co., 1966.

Kelley, William M. *A Drop of Patience.* New York, Doubleday and Co., 1965.

King, Martin Luther, Jr. *Where Do We Go from Here: Chaos or Community?* New York, Bantam Books, Inc., 1968.

Lester, Julius. *Look Out, Whitey—Black Power's Gon' Get Your Mama!* New York, Grove Press, Inc., 1968.

Malcolm X. *The Autobiography of Malcolm X.* New York, Grove Press, Inc., 1964.

Moody, Anne. *Coming of Age in Mississippi: An Autobiography.* New York, The Dial Press, Inc., 1968.

Rowan, Carl T. *South of Freedom.* New York, Alfred A. Knopf, 1952.

Walker, Margaret A. *For My People.* New Haven, Yale University Press, 1942.

Williams, John A. *The Man Who Cried I Am.* Boston, Little, Brown and Co., 1967.

Wright, Richard. *Native Son.* New York, Harper & Brothers, 1940.

Young, Whitney M., Jr. *To Be Equal.* New York, McGraw-Hill Book Company, 1964.

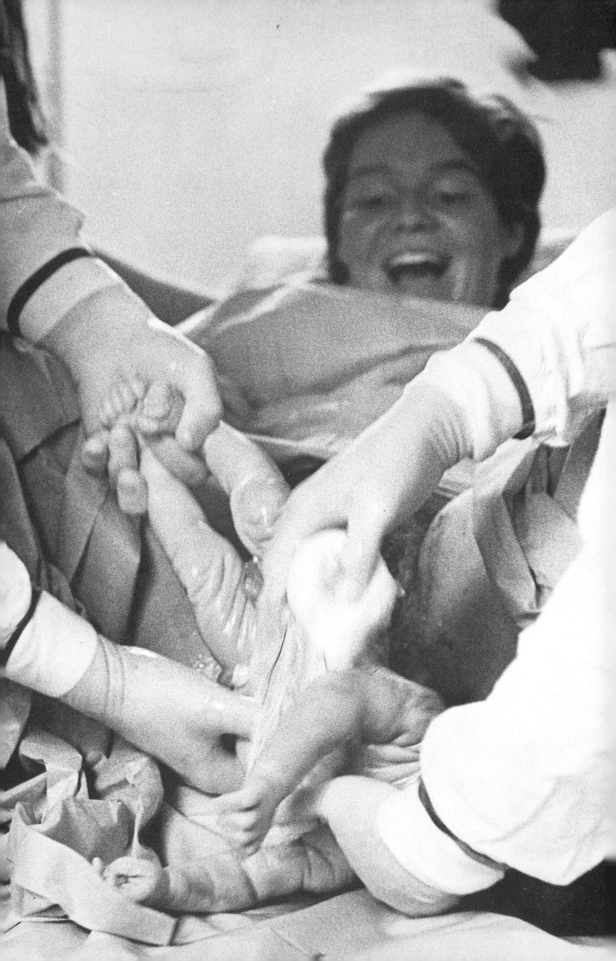

CHAPTER 6

Attitudes and Behavior That Kill

In 1970, at a forum sponsored by the Southwest Intergroup Relations Council in Austin, Texas, Theodore Freedman stated that (1) over one-third of the United States population is anti-Semitic and (2) the majority of the other two-thirds is apathetic toward Jews. Freedman's conclusions were supported by several studies, including one conducted by the Survey Research Center of the University of California.

The declining support for overt anti-Semitic discrimination and the continuing acceptance of anti-Semitic beliefs is a pattern found in most cities throughout America. This is true even in black neighborhoods where Jews have been ardent civil rights supporters. Equally disturbing are the findings of the Southwest Intergroup Relations Council that the religiously devout are on the average more bigoted, more authoritarian, and more antihumanitarian than the less devout. Many religiously devout Protestants and Catholics exhibit prejudice against Jews.

With a population of over six million persons, Jews are the second-largest minority group in America. Only the blacks, with a population of twenty-two million, are more numerous. Even though many people harbor negative attitudes toward Jews, few have had intimate contact with them. As will be shown in this chapter, negative attitudes can set in motion behavior that will socially or physically kill the objects of these attitudes.

Attitudes

A *social attitude* is a degree of readiness to behave in a given manner toward an object or situation.[1] Much

---

[1] William B. Ragan and George Henderson, *Foundations of American Education* (New York, Harper & Row, 1970), 236.

Attitudes could be added to this definition to make it more scientifically precise, but it is adequate for the field of human relations. Let us examine the implications of this definition.

1. "A *social attitude* is a degree of readiness . . . ." This is a vague statement. However, if we think of it as (a) an individual's ability to perceive certain objects and situations and (b) his quickness to respond, his motivation to respond, and his experience in responding, then "degree of readiness" can stand the test of further scrutiny. An example of this process is a white congregation that interviews a black minister and then experiences anxieties growing out of the thought of employing a nonwhite as its pastor.

2. "A *social attitude* is a degree of readiness to behave in a given manner . . . ." It should be made clear at the outset that an attitude is not an overt response. It is a response, to be sure, but an implicit or mental one. Therefore, an attitude is a readiness to act but is not an act itself. The crucial human relations question that arises here, then, is, Under what conditions does an attitude elicit overt expression?

Even the most general answer must include at least two variables. First, an attitude is likely to result in overt expression in direct proportion to rewards and in inverse proportion to punishments. We cannot, however, always predict an individual's behavior from his known attitudes, nor can we always predict behavior on the basis of whether it will be rewarded or punished. For example, even though a white woman is aware that her parents are segregationists, she may date a black man. It is also true that a weakly held attitude will produce action if the social gratifications for doing so are great enough. Consequently, many initially dubious employers have become outstanding equal-opportunity employers because of monies received through federal contracts requiring the hiring of minorities rather than because of an initial commitment to equal opportunities for minorities.

A second condition in which an attitude is likely to result in overt behavior has already been described: a degree of readiness. Some individuals will act out their attitudes no matter how negative the reactions to their behavior. These individuals become martyrs to various causes, such as antiwar and women's liberation movements. On the other hand, there are individuals who cannot—under any circumstances—muster sufficient readiness to act out their attitudes. Often we hear people say, "I know I should, but I can't." Technically, the degree of readiness must rise and resistance must lower to a crucial point before an attitude will manifest itself in action. Specifically, we are speaking in terms of thresholds at which the degree of readiness (perception, motives, and response) must be sufficiently developed and the situation must be sufficiently rewarding or permissive for at least part of the attitude to result in overt behavior. Millions of "sinners," for example, have become Christians following near-death experiences.

It is important to realize that "overt behavior" can mean anything from making marks on an attitude questionnaire to dying for a cause. It is generally assumed in psychological experiments that, when most variables in a situation are held constant, the degree of action taken toward an object is a function of *motivation*, the desire to achieve a goal. Although this assumption may be correct in most instances, it must be remembered that there is more to the degree of readiness than motivation; there is also a *response system*, the means used to achieve the goal. For example, two individuals, X and Y, may be equally well motivated to succeed in school, but the response of X may be to go to the library to study, while Y may try to obtain the notes of former students who achieved A's in the courses in which he is presently enrolled. In a similar manner, two women may be equally motivated for international peace, but the behavior of one involves only a verbal response whereas the other joins picket lines, writes letters to legislators, and votes for peace candidates. Thus there are talkers, doers, and talkers who are doers.

3. "A *social attitude* is a degree of readiness to behave in a given manner toward an object or situation." Here "object" and "situation" are used in the broadest terms. Object refers not only to individuals but also to their beliefs. Within this definition any group of people or their behavior is considered socially significant and may become embodied in social attitudes. A social attitude, then, is a degree of readiness to behave in a given manner toward some perceived aspect of our environment. Whether this readiness will result in overt behavior is determined by certain conditions internal and external to the individuals involved. With this basic foundation, let us now turn to the problem of how social attitudes are formed.

We Learn to Hate

The following theories about attitudes are now generally accepted:

    1. Attitudes are learned.

    2. Attitudes are learned mainly from other people.

3. Attitudes are learned mainly from other people who have high or low prestige for us.

4. Once attitudes have been learned, they are reinforced.

The first three theories have to do with perception of social objects and the development of motivational and response systems appropriate for our perceptions. The fourth theory suggests that motives not directly related to a particular social object may, however, be used to perpetuate an attitude toward it. These theories should become clearer with the following illustrations.

1. *Attitudes are learned*. Attitudes are learned; they are not innate. The mother of a gentile child, Tina, who exhibited prejudice against Jewish children, said, "Tina has always played with gentile children. She never plays with Jewish children; I didn't have to teach her that." The assumption here seems to be that powerfully held attitudes, such as religious prejudices, must be part of the individual's physical being. The mother apparently believed that she did not have to teach her daughter to discriminate against Jews. But there is much evidence to the contrary.

Anti-Christian and anti-Jewish attitudes have been detected in children as young as three years old.[2] However, studies have shown that even these attitudes are not very well developed until age ten or eleven in most children. Young children begin to use hate words before they fully understand the connotations. Social scientists have documented thousands of cases illustrating that attitudes are learned. The mother quoted earlier, for example, believed that Tina knew instinctively not to associate with Jews ("I didn't have to teach her that"). But her third-grade son suggested other reasons for the attitude: "Mother told me not to play with them [Jewish children] because they are different. . . . I had a Jewish friend in school. I liked him, but Mother didn't want me to play with him." The mother had taught her children to reject Jews.

The learning of attitudes is also seen when adults change their commitments as they move into situations in which new attitudes are more functional, for example, when they join a church or move into a new neighborhood. Thus attitudes are part of a wide range of adjustment devices which every human being acquires. Attitudes of acceptance must be learned in much the same manner that we learn to reject people.

[2] Bruno Lasker, *Race Attitudes in Children* (New York, Holt), 1929.

It is sad that most American children are taught to hate rather than to love those who are culturally different.

Researchers who compare children's and parents' versions of attitudes note that as children grow older they tend to forget that they were instructed in attitudes by their parents. By about the age of ten most children regard their racial attitudes as their own. Seldom do they recall having been coached by their parents. *Attitude amnesia* develops, and elaborate rationalizations are presented to account for the learned attitudes, with the result that most people believe that they came by their attitudes "naturally."

2. *Attitudes are learned mainly from other people.* We learn most of our attitudes from other people. As ego-deflating as it may be to accept, the fact is that few of us invent our attitudes. An attitude is a complex perceptual invention, and most of us are not perceptual inventors. Consider, for example, a seemingly simple perception: "That man is called a Puerto Rican, and, therefore, he is inferior to me." Such a straightforward attitude as this—including the man and his label—requires considerable rationalizing. Individuals who perceive Puerto Ricans as inferior have to think beyond individual Puerto Ricans, who may be adequate by every objective standard, in order to define the group "Puerto Ricans" as inferior.

The superiority or inferiority of a group (as contrasted to that of an individual) is not obvious; not many casual observers can perceive significant group differences. To illustrate: The existence of war or of nationality as a social institution is by no means obvious. Most men simply cannot think of liking or disliking war per se but only of liking or disliking particular wars; nor can they think of accepting or rejecting nationalities per se but only of accepting or rejecting specific nationalities. Before an attitude can be formed about an object, something must be perceived as its characteristic. Since most of us are not very adept at inventing new ways (or even old ways) of perceiving our world, there seems to be a sound basis for believing that attitudes, like most things, are invented by only a few and used by many.

There are other reasons for assuming that attitudes are learned largely from other people. Autobiographies and case histories illustrate that an individual's attitudes tend to be those of his relatives, sex group, peers, office mates, school group, region, religion, and nationality.[3] Certainly, we develop some attitudes independently of our friends, but our friends are the foremost determinants of most of our social attitudes. The

3 Lloyd Warner et al., *Social Class in America* (Chicago, Science Research Associates, Inc., 1949).

tendency of individuals to hold the same attitudes as the people with whom they interact is so consistent as to make the independent acquisition of most attitudes seem unlikely. This does not necessarily mean that an individual learns his attitudes only from the individuals or groups with whom he lives.

No doubt some readers will ask, "Is it true that we hold the same attitudes as those with whom we live simply because we are all exposed to similar conditions?" In other words, do we learn the same attitudes independently simply because we all have the same experiences? Of course not. While all of us may look at the same phenomenon, we depend on a few "important" people to tell us what we have seen. Thus stereotyped attitudes toward various ethnic groups are found among people who have had no contact with them. Further, it has been found that initial attempts to change negative social attitudes through personal experience are not very successful.

The unlikelihood that individuals will invent attitudes for themselves, the correlation of their attitudes with those of the people with whom they live, and the low level of correlation between attitude and personal experiences—all of these factors point to the conclusion that attitudes are learned from other people. But attitudes are not learned from just any people.

3. *Attitudes are learned mainly from people who have high or low prestige.* Investigators have been testing this hypothesis for years. In a typical experiment subjects respond to one or more attitude scales. Then they are told the attitudes of 98 per cent of the nation's leading educators, of certain authorities, or of the majority of their own reference group on the same scales. Later they are retested with equivalent tests. In most cases the retest scores move significantly in the direction of the educators, authorities, and peers. We can only conclude that we tend to match our attitudes with persons or groups important to us who have high prestige.[4] There are, of course, exceptions. Some individuals will not shift their attitudes to match those of an admired person if the attitude attributed to the latter is diametrically opposed to theirs. There is, nevertheless, a strong tendency for us to reinterpret our models' statements in line with our own views rather than admit that the models are wrong. "The press distorted his views," a son replied when asked about a direct quote attributed to his father, whom he worshiped.

The second part of the hypothesis is that we tend to adopt attitudes

---

[4] Leon Festinger, "Informed Social Communication," *Psychological Review*, Vol. 57 (September, 1950), 273.

"If they had crowned George Washington king, none of this would be happening now."

Artist: Henry Martin. Copyright 1971 Saturday Review, Inc.

opposite to those of persons with low prestige. Such attitudes are likely to be held for one of two reasons: (a) certain people have low prestige because they have rejected us and we adopt attitudes opposite to theirs as a means of rejecting them in turn or (b) certain people are poor role models for us, and thus we elect not to imitate them.

4. *Once attitudes have been learned, they are reinforced.* If we assume that the first three theories are correct, the initial formation of attitudes is the result of a desire to be like individuals whom we hold in high esteem. Once formed, however, the attitude may serve various other motives, such as economic or nationalistic ones. Thus, although most blacks in a community may learn negative attitudes toward whites from their community leaders, the attitudes of only a few blacks center on economic motives. On the other hand, successful white businessmen, for example, may initially adopt antiblack attitudes in order to conform to social pressures and may maintain these attitudes in order to exclude black competitors.

The economic motives that reinforce attitudes are relatively obvious. Clearly, in the short run, it is economically advantageous for one group to exclude others from certain classes of work, to deny them adequate legal protection in bargaining for their labors, to keep their aspirations low, or even on occasion to exterminate them. The questions which economic interpretations of social attitudes fail to answer, however, are these: Why are repressive methods used against one minority group but not another? And why are certain attitudes enforced even to the point of national disaster?

How Attitudes Are Formed

There are several ways in which attitudes are formed. If we are aware of these processes, we are better able to alter attitudes. Some popular ideas about how attitudes are formed have been refuted by experiment.

Attitudes are seldom formed by logic. It is very difficult to find circumstances in which attitude change has come about as a result of logical argument or additional information. When students in classroom experiments are confronted with logic or with new information, they do not tend to change their attitudes. For example, students who receive intensive instruction in anthropology do not as a rule abandon their belief in innate racial differences. Those who register changes in attitude because of such information consistently fail to maintain the new attitudes as the prestige of the person presenting the logical arguments or imparting the information decreases. Therefore, not simply *what* is said but also *who* says it is an important variable influencing whether an argument or information will change attitudes.[5]

There is also the general finding that attitudes acquired by logical arguments are not acted out very logically. For example, white students' attitudes toward blacks may become more tolerant during a course in race relations but show very little carry-over into other classes. In fact, many students adopt what they perceive to be the "correct" attitude in order to pass a course but revert to a polar attitude in other classes. Even more to the point is the finding that students can learn to be highly proficient in detecting the propaganda of other nations but show very little transfer of their training to recognize their own nation's propaganda.

Not only is there little evidence that important attitudes are changed by logical-information inputs, but there is even considerable evidence that a great amount of information, particularly on controversial topics, actually hardens or freezes whatever attitude is already in the making. Male chauvinists, for instance, tend to be even more committed to unequal treatment of women after they are confronted with data proving such treatment. Techniques such as an exceedingly emotional religious appeal or a relatively unstructured course in human relations often are more effective than highly structured scientific lectures. Elaborate brotherhood conferences or professional seminars with "experts"—situations in which opposing interests are presented in great detail—tend to produce little shift in attitude but, instead, to add to the confusion about what attitude should be taken. The unqualified assumption that information will improve attitudes in one way or another is based on the questionable assumption that what is true and what is desirable are one and the same.

Important attitudes are seldom influenced by logic because in most cultures, including our own, logic is valued as a *means* but seldom as an *end* of life. The desired end tends to culminate in some visible sign of success, and when the choice is between logic and success, success gen-

---

[5] Ragan and Henderson, *Foundations of American Education*, 238.

erally prevails. This is not to imply that most of us want to appear illogical. On the contrary, most people would like to project an image of being very logical—but not if such an image will cause them to fail to achieve certain goals, especially economic goals. Most people are less powerfully motivated by logic than by certain nonlogical values.

The reader can easily test the power of logic (and information) by following these simple steps: (1) select an individual who is fairly neutral toward you, (2) determine an attitude which he holds with considerable strength but which happens not to be based on logic and fact, (3) objectively and unemotionally try to alter his attitude by pointing out the illogical aspects of it, and (4) observe your effect. This exercise is likely to illustrate that logic and information have little to do with attitude formation. There are, however, at least two special instances in which this may not be the case. Attitudes may be formed by logic and information if the attitude to be formed or changed does not conflict with motives more powerful than the desire to be logical or if the individual in whom the attitude is to be formed or changed is one of those rare persons for whom "having it right" is more important than "having it his way."

The first condition is important if we are trying to develop an attitude for which no powerful counterattitude exists. This might be the case when laws are proposed for a community in which no powerful antiattitudes have been developed, such as new zoning regulations. The second condition is important in several ways. Being logical may be as much a part of an individual's reward system as "having it his way."

Attitudes are seldom formed as a function of intelligence. In this day of loose and careless logic, it has been claimed that people become radicals (or liberals) because they are more (or less) intelligent than conservatives. Upon reading about studies investigating intelligence and attitudes, one learns that the correlation between intelligence and liberalism (or conservatism) ranges from low positive correlation to no correlation at all.[6] That is hardly scientific support for attributing attitudes to intelligence. Interestingly, there is a tendency for us to believe that all people who share our values are intelligent and that those who do not are stupid.

Attitudes are seldom formed by personal experience. Often we hear that racial integration would become our way of life if people of the various races would only see more of each other. Placing bodies together is not enough. We are also told that some blacks have antiwhite attitudes because they have been treated brutally by whites. Yet many blacks who have rarely

6 Robert Rosenthal and Lenore Jacobson, *Pygmalion in the Classroom: Teacher Expectation and Pupils' Development* (New York, Holt, Rinehart & Winston, Inc., 1968), 181–82.

seen whites, much less been physically attacked by them, hold much the same antiwhite attitude. In still another area many pacifists believe that firsthand experiences with war would cause people to want world peace. Pacifists find it difficult to explain why members of veterans' organizations tend to be more committed to wars than nonveterans.

One factor that reduces the importance of personal experience on attitude formation is the tendency of people to perceive and remember only what they are socially and psychologically prepared to see and recall. Communists, for example, tend to see capitalists as evil, and vice versa. Our friends tend to predetermine not only how we react to a given stimulus but indeed whether we perceive it in the first place. Consider, then, the difficulty of changing the attitude of whites toward blacks by "getting them together," if the whites are prepared to see only negative characteristics in blacks.

A second factor that may reduce the importance of personal experience in shaping attitudes is the possibility that personal experiences may actually reinforce the attitudes which they are supposed to change. Continuing with the black-white example, the prejudiced white man will not develop a problack attitude when he interacts with blacks if their behavior happens to fit his stereotyped beliefs about them. It is difficult for many social reformers to accept the fact that some members of ethnic minorities actually reinforce the very attitudes which the reformers are eager to eradicate.

Does all of this mean that intercultural or interracial contacts are entirely without value? Certainly not. Attitudes can be formed or changed by personal experience (1) if the attitudes are not in conflict with more powerful motives, (2) if the experience is carefully selected to represent an institution or group in the best (or worst) possible light, and (3) if the persons who are to experience changed attitudes are prepared to experience the best (or worst) in the situation—or (4) if the attitude involves perceptions that are so simple as to be obvious examples of empirical contradiction.

Studies indicate that white schoolchildren tend to develop pro-Chinese attitudes after personal experience with outstanding Chinese children but are not as likely to develop problack attitudes following experience with outstanding black children. From this observation, can we assume that some inherent fact about the two ethnic groups explains this difference? Not really. We may assume with ample justification that white children tend to acquire strong motives for disliking blacks and probably insignificant motives one way or another as far as Chinese are concerned.

Although it may seem that only unimportant attitudes can be changed, that is not the case; it only means that new attitudes can be learned by rewarding experiences, providing that more punishing experiences will not follow. When a white child's parents, peers, and others within the community punish him for his change in attitude by calling him "nigger lover," he is less likely to accept blacks, even friendly, cultured blacks.

Experimenters testing white college students for their attitudes toward nonwhites have found a statistically significant shift in attitudes in a favorable direction if the situation is pleasant and the subjects can identify with nonwhites, that is, middle-class nonwhites.[7] It has been shown, in a carefully structured experience, that the risk that contact might actually reinforce negative attitudes is minimized. The extent to which the subjects are prepared to change their attitudes is also important. This is, of course, in the language of card players, stacking the deck in favor of the dealer (the researcher). We are not often able to achieve such "stacking" in everyday life.

The following paper offers some additional suggestions for changing attitudes and behavior.

Processes for Attitude Change[8]

One of the most important historical examples of attitude change is Adolf Hitler's horribly effective and efficient program, in which every detail was used for the benefit of the propagandist:

> Meetings were not just occasions for people to make speeches, they were carefully planned theatrical productions in which settings, lighting, background music, and the timing of entrances and exits were devised to maximize the emotional fervor of an audience already brought to fever pitch by an hour or more given over to singing and the shouting of slogans.[9]

In his *Discourses*, Niccolò Machiavelli discussed the characteristics of a communicator, the disguised intent of the persuader, and the use of prestige effects. On the characteristics of a communicator, Machiavelli wrote:

> . . . [the] man of authority . . . should present himself before the multitude

[7] Roger I. Yoshino, "Children, Teachers, and Ethnic Discrimination," *Journal of Educational Sociology*, Vol. 34, (May, 1961), 391–97.

[8] By Diane Roether, graduate student, University of Oklahoma. Used with permission. Subsequent footnotes in this chapter are Miss Roether's.

[9] Terence H. Qualter, *Propaganda and Psychological Warfare* (New York, Random House, 1962), 112.

with all possible grace and dignity, and attired with all the insignia of his rank, so as to inspire the more respect.[10]

On the disguised intent of the persuader, Machiavelli wrote:

> For he who for a time has seemed good, and for purposes of his own wants to become bad, should do it gradually, and should seem to be brought to it by the force of circumstances; so that, before his changed nature deprives him of his former friends, he may have gained new ones, and that his authority may not be diminished by the change. Otherwise his deception will be discovered, and he will lose his friends and be ruined.[11]

On the use of authority Machiavelli wrote:

> . . . there are many good laws, the importance of which is known to the sagacious lawgiver, but the reasons are not sufficiently evident to enable him to persuade others to submit to them; and therefore do wise men, for the purpose of removing this difficulty, resort to divine authority.[12]

In his book *Mein Kampf*, Hitler told how to tailor a message to the audience and how to use emotional appeals:

> . . . all effective propaganda must be confined to a very few points which must be brought out in the form of slogans until the very last man is enabled to comprehend what is meant by any slogan. . . . An immense majority of the people . . . are governed more by feeling and sentiment than by reasoned consideration.[13]

In literature, Mark Antony's funeral oration in Shakespeare's *Julius Caesar* is an example of a successful attempt to change a group's attitude and behavior by subtly discrediting one's opponents. Cassius and the conspirators had persuaded Brutus to help them kill Caesar in order to capitalize on Brutus' good reputation with the citizens. At Caesar's funeral Brutus defended the assassination as a necessary act, carried out "not from loving Caesar less but from loving Rome more." The audience, swayed by the speech, was prepared to oppose Mark Antony, should he give a pro-Caesar or anti-Brutus speech. Mark Antony, however, began with an introduction which mystified the crowd by agreeing with their position. He had not come to praise Caesar, he said; his function was merely to bury the slain ruler. Mark Antony, like the crowd, praised Brutus as an honorable man. Having established agreement with the crowd, he then

---

[10] Niccolò Machiavelli, *Discourses* (trans. by L. J. Walker), (New Haven, Yale University Press, 1950), 251.

[11] *Ibid.*, 225.

[12] *Ibid.*, 147.

[13] Adolph Hitler, *Mein Kampf* (trans. by E. T. S. Dugdale), (Cambridge, Mass., Riverside Press, 1933), 77–78.

effectively used emotional appeals against Brutus, and by the end of his speech he had succeeded in getting the crowd to conclude that Brutus and the other conspirators were traitors and murderers who should be punished.

Mark Antony's technique has been experimentally validated. Ewing observed that an anti-Ford-automobile speech, presented to a pro-Ford audience, was more influential in producing anti-Ford attitudes in the group when the speaker began by defining himself as pro-Ford. This approach was considerably more effective than an almost identical speech which omitted the initial establishment of a common foundation of agreement with the audience.[14]

In religion, mass revivalists such as Billy Graham use the technique of public commitment—physically "coming forward." Revival audiences do not have to "believe" in Jesus Christ before coming forward. The fundamental psychological principle is that an attitude can change after a behavior change which negates the original attitude; that is, in many instances attitude change follows behavior change.

In law, successful trial lawyers pay attention to many factors and to seemingly trivial details which will persuade a jury to agree with their conclusion and reject that of their opponents. On this subject Louis Nizer has written:

> The plaintiff has a decided advantage in summing up last. He can analyze the argument just heard by the jury and point out the facts it omitted and the omissions in proof it assumed existed. . . . When I am required to sum up first, I endeavor to prepare the jury so that it will not yield to . . . my adversary. I remind the jury that he will have the last word and that I will not be permitted to reply. I tell them that I must depend on their recollections to correct any misstatement of fact which my opponent, who follows me, may make. I must rely on their discriminating judgment to reject any false arguments. Then, as I proceed to build my own case, I anticipate the contentions of my adversary. I announce his slogans and attempt to destroy them, asking the jurors to become my watchmen when they hear such sophistry, and reject it as an insult to their intelligence. . . . It is interesting to observe the bland look on a juror's face when you begin, perhaps even a cynical smile, and how he is caught up in the drama of your recital, his face responding properly with varying emotions of sympathy or resentment as the arguments make inroads upon him.[15]

Demagogues, debaters, revivalists, and attorneys all learn that certain attitudes and values are often so widely accepted in a given culture that they are virtually truisms for all members of that culture and that rarely, if ever, are contrary views presented. A leader who is unaware of, or misperceives, cultural

[14] T. A. Ewing, "A Study of Certain Factors Involved in the Study of Changes of Opinion," *Journal of Social Psychology*, Vol. 63 (1964), 63–88.

[15] Louis Nizer, *My Life in Court* (New York, Pyramid Publications, Inc., 1961), 42, 432–34.

variables will find it difficult or impossible to effect attitude change. Johann H. Bernstorff wrote that, during World War I, German propaganda

> showed a complete lack of understanding of American national psychology. The American character . . . is by no means so dry and calculating as the German picture of an American businessman usually represents. . . . There is no news for which a way cannot be guaranteed through the whole country, if clothed in a sentimental form. [England and France] exploited this circumstance with the . . . case of the German invasion of "poor little Belgium"; . . . and other incidents. Those who had charge of the Berlin propaganda, on the other hand, made very little of such occurrences on the [Allied] side, e.g., the violation of Greece, the bombing of the Corpus Christi procession in Karlsruhe, etc.[16]

In social psychology there are two main approaches to attitude change. The *formal attitude-change approach* is based on learning theory and assumes that man is a rational, information-processing being who can be motivated to listen to a message, learn its contents, and include them in his responses when his learning is rewarded. The means of change is a formal, structured communication, and the reason for change is either the actual or the expected reward for concurrence with the communicator.

The *group dynamics approach*, based on Kurt Lewin's field-theory orientation, assumes that man is a social being who needs people as a basis of self-knowledge, learning proper responses to environmental demands and channeling and controlling present behavior through the operation of group norms. The means of change is group norms, which may be communicated informally and which may be different from the individual's attitude or behavior.[17] Both approaches center on communication.

Communication variables which have been experimentally validated are those dealing with credibility, specifically with expertise and trustworthiness. In other words, the target of change is concerned with the amount of information the change agent has that is applicable to the topic and his ulterior motives in supporting a particular position. Variables which have not been as rigorously validated but appear to have some effect on the target of change are social status, age, physical appearance, and speaking ability.[18]

Other communications variables have been studied, including the order or presentation of the arguments, one-sided versus two-sided presentation, and explicit versus implicit conclusion drawing. Of course, audience characteristics

16 Johann H. Bernstorff, *My Three Years in America* (New York, Charles Scribner's Sons, 1920), 53.

17 See Kurt Lewin, *Field Theory in Social Science* (New York, Harper & Row, 1951).

18 Philip Zimbardo and Ebbe B. Ebbeson, *Influencing Attitudes and Changing Behavior* (Reading, Mass., Addison-Wesley Publishing Co., Inc., 1969), 17–19.

include the ability to understand the message, personality traits important to acceptance of the message, and general motivational traits.

Most communications studies conclude that change in attitude is a combined function of the individual's initial position, his attention to the message and to the communicator, his understanding of the message, and his acceptance of the message. Studies of the process of attention differentiate between factors necessary for attention getting and attention holding. The unique characteristics of the speaker—his voice and appearance—and the way he is introduced have an effect on attention getting, as do the novelty of the message and the channel through which it is presented. To hold attention, the message must not be so simple as to bore an audience or so complex as to be incomprehensible. Summaries, restatement, rehearsal opportunities, and the use of the audience's language also exert some influence on message comprehension.

Depending on the motivational basis for the individual's initial attitude, acceptance of a message may be affected by new information which disproves his existing beliefs, by rewards for accepting the message, and by awareness of irrational aspects of his initial attitude. The individual's consciousness of the manipulative intent of the speaker is often sufficient to make the attempt ineffectual. Instead of accepting the message, he may refuse to listen to the message, he may refuse to do the mental work necessary to comprehend the message, or he may expend much effort silently rehearsing counterarguments during the speech.

By understanding the dynamics of persuasion, a leader is in a better position to evaluate and manipulate variables to produce changes in attitude and behavior. It is our hope, however, that individuals in leadership positions will not use their power to destroy or unmercifully manipulate their followers as did Hitler and Machiavelli.

The Power to Change

Power is the capacity to carry out, by whatever means, a desired course of action despite the resistance of others and without having to take into consideration their needs. Many of today's problems involving human relations are centered in political power. When power is institutionalized into a system, it is referred to as *authority*.

Power is a universal experience; practically every person has had a measure of it, great or small, for a brief moment or for an extended period of time. Whether it is held by a leader or a follower, power is an integral

aspect of most social arrangements. In fact, it is one of the most prevalent factors influencing attitudes and behavior. Power has become both a desire and a social necessity. Ancient writers often regarded it as an evil subject and the desire for its possession as an evil emotion. Even today some writers use the phrase "the power elite" in an uncomplimentary sense.

Despite negative connotations the desire for power is growing, not diminishing. Racial minorities, participants in the women's liberation movement, college students, and union members are but a few examples of the many groups trying to increase their power. They all have one desire in common: to gain enough control to alter their chances for realizing personal goals. There are five "natural laws" of power:

1. Power invariably fills any vacuum in human organizations.

2. Power is invariably personal. There is no such thing as "class power," "elite power," or "group power," though classes, elites, and groups may form into organizations in which power is lodged in individuals.

3. Power is invariably based on a system of ideas or a philosophy.

4. Power is exercised through and depends on institutions. By their existence institutions assume control and eventually confer or withdraw power.

5. Power is invariably confronted with and acts in the presence of a field of responsibility.

In the politics of extremism violence breeds more violence until a vicious circle of terror is established. Most politicians are afraid of power, and yet they need it; those who claim exemption from that need are themselves in danger of falling victims to the nearest tyrant. Even ultimate freedom, as expressed in the writings of the Marquis de Sade, is enjoyed by totally subjecting others to our will. This is not unlike the despotism surrounding a Maoist ruling order which claims absolute rights over the minds and bodies of its subjects. The history of politics is largely a chronicle of the struggles of rulers to increase their power and of those being ruled to decrease it.

Between the nightmares of totalitarianism and the pleasant dreams of democracy lies an infinite range of frustrations and anxieties, all representing untidy realities. Sometimes we forget that social systems are people. Political systems are neither good nor bad; people are good or bad. If freedom is to have any meaning for significant numbers of citizens, the weak must be protected from the strong. This goal is more likely to be achieved under the rule of law. When the laws are not fair *and* just, the strong and the unscrupulous tend to rob, maim, torture, and kill the weak. This was true in the lawless West and it is true today in the lawless inner cities.

The humane control of power is achieved only when the possessors of power regard it as a sacred trust to be exercised for the general welfare rather than as a means of achieving selfish ends. Humane leaders are men and women of good will and integrity; they employ democratic principles to guide them in their actions. As we approach the twenty-first century, it is evident that we must get on with the business of fostering attitudes and behavior that reflect our democratic creed.

Suggested Reading

Adorno, T. W., et al. *The Authoritarian Personality*. New York, Harper & Row, 1950.

Allport, Gordon W. *The Nature of Prejudice*. New York, Doubleday & Company, Inc., 1954.

Arnspiger, V. Clyde. *Personality in Social Process*. Chicago, Follett Publishing Company, 1961.

Axline, Virginia M. *Dibs in Search of Self*. New York, Ballantine Books, Inc., 1964.

Bettelheim, Bruno, and Morris Janowitz. *Social Change and Prejudice*. New York, The Free Press, 1964.

Blake, Robert R., and Glenn V. Ramsey. *Perception: An Approach to Personality*. New York, The Ronald Press Company, 1951.

Boas, Franz. *Race, Language, and Culture*. New York, The Macmillan Company, 1940.

Boulding, Kenneth E. *The Image: Knowledge in Life and Society*. Ann Arbor, University of Michigan Press, 1956.

Clark, Kenneth B. *Prejudice and Your Child*. Boston, Beacon Press, 1955.

Cofer, Charles N., and M. H. Appley. *Motivation: Theory and Research*. New York, John Wiley & Sons, Inc., 1964.

Cohen, Arthur R. *Attitude Change and Social Influence*. New York, Basic Books, Inc., 1964.

Dye, Thomas R., and Brett W. Hawkins, eds. *Politics in the Metropolis: A Reader in Conflict and Cooperation*. Columbus, Ohio, Charles E. Merrill Publishing Co., 1967.

Etzioni, Amitai, and Eva Etzioni, eds. *Social Change*. New York, Basic Books, Inc., 1964.

Festinger, Leon. *A Theory of Cognitive Dissonance*. Stanford, Stanford University Press, 1957.

Fiedler, Fred E. *Leader Attitudes and Group Effectiveness*. Urbana, University of Illinois Press, 1958.

Ginzberg, Eli, et al. *Effecting Change in Large Organizations*. New York, Columbia University Press, 1957.

Goodwin, Mary E. *Race Awareness in Young Children*. Rev. ed. New York, Collier Publishing Company, 1964.

Suggested Reading (continued)

Howe, Reuel L. *The Miracle of Dialogue*. New York, The Seabury Press, Inc., 1963.

Insko, Charles A. *Theories of Attitude Change*. New York, Appleton-Century-Crofts, 1967.

Jahoda, Marie, and Neil Warren, eds. *Attitudes: Selected Readings*. Baltimore, Penguin Books, Inc., 1966.

Janis, Irving, et al. *Personality and Persuasibility*. New Haven, Yale University Press, 1959.

Kiesler, Charles A., B. E. Collins, and Neal Miller. *Attitude Change: A Critical Analysis and Theoretical Approaches*. New York, John Wiley & Sons, Inc., 1969.

Kroeber, Alfred L. *The Nature of Culture*. Chicago, University of Chicago Press, 1952.

Lasker, Bruno. *Race Attitudes in Children*. New York, Holt, 1929.

Lewin, Kurt. *A Dynamic Theory of Personality*. Trans. by D. K. Adams and K. E. Zener. New York, McGraw-Hill Book Company, 1935.

Lynd, Helen M. *On Shame and the Search for Identity*. New York, Harcourt, Brace & World, Inc., 1958.

Machiavelli, Niccolò. *Discourses*. Trans. by L. J. Walker. New Haven, Yale University Press, 1950.

Marrow, Alfred J. *Changing Patterns of Prejudice*. Philadelphia, Chilton Book Company, 1962.

Maslow, Abraham. *Self-Actualizing People: A Study of Psychological Health*. New York, Brooklyn College, 1951.

Megargee, Edwin I., and Jack E. Hokanson. *The Dynamics of Aggression*. New York, Harper & Row, 1970.

Piaget, Jean. *The Moral Judgment of the Child*. New York, The Free Press, 1965.

Qualter, Terence H. *Propaganda and Psychological Warfare*. New York, Random House, Inc., 1962.

Ragan, William B., and George Henderson. *Foundations of American Education*. New York, Harper & Row, 1970.

Reymort, M. K. *Feelings and Emotions*. New York, McGraw-Hill Book Company, 1950.

Rose, Peter I. *They and We: Racial and Ethnic Relations in the United States*. New York, Random House, Inc., 1964.

Rosenthal, Robert, and Lenore Jacobson. *Pygmalion in the Classroom: Teacher Expectation and Pupils' Intellectual Development*. New York, Holt, Rinehart & Winston, Inc., 1968.

Rothman, G. *The Riddle of Cruelty*. New York, Philosophical Library, 1971.

Rubin, R. I. *The Angry Book*. New York, The Macmillan Company, 1969.

Schmidt, W., and Richard Beckhard. *The Fact-Finding Conference*. Washington, D.C., Leadership Resources, 1961.

Sherif, Carolyn, et al. *Attitudes and Attitude Change*. Philadelphia, Saunders, 1965.

Stock, T. *Emotional Dynamics and Group Culture*. New York, New York University Press, 1969.

Stogdill, Ralph M. *Individual Behavior and Group Achievement: A Theory, the Experimental Evidence*. New York, Oxford University Press, 1969.

Summers, G. F., ed. *Attitude Measurement*. Chicago, Rand McNally & Co., 1970.

Triandia, Harry C. *Attitude and Attitude Change*. New York, John Wiley and Sons, Inc., 1971.

Van den Berghe, P. L. *Race and Racism: A Comparative Perspective*. New York, John Wiley & Sons, Inc., 1967.

Whiting, John W. R., and Irvin L. Child. *Child Training and Personality: A Cross Cultural Study*. New Haven, Yale University Press, 1953.

Young, Whitney M., Jr. *Beyond Racism*. New York, McGraw-Hill Book Company, 1969.

Zimbardo, Philip G., and Ebbe B. Ebbeson. *Influencing Attitudes and Changing Behavior*. Reading, Mass., Addison-Wesley Publishing Company, Inc., 1969.

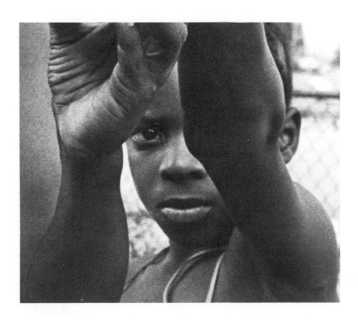

CHAPTER 7

Beyond Words

Those of us concerned about and committed to improving human relations must guard against accepting and perpetuating such clichés as, "I'm not prejudiced," and, "I treat all people the same." This point was vividly illustrated not long ago. After giving a talk on black-white relations, I asked for questions or comments. A slightly built middle-aged lady raised her hand and said, "I'm glad you told these people what you did. I've never had a problem. I've always had niggers for friends."

Even the most "liberal" individuals do not treat all people the same. As painful as it may be to admit, we are all prejudiced *for* or *against* other people. Some parents, for instance, firmly believe that children of one sex are "better" than those of the other. People who believe that they are not prejudiced are not likely to correct their prejudicial behavior. In most instances the first step in solving a problem is to recognize it.[1]

Focusing on People

Because we are creatures of culture, our attitudes, feelings, and values make objective thinking difficult. However, *it is behavior, not attitudes, that comprise*

[1] George Henderson and Robert F. Bibens, *Teachers Should Care: Social Perspectives of Teaching* (New York, Harper & Row, 1970), chap. 2.

the major human relations problems confronting us. There are many laws against discriminatory behavior, but there are none against prejudicial attitudes. Some human rights activists maintain that it is not what we think about others that hurts or helps but how we act out these thoughts. Many Americans act out their race prejudices. Many whites, for example, are blatantly prejudiced against nonwhites, and many nonwhites are blatantly prejudiced against whites. Because most writings, not to speak of the news media, focus on black-white conflicts and confrontations, prejudices involving other groups are inadequately reported.[2]

Of course, prejudice is not limited to color. Social-class prejudice is a problem, too. Some individuals, for instance, are attracted to upper- and middle-class people and repelled by those of the lower classes. Lately national attention has been focused on still another type of prejudice—prejudice against women. And to this long list of prejudices we could add prejudice against the mentally and physically handicapped.

Prejudice is a prejudgment, a conclusion drawn without adequate knowledge or evidence. Prejudice has a way of multiplying and spreading to areas unrelated to the initial object of concern. Whites prejudiced against disadvantaged nonwhites, as an illustration, find it relatively easy to reject disadvantaged whites, especially the handicapped, welfare recipients, and members of another religious group. The bigot blames others for various social misfortunes: floods, high taxes, inflation, wars, and—interestingly—racism. Such prejudgments are easier to make than objective judgments, which require more energy, knowledge, integrity, and time. In their efforts to make expedient decisions, bigots react to concepts rather than to people.

To abate their prejudices, individuals must have knowledge of their own strengths and weaknesses, an understanding of how people become prejudiced, and empathy with the many minorities that are targets of prejudicial behaviors. In short, they must understand not only their own prejudicial behavior but also the prejudicial behavior of others. We usually get back the kind of human relations we give to others—acceptance fosters acceptance, and rejection brings rejection. Because each individual's personality reflects his intrapersonal and interpersonal experiences, some personalities can be described as ugly and stunted, while others are beautiful and dynamic.

Effective human relations result when each individual accepts and

---

[2] Earl Raab and Seymour M. Lipset, *Prejudice and Society* (New York, Anti-Defamation League of B'nai B'rith, 1959).

respects the differences of others. This basic principle of human relations is frequently taught but seldom practiced. Whether positive or negative, social behavior spreads in a contagious manner. Unfortunately, only a few people living in socially and ethnically heterogeneous environments realize that their differences are an asset which provides them with an opportunity for learning from others. Most people waste the major portion of their lives rejecting potential friends of different ethnic, religious, sex, and social backgrounds.

Ethnic Relations

Daily we are exposed to mass-media programs which characterize our nation as a country dominated by white Anglo-Saxon Protestants (WASPs). Minorities who accept this exaggerated view of America become willing parties to a prophecy that fulfills itself; they become losers by default.[3] When this happens, the WASPs do inherit positions of power and pass on the socially myopic prophecy from one generation to the next. For these and other reasons race prejudice is one of the most pressing human relations problems in our society. The ethnic prejudices we find in our neighborhoods, schools, and jobs come from two main sources: first, the values and attitudes we learn from others and, second, the tensions and frustrations all of us experience while trying to cope with other people, especially strangers.

Black Americans

The visible effects of prejudice can be seen in the plight of the black Americans. Specifically, segregation and discrimination in employment, education, law enforcement, and housing have created a vicious circle from which few blacks can escape.

Nearly one-half of the nation's twenty-two million blacks are concentrated in fifty cities, the largest numbers living in New York City, Chicago, Detroit, Philadelphia, Washington, Los Angeles, Baltimore, Cleveland, and New Orleans. The 1970 census data show that blacks continue to be clustered at the lower end of the wage scales in most jobs. Contrary to popular opinion, Americans of Spanish origin have higher incomes than blacks. In 1970 the median family income of Spanish-Americans was $7,330, compared with $6,280 for black families and

---

[3] Gordon W. Allport, *The Nature of Prejudice* (Cambridge, Mass., Addison-Wesley Publishing Co., Inc., 1954).

$10,240 for white families. Black families headed by women are the poorest of all.

Although the percentage of black women who head households and work is the same as that of their white counterparts, black women earn considerably less than white women. Nearly 60 per cent of working black mothers earn less than three thousand dollars a year, compared with 30 per cent of white female family heads who earn less than that amount. As a group, black male wage earners also earn less than their white counterparts.

In June, 1971, the over-all unemployment rate was 15.1 per cent for black veterans of the Vietnam War and 12.9 per cent for nonveteran blacks between the ages of twenty and twenty-nine. The unemployment rates were 10 per cent for all veterans and 7.5 per cent for nonveterans. The unemployment figure was much bleaker for blacks under age twenty-four: 20.9 per cent for veterans and 17.4 per cent for nonveterans. The unemployment rates were 14 per cent for all veterans and 10 per cent for all nonveterans under twenty-four. Conditions have changed little since 1971. Whether veterans or civilians, blacks currently have higher rates of unemployment than their white counterparts.

To date, school-desegregation efforts have been characterized by the closing of predominantly black schools, accompanied by dismissals and demotions of black teachers, athletic coaches, and administrators (some white school-board members have referred to these discriminatory practices as "deniggerizing the schools"). Other practices include maintaining segregated social clubs and homecoming celebrations (presided over by white queens and attendants) and allowing "Dixie" to be played but not the Negro National Anthem ("Lift Every Voice and Sing"). More than 400,000 white students are attending segregated private schools in eleven southern states. Interestingly, however, the desegregation efforts of the South have been more successful than those of the North and West. Approximately 45 per cent of the black students in the South attend desegregated schools, while less than 30 per cent of the black students in the North and West attend desegregated schools.

Recent debates about school busing have obscured the real issue in education. Under ordinary circumstances there is nothing special or socially offensive about busing. Currently, approximately twenty million school children are bused over two billion miles a year, and most of this occurs in predominantly segregated-school areas. It seems, then, that busing becomes special and socially offensive to most people when it is used to bring black and white children together.

Few blacks would suggest that busing per se guarantees quality education. There is no educational magic in sitting next to white children. On the contrary, black leaders have been saying for years that quality education must go beyond busing—it requires more money and a more equitable manner of financing schools; more qualified teachers and administrators; more relevant curricula; and more community control of schools. At best, busing is only a stop-gap, which must ultimately be supplemented in some communities and replaced in others with programs for bringing better education to where the children are.

In those districts where busing is used to improve the quality of education, it is fair for both whites and blacks to be bused. Few whites—northern or southern—seem willing either to desegregate the public schools or to provide the necessary resources for upgrading predominantly black schools. Thus most black children in the 1970's are likely to attend schools similar to those cited in the 1954 Brown case—schools that are racially segregated and educationally unequal.

Racial tension also threatens to split police ranks. Since 1968 organizations representing black police officers have been formed in several major cities, including Chicago (the Afro-American Patrolmen's League), San Francisco (the Officers for Justice), New York City (the Guardians), and Pittsburgh (the Guardians). These organizations grew out of on-the-job confrontations between black and white policemen. Perhaps police departments in major cities will attack the problem of racism in the same manner as the Department of Defense did in 1971. In addition to accelerating recruitment and promotion of members of minority groups, the Department of Defense instituted compulsory education in race relations for all of its personnel. The police are not unlike the military—harmonious relations are needed within ranks so that organizational efficiency will not be impaired by racial unrest.

Four agencies ensure or regulate banks and savings-and-loan associations and make 80 per cent of the annual home loans. On March 7, 1971, thirteen civil rights and public interest organizations filed petitions asking the controller of the currency, the Federal Home Bank Board, the Federal Reserve System, and the Federal Deposit Insurance Corporation to stop supporting racial discrimination in the private sector of home-mortgage financing.

Public housing is also segregated housing in most cities. High-rise public housing units are vertical racially segregated reservations for low-income aged persons and for younger people with large families. The aged are forgotten, and the young become angry. Young or old, most black residents of public housing are almost completely cut off from people outside their housing projects. Without a doubt, their poverty of spirit is much more detrimental than their poverty of income. Such people live in crowded social, physical, and psychological boxes that become more crowded each year. Apathy, civil disobedience, and race hatred are predictable behavior when people are kept in such vertical "reservations."

Puerto Ricans

There are over a million Puerto Ricans in the continental United States, most of them living in New York City's Spanish Harlem. They are neither black nor white. Ramón Vélez, executive director of the Hunts Point Multi-Service Center, and Joseph Monserrat, director of the Office of the Commonwealth of Puerto Rico in Manhattan, have been two of the most articulate spokesmen for Puerto Ricans. In 1971 they pointed out that Puerto Ricans are last in housing, education, employment, and income when compared with other minorities in New York City.

Since most companies provide employment application forms in English only, Spanish-speaking Puerto Ricans are excluded from any job opportunities. In addition, few personnel officers speak Spanish. The final blow comes from the fact that the agrarian background of most Puerto Ricans does not provide skills with which even those who speak English can qualify for the highly automated industrial jobs. There are relatively few training programs for unemployed and underemployed Puerto Ricans.

The average sixth-grade Puerto Rican child is three years behind the average English-speaking child and one year behind the average black child in verbal ability, reading comprehension, and mathematics. The gap narrows between Puerto Rican and black children in the higher grades, but it widens between English-speaking and Puerto Rican children. Most Puerto Ricans drop out of school before reaching high school. Even though bilingual education has proved helpful in improving the quality of education, as well as increasing the school retention rate of Puerto Rican children, most school systems do not provide funds for bilingual education. (See the discussion below pertaining to bilingual education for American Indians and Mexican-Americans.)

The housing problems of Puerto Ricans are more acute than those of most slum dwellers. Their housing is generally substandard and dilapidated. Poor housing, in turn, negatively affects their health, and many are afflicted with tropical diseases that American doctors are not trained to diagnose. As is true in other ethnic groups, there is a shortage of Puerto

Rican doctors. Furthermore, hospitals have done little to hire Spanish-speaking professionals and paraprofessionals. But this condition is not unique to hospitals; most education, health, and welfare agencies have been negligent in employing Spanish-speaking personnel.

The plight of Puerto Ricans is periodically romanticized in such theatrical productions as the Broadway musical *West Side Story*. But life in the barrio is generally grim and marginal. Joining with blacks and Mexican-Americans, Puerto Ricans are gaining more control over their community resources. They are becoming more committed to direct action as a means of gaining power for themselves.

American Indians

Until the 1970 United States census Indians were not even listed as an identifiable ethnic group. Approximately 450,000 of the 650,000 American Indian population live on fifty-six million acres of reservations in twenty-six states. Part of their frustration can be explained by the following statistics: Indians have ninety million *fewer* acres of land today than they had in 1887; their average life expectancy is forty-four years; more than 40 per cent of Indian schoolchildren—almost double the national average—drop out before completing high school; nearly 60 per cent of the adult Indian population has less than an eighth-grade education; infant mortality—twenty-six deaths per thousand—is more than ten points above the national average; 50 per cent of Indian families have annual incomes below two thousand dollars; their unemployment is almost fifteen times the national average.

More than half of American Indian children attend public schools. Many others are required to leave their communities to attend government schools, often hundreds of miles from their homes. In Oklahoma the Chilocco Indian School has a large number of students from Alaska, and most of the students at the Fort Sill Indian School at Lawton are Navahos from Arizona and New Mexico.

A severe problem for most Indian pupils is their inadequate English language background before entering school. Because the curriculum is based on the premise that children can speak and understand English, the reservation Indian pupils in particular need to learn the significance and meaning of English words as they relate to cultural concepts. Indian children who do not understand English or those who speak and use it haltingly need additional training before the public school curriculum can be of benefit. Preschool education in the "alien" culture is a necessity for academic success. Studies of Indian students are characterized by low test scores with marked deficiencies in English and math and high dropout rates.

The use of bilingual language materials and the employment of dedicated teachers appear to be the best approaches to improving the quality of instruction for Indian and other minority-group students. Teaching English as a Foreign Language (EFL) is one of the most widely used programs. However, owing to the English-Spanish emphasis of these programs, most Indian children are not benefiting from them. The sounds that are difficult for a Spanish child to produce are frequently not the sounds difficult for an Indian child.

The first concern for those teaching a language should be the sound systems, and the second concern should be the basic sentence structure. Navaho sentence structure, for example, differs significantly from either English or Spanish:

English: I gave the ball to the boy.
Spanish: Him I gave the ball to the boy.
Navaho: Boy ball I gave.

The English verb tenses are completely different from the Navaho's conception of time. To him, time is like the air, something flowing through everything and existing in abundance. A language program needs to be developed that will compensate for the difference between Navaho and English.

When we succeed in teaching Indian pupils English, we increase the possibility of successes similar to that of N. Scott Momaday. In 1969, Momaday, a Kiowa, became the first American Indian to win a Pulitzer Prize, for his novel *House Made of Dawn*.

The American Indians have many outstanding contemporary leaders, among them Wendell Chino, a member of the Mescalero Apache tribe of New Mexico, who was the first president of the National Congress of American Indians (the first all-Indian nationwide organization); Dan Kachongeva, a member of the Hopi tribe of northern Arizona, who encouraged his followers not to abandon their desert-culture heritage; Robert Smallboy, a member of the Cree tribe in Alberta, Canada, who led 150 members of his tribe of the Hobbema Reserve to the Kootenay Plains of the Rocky Mountains, where they are relearning how to live off the land and also how to govern themselves; and Vine Deloria, Jr., a member of the Standing Rock Sioux tribe of North Dakota, whose writings—especially *Custer Died for Your Sins: An Indian Manifesto*—encourage Indian self-pride and self-determination. The late Tom Segundo, a member of the Papago tribe of southern Arizona, abandoned his law practice and returned to his reservation to design and promote new economic and social programs; and the late Clyde Warrior, a member of the Ponca tribe of Oklahoma, who was one of the most militant of the "young warriors."

Virtually none of the elementary and secondary school textbooks adequately portray the life and heritage of native Americans. Despite accelerated efforts toward improvement, most textbooks still contain misinformation, distortions, or omissions of important facts about American Indians. Too many textbooks claim that America began with Columbus' "discovery." Too many textbooks use demeaning terms, such as "primitive," "filthy," "warlike," and "savage," to describe native Americans. Little wonder that alienation is growing among the tribes of America.

In 1970, Indians began expressing a growing mood of militancy. They staged mass protests in Denver and Cleveland, seized Alcatraz Island, stormed Fort Lawton outside Seattle, and tried to take over Ellis Island. Navaho Indians acted out their frustrations with the "white man's way" by starting their own schools in Ramah, New Mexico, and the Salt River and Zuñi tribes won approval for control of their federal programs.

On January 12, 1972, Indian Commissioner Louis R. Bruce announced that the following five-point program would be implemented by the Department of the Interior:

1. Accelerated reservation-by-reservation development programs in which the Bureau of Indian Affairs would adjust its program to assist tribes that have comprehensive plans for economic and social development.

2. Redirection of the $42 million employment assistance program to train Indians on reservations for jobs in their own communities. Supervision of the program would be transferred to area officers, and more on-the-job training funds would be allocated.

3. Resources protection under the direction of the Indian Water Rights Office to protect Indian water and land rights from encroachment by federal and private interests.

4. The $30 million allocated for road construction on Indian reservations to be doubled in the next fiscal year.

5. More tribal control of education programs in order to make Indian education more responsive to the needs of Indian children and their parents.

In principle, this program was certainly a redirection of federal policy and programs and if implemented would give Indians more control of their own affairs. It remains to be seen how much of this program will in fact be implemented.

Mexican-Americans

Spanish explorers had arrived in the New World and founded communities many years before the Pilgrims landed on Plymouth Rock. Juan Ponce de León landed on the southern coast of Florida in 1513, Spaniards founded St. Augustine, Florida, in 1565, and Juan de Oñate explored what later became the American Southwest in 1598. Although Spanish-speaking people can trace their American heritage back over 450 years, they have yet to achieve the socioeconomic status accorded Anglo-Americans.

A growing number of the more than five million Mexican-Americans (or Chicanos, as many prefer to be called) are stirring to the call of Brown Power. Their increased awareness of their self-identity and proud heritage is a recent phenomenon. Slowly the ethnic stereotype that the Chicanos are too drowsy and too docile to carry on a sustained fight against poverty and discrimination is changing.

Chicanos are a distinctive minority separated from the dominant "Anglo" culture by poverty and by differences in language and culture. Over 90 per cent of the Mexican-Americans are concentrated in the southwestern states of California, Texas, Colorado, New Mexico, and Arizona. Some Chicanos claim descent from Spanish explorers. Others say that they are descendants of the ancient Aztecs. But the vast majority describe themselves as mestizos, people of mixed Spanish and Indian blood. Pride in their heritage discourages the Chicanos from integrating with white American culture. Most of them voluntarily live inside the barrio.

Even though they have been economically and politically dominated by Anglos, Mexican-Americans have maintained their language pattern and strong sense of ethnic pride and unity. The price they have paid to maintain these cultural traits can be measured in terms of their low level of education, high rates of poverty, substandard housing, inadequate health care, and low self-esteem. These are the conditions that are sparking Brown Nationalism.

As brown nationalism grows, more Mexican-Americans are becoming aware of their cultural heritage. This appeal to *la raza* ("the race") is a rallying cry common to almost all political and economic activities of militant Chicanos. In more specific terms militant Chicanos are seeking the preservation of "the race" within the dominant American culture.

The tactics of Mexican-American leaders range from nonviolence to violence. César Chávez, organizer of the 1965 grape pickers' strike, is a leader committed to nonviolence. His name, picture, union banner, and slogans are injected into a wide range of Spanish-speaking causes, including those which focus on bilingual education, voter registration, and improved law enforcement. Chávez' United Farm Workers Organizing Committee is known from coast to coast.

In contrast, Reies López Tijerina ("King Tiger"), founder of the Alianza Federal de Mercedes (Federal Alliance of Free City States), is dedicated to using whatever means are necessary—including violence—to free Spanish-Americans from the Anglos. Tijerina's primary goal is to reclaim the millions of acres of communally owned land in northern New Mexico and southern Colorado allegedly taken away from Spanish-Americans by the United States government through legal trickery, in violation of the Treaty of Guadalupe-Hidalgo of 1848. In 1967, Tijerina and a few followers raided a courthouse in northern New Mexico in an attempt to arrest the district attorney for violation of Chicanos' civil rights.

Rodolfo ("Corky") Gonzáles, founder of the Crusade for Justice, is a leader of the legal-defense approach to Mexican-American freedom. In 1968 the Mexican-American Legal Defense and Educational Fund was organized by the Ford Foundation to supplement the work begun by the Crusade for Justice. In the same year the Ford Foundation also provided funds for the creation of the Southwest Council of La Raza, a coordinating body for grass-roots efforts in community organization.

To state simply that Mexican-Americans desire the best of both cultures is to overlook the questions raised by Chicano leaders: Is it possible to obtain the best of both cultures? Will Anglos assimilate with a large number of Mexican-Americans whom many believe to be socially inferior? Will assimilation cost Mexican-Americans their cultural identity? While these questions are being pondered, most Chicanos are receiving inferior education. In 1970, a United States Commission on Civil Rights study of 532 school districts in Arizona, California, Colorado, New Mexico, and Texas concluded that in most schools surveyed "suppression" and "strict repressive measures" are applied to enforce a ban on the use of Spanish in the classroom; fewer than 10 per cent of the schools offered courses in Mexican-American history; many textbooks reflected an Anglo-American bias; and only sixty out of one hundred Chicanos who entered the first grade graduated from high school, compared with eighty-six out of one hundred whites. The one-hundred-page report, *The Unfinished Education*, also paints a bleak picture of education for Indians and blacks.

Asian-Americans

In 1970 the total Asian-American population was approximately 1.5 million. Of this number Japanese-Americans comprised 600,000; Chinese-Americans comprised 435,000; and Filipinos comprised 345,000. More than 80 per cent of the Japanese-Americans live in Hawaii and California, while Washington, Illinois, and New York each have 3 per cent. Forty per cent of the Chinese-Americans live in California, 20 per cent live in New York, 12 per cent live in Hawaii, and a total of 6 per cent live in Illinois and Massachusetts. Nearly 40 per cent of the Filipinos reside in California, 30 per cent live in Hawaii, and a total of 9 per cent live in New York, Illinois, and Washington.

Asian-Americans, especially Chinese-Americans and Japanese-Americans, are joining other minority groups in reacting to what they believe to be white Americans' patronizing and racist behavior. In essence, theirs is a rebellion against the Oriental stereotype of the slant-eyed, pig-tailed "Chinaman" or "Jap," who habitually smiles and says, "Ah-so." Radical young Chinese periodically form organizations, such as the Boxers and the Red Guard, whose major purpose is to stop tourists from treating Orientals like freaks in a sideshow.

Many non-Orientals still think of Chinese-Americans and Japanese-Americans as people who work primarily in laundries and gardens. In academic circles the equally patronizing stereotype of the earnest, bespectacled young Oriental scholar is replacing the older stereotype of the pig-tailed coolie. The new stereotype has grown out of the national reputations achieved by such men as I. M. Pei and Minour Yamasaki, architects; Gerald Tsai, head of the Manhattan Fund; Tsung Dao Lee and Chen Ning Yang, winners of the Nobel Prize in physics; Samuel I. Hayakawa, president of San Francisco State College; Daniel Inouye, United States senator from Hawaii; Toyohiko Takami, dermatologist; and Hideyo Noguchi, bacteriologist.

Japanese-Americans are sometimes held up by white Americans as the "model American minority," primarily because they have achieved a high level of economic and social success without rebelling. In California, for example, Japanese-Americans have a higher median family income than any other group except white Americans, and they are the best educated of all groups. Japanese-Americans have the lowest rates of adult crime, juvenile delinquency, and mental illness.

The socioeconomic problems of Chinese-Americans are vividly illustrated in the following San Francisco Chinatown statistics: More than one-third of Chinatown's families are poverty-stricken; three-fourths of all housing units are substandard; rents have tripled in the past five years; more than half the adults have only a grade-school education; one-third of the core city residents are more than sixty-five years old; juvenile delinquency is increasing; and the suicide rate is three times the national average. These statistics are compounded by an influx of Chinese immigrants who cannot speak English. There are few programs to help non-English-speaking people of any group, especially Chinese.

Feeling less secure and subject to greater internal pressures to maintain an identifiable community, Chinese-Americans have organized schools for teaching Chinese after the regular school day and on weekends. In these schools the children read newspapers, books, and poetry in Chinese so that they can maintain their cultural identity. Racial integration of the public schools is opposed by many Chinese-American parents because non-Chinese children are less likely to adhere to the basic philosophical guides taught in Chinese schools: one should respect older people, deal with others peacefully, observe proper manners, and remember that making money is not the only purpose of education.

Like the Chinese-Americans and the Japanese-Americans, the great majority of Filipinos live in urban areas. Recent migrants from the Philippine Islands are well educated; many are doctors, engineers, lawyers, nurses, and teachers. While they differ from their predecessors, who were poorly educated, their employment opportunities are similar. Many professionally trained Filipinos are underemployed and unemployed. Language is not the problem, for English is taught in the public schools in the Philippine Islands. Filipino leaders maintain that they are discriminated against because they are nonwhite, not because they lack skills or the ability to speak fluent English.

Sex Discrimination

At no time in our history have traditional sex roles been so seriously challenged as they have in the past decade. The major purpose of the women's liberation movement and the homosexual liberation movement is to redefine behavior that has been taken for granted as "correct" for men and women. While there is much similarity in the two movements, their goals are not the same. Women are concerned with gaining economic, sexual, and social equality with men in socially acceptable activities, while male and female homosexuals are concerned with redefining patterns of sexual gratification that are now socially unacceptable.

"Male-chauvinist pig!"

Women's Liberation

Throughout most of America's history, women have been subservient to men. Although they comprise 53 per cent of the nation's population, women remain the one group which does not enjoy the full protection of the United States Constitution. Some state statutes have separate provisions for qualifying women jurors; several states deny women the right to start an independent business without court approval or, if they are married, their husbands' approval; in most states, community property laws allow husbands complete control and management of community property but do not give wives the same rights; and "protective" laws, especially restrictive labor standards, discriminate against women. These are but a few reasons for the revival of the Women's Liberation Movement, which began in the late 1800's. In 1837, Susan B. Anthony, a seventeen-year-old teacher, started the women's rights movement when she demanded equal pay for women teachers, coeducation, and higher education for women. In 1848, Elizabeth Cady Stanton and other women abolitionists held the first American women's rights convention in Seneca Falls, New York. The convention asserted in a declaration of principles that "all men and women are equal" but that men had established "absolute tyranny" over women.[4]

In the early twentieth century the women's rights movement was led by social leaders such as Ann Morgan and Mrs. Oliver H. P. Belmont; social workers such as Jane Addams and Frances Perkins; and Rose Scheiderman, president of the Women's Trade Union League. In those years women were primarily concerned with securing the right to vote and equal employment opportunities. Finally, in 1920, women won the right to vote—fifty years after the Negroes won suffrage. Under the prodding of the women's rights leaders, during World War I the federal government accelerated efforts to promote equal pay for equal work, and in 1920 the Women's Bureau of the Department of Labor was created. In 1923 the Civil Service Reclassification Act barred sex discrimination in federal government service. Further strides in equal pay for equal work were made during the Depression and World War II.

The mid-1960's brought a new mood of feminism which quickly gained the label "women's liberation movement." The contemporary movement appears to have sprung from two sources: the frustrations of working women and the resentments of young women active in civil rights and radical movements.

When Betty Friedan published *The Feminine Mystique* in 1963, she became a spokeswoman for women who wanted or needed to work. In 1966 she was instrumental in forming the National Organization of Women (NOW). NOW was an effort to implement the Civil Rights Act of 1964, which barred discrimination in employment on the basis of sex. (The addition of the word "sex" to Title VII of the act had been made in an effort to defeat the bill. The insertion of "sex" in the act was accompanied by much joking and laughter in the House of Representatives.)

NOW adopted the following national goals:

1. Equal rights under the Constitution
2. Enforcement of the Civil Rights Act of 1964
3. Maternity-leave rights in employment and equal social security benefits

[4] See "Special Issue: The American Woman," *Time*, March 20, 1972.

4. Tax-deduction provisions for home- and child-care expenses
5. Day-care centers for children
6. Equal and unsegregated education
7. Equal job-training opportunities and allowances for women in poverty who must support their families
8. The right of women to control their reproductive lives

A second source of ferment in the 1960's was the discontent of women active in radical left movements. Some of these women, white and non-white, began to feel that they were working for everyone's liberation except their own. Others felt excluded from the meaningful work of their civil rights organizations. They resented wisecracks of male leaders like Stokely Carmichael, who suggested to members of SNCC that "the position of women in our movement should be prone." For the most part, efforts by women members of SNCC and Students for a Democratic Society (SDS) to promote serious consideration of the problems of women were greeted with laughter. By the late 1960's radical women were forming their own groups or organizing caucuses within existing liberation organizations.

Some captured headlines by burning their bras and staging protest marches. Others dramatized their plight in verse and prose. They encouraged other women to recognize that their problems are societal—not personal—and to seek social solutions in cooperation with their oppressed sisters throughout the world.

Black women have been slow to identify with the goals of the women's liberation movement. Most black women are committed to giving black liberation top priority. They believe that if women suddenly achieved equality with men black women would continue to carry the major burden of their families. The consensus among black women is that their first task is to liberate the black male. A few outspoken black women downgrade women's lib as nothing more than an attempt on the part of whites to live according to stereotypes of poor blacks without the disadvantages of being black. To illustrate their point, they cite common-law marriage, children out of wedlock, sexual "freedom," and families without men.

Tongue-in-cheek, blacks in the Women's Liberation Movement note that black women have always been "liberated to work": they have been liberated to labor in the fields; to clean and cook in white women's homes; to nurse and rear white babies; to perform menial industrial jobs; and to return to their slum homes at night to perform many of the same tasks all over again. Liberation for these women may well consist of being able to experience the "boredom" against which affluent white women are rebelling.

There are philosophical differences within the movement. A major split centers on where to place the blame for women's subservience. Is the enemy capitalism, which spawns the twin evils of racism and sexism? Or is the enemy "the Man,"—all men—who are the creators of capitalism, communism, and male-dominated social systems?

Much of the recent women's lib commentary is aimed at the limitations placed upon women because of cultural convenience and not on the basis of facts. Through the years males have justified stereotyped female roles because of women's so-called biological nature (their childbearing function), physiological nature (their weaker muscles), and psychological nature (their passivity and dependence). With considerable scientific data to back them up, the women's liberationists reject this explanation. They say that if women are immobilized by childbearing and child rearing, if they are physically weak and need the protection of men, if they are psychologically submissive and dependent, society has taught them to be this way.

Facts support the women's lib assault on the traditional wife, companion, and wage-earner roles assigned to women. Men lose more days from work each year than women; the average housewife works ninety-six hours a week; women drivers have fewer accidents than men do; women college graduates earn half as much as male college graduates; one in eight women who work are the sole support of their family. Even so, fields of study still reflect male-female roles. Science, engineering, law, and business are defined as "men's" fields, while teaching, nursing, social work, and the culinary arts are "women's" fields.

Of course, there has been progress since 1837. A few industries have altered their employment practices to provide equal opportunity for women, state laws and local ordinances are being changed to extend equal protection to women, and the news media have begun to focus on the problems of women. Even Congress reflects a trend toward more power for women. The dozen women serving in Congress in 1972 exercise considerably more power than their predecessors, especially Jeanette Rankin, who in 1917 was the first woman to win a seat in Congress. Historians seem certain to mention Senator Margaret Chase Smith, the first woman to serve in both houses of Congress, and Representative Shirley Chisholm, the first black woman to serve in Congress and also the first black woman to be a presidential candidate. In many ways the lines of a Bob Dylan song are prophetic of women's rights: "For the times they are a-changin'."

Traditional female roles have forced generation after generation of women to be submissive, conceited about their appearance, less competitive with and dependent on men. The 1970's are likely to witness the growth of women's organizations dedicated to redefining the role of women, raising it from that of servants to peers of men.

Homosexual (Gay) Liberation

Since 1950 a dozen or so organizations of homosexuals have been created. The gay liberation movement, as it is called, utilizes public forums, newsletters, journals, and legal aid to alter society's negative definition of homosexuality. Within the past decade homosexuality has become more open and socially visible, especially among an increasingly large number of youth, who regard homosexuality as an alternative life style. On May 10, 1971, the Gay People at Columbia, a group of homosexual male students at Columbia University, established the first homosexual lounge on an American campus.

Despite several theories that seek to explain the alleged increase in homosexuality, there have been few scientific studies of homosexuality.

Many writers have concluded that homosexual behavior in America has not increased very much since the 1953 Kinsey report. Kinsey estimated that only 4 per cent of American males are exclusively homosexual and that only 2 per cent of American females are exclusively homosexual. However, Kinsey concluded that a large number of both sexes engage in some form of heterosexual and homosexual behavior.

It is of interest to note that in the Judeo-Christian culture attitudes differ with regard to male homosexuality and female homosexuality. Male homosexuality is seen as a barrier to reproduction and, therefore, wasteful of semen, while homosexuality in the female does not affect her value as a wife or her ability to reproduce. Historically, female homosexuality has not intruded itself on the public consciousness as much as male homosexuality.

Most of the problems encountered by homosexuals mirror society's predominant attitudes and values. Men and women who show overt signs of physical attraction to members of their own sex are likely to be labeled "queer." Little children quickly learn that it is socially "bad" to be queer, long before they understand the implications of the term. Besides, such reasoning continues, males should be "masculine"and females should be "feminine." Role reversals are frowned upon.

Aware of the social and legal penalties imposed on known homosexuals, most of them elect to hide their sexual preference from nonhomosexuals. Hiding their sexual preference only serves to compound the self-contempt, guilt, and shame many homosexuals experience. Together with women's liberation and radical black groups, leaders of the gay liberation movement believe that their oppression will end only when the present social institutions are drastically altered or overturned.

The need for population control to ensure species survival may nonviolently and quickly alter society's attitudes toward homosexuality. If the survival of the human species no longer requires that all adults be procreative, then perhaps sexual intercourse with members of one's own sex may come to be socially "better"—or at least safer than medication—to prevent pregnancy. In any case, homosexuality has ceased to be a topic openly discussed only by comics in nightclubs.

Social Class

Even though an individual's exact income may be unknown, we are able—by his job classification, clothes, and home address—to place him in a social class. In our status-conscious society there are few places where lower-class people can find either well-paid employment or outstanding recognition. The activities of most formal and informal organizations are geared to middle-class-oriented people. On jobs and in schools the accepted norms of behaviors reflect what is often described by social scientists as a *middle-class bias*. Clubs, holiday parties, and other business-related social activities are designed for middle-class participants. People of the lower class respond by avoiding such activities, a reaction which in turn intensifies their disadvantages.[5]

In the world of work the few high-status employees take active part in the prestigious activities related to their jobs, while most low-status employees share in none at all. Acting as gatekeepers of job-related organizations, high-status employees resist broadening the base of participation to include low-status employees. "They need the time to improve their work skills," and "They wouldn't be happy with *our* crowd," are reasons frequently given for restricting the base of participation. Thus lower-level employees are forced to form their own job-related organizations.

Feeling left out and powerless, most lower-class people spend as little time as possible interacting with people of higher status. Under

[5] John Dollard, *Caste and Class in a Southern Town* (New Haven, Yale University Press, 1937).

extreme conditions of alienation (feelings of isolation, powerlessness, or normlessness) they drop out of school or quit their jobs. Dropout statistics present only a part of the picture, since physical withdrawal from school or job is anticlimactic. Many school-age children are psychological dropouts by the time they are in third or fourth grade. Some middle-class writers arrogantly assume that, by dropping out, lower-class people are proving that they are only happy with "their own kind."

A major complaint of minority-group dropouts is that their teachers or supervisors, mainly through ignorance, insensitivity, or premeditated malice, addressed them in offensive ways ("you people," "boy," "girl"). Not only can such labeling embarrass minority-group people but it may in some instances cause them to become hostile. The most detrimental slip of the lip occurs when a teacher or supervisor refers to minority-group individuals as "you people." This sets up an "us-them" dichotomy which convinces minority-group individuals they must be defensive and paranoid to survive.

Explicit differences between social classes show up in dress and speech. In some business organizations supervisors get needlessly upset about an employee's life style. What difference does it make whether an individual has an Afro haircut or a crew cut? prefers jazz to classical music? says "ya'll" instead of "you-all"? The more effective supervisors acknowledge that they themselves are not paragons of cultural refinement. Furthermore, they realize that there is little relationship between physical

appearance and academic, athletic, or mechanical abilities. Most employers and supervisors, however, have yet to learn what most professional athletic coaches know: It does not matter that an athlete's hair is a bit long or his clothes are flashy; what does matter is his performance.

Elementary and secondary schools are also strongholds of social-class snobbery. To the lower-class student school is a place of many contradictions. He is encouraged to display initiative and curiosity about a subject while passively submitting to his teacher's authority. In some situations he is challenged to be creative but receives an inferior evaluation if his creative efforts do not fit a norm of behavior. He is told to interact with other students but not to be too aggressive. Finally, he is urged to speak *only* "proper" English. Middle-class children are able to follow these codes with a minimum of discomfort. After all, school under these terms is their game. The social-class difference was clearly illustrated in the following situation:

> Mrs. B. was standing at her desk taking roll. Two well dressed, physically attractive girls entered the class talking loudly. Without looking up, Mrs. B. said:
> "Michele and Faith, please take your seats and be quiet. The tardy bell has rung and you're late. I hope you'll tell me after class what was so interesting that you couldn't get to class on time."
> A few seconds later another student entered the room. He was shabbily dressed and his stringy black hair was uncombed. Mrs. B. stopped taking attendance, looked up, and frowned:
> "Didn't you hear the bell, Roland? You people act as if this school operates on mañana time. I'm going to mark you tardy and report you to the office."
> Roland shrugged, never stopped walking until he reached his seat. He slipped quietly into it and began staring out of the window.[6]

Much has been written about middle-class school standards. There is nothing wrong with middle-classness if all children are given an opportunity to achieve it. The most negative aspect of such standards is that few lower-class children can live up to them. Teachers do an inadequate job of teaching school standards to lower-class children. Most middle-class students easily adopt acceptable behavior but selfishly refuse or thoughtlessly fail to help their lower-class classmates achieve it.

Children who do not learn to cope with school norms become frustrated. For the extremely frustrated child dropping out of school is often

[6] Henderson and Bibens, *Teachers Should Care*, 90–91.

better than staying in school and having his ego defenses painfully torn from him, one psychological layer after another. Many children who fail in school learn to hate middle-classness. Their hatred may spread beyond the school to other social systems representing what he believes to be a repressive middle-class society. Many work situations are very similar to school situations; workers who fail to become functional members of their organization may become ardent haters of the organization.

In summary, the most ineffective school and job programs continue to be based on pious, middle-class, snobbish assumptions about *who ought not to be involved* in activities rather than *who needs to be involved*. All members of an organization need to be involved in a wide range of its activities. Job and school projects which require cooperative efforts are especially appropriate for broadening the base of participation, as well as for learning good human relations.

Heterogeneous groupings have the greater potential for behaving democratically than homogeneous groupings. But putting the bodies together does not ensure a democratic grouping. It takes considerable work and planning to make democracy a reality. "There's no need to waste our time working with those people," a high school teacher concluded. "Once a poor nigger always a poor nigger." He was talking about lower-class Negroes, but he could just as well have been referring to Indians, Mexican-Americans, Puerto Ricans, or other deprived minorities. In a democratic society it is imperative that formal and informal organizational activities do not become exclusively social-class or racially determined.

The following article clearly illustrates the need to become consciously aware of the effects of our behavior on other people. But being aware is not enough. We must act to prevent doing harm to others.

Wanted: A Human Relations Approach to Education[7]

Although many phases of American society might fittingly be described by the phrase "man's inhumanity to man," none seems more worthy of this designation than our public schools.

Six years ago I would not have made that statement; then, I would have denied it vehemently. But then I was a young, first-year high school teacher, glossy and polished with the pride and confidence that I would be the best teacher my students had ever known. Now I am older and wiser, dulled by a system that doesn't really care but only pretends to, a system in which textbook is topdog and student is underdog, a system which dehumanizes humans.

[7] By Jacquelene Peters, graduate student, University of Oklahoma. Used by permission.

The Past.

I entered my first teaching assignment never questioning that I knew what education was all about. I had been trained to teach the English language; that was what the students needed, and that was what they were going to get. (Never did I stop to consider then that many of them had a fourth-grade reading level or a hatred for school or alcoholic parents or little money with which to buy a notebook.)

So English I taught—from informal essays to Shakespearean drama, from short stories to the medieval sonnet. I followed the traditional school rules of, "Below 70, give an F," and, "Fix all grades in an accurate curve" without question. I lowered averages for talking, for acting up in class, for failing to get homework, and for chewing gum.

One time an overweight, self-conscious sophomore girl refused to stand up in front of the class and practice our unit on etiquette (etiquette! to a class whose meals meant jelly glasses rather than china and crystal, to students whose, "May I introduce. . .," would receive derisive laughter at home). So I *forced* her to participate, saying that it was her *duty* to the class and to me to do what the rest of the students were doing! When a freckle-faced, implike boy talked back to me, I made him stand up for fifteen minutes while the class and I sat and looked at him.

For four years I taught this way, really feeling that I was a good teacher, not knowing then that I was playing a big part in the "man's inhumanity to man" role. I liked my students, but I didn't try to get close to any of them; my main aims were to keep them relatively quiet and to finish the textbook by the end of the year. These were the criteria absorbed from my teacher-education classes, and doubting them never entered my mind.

Now I know I was wrong.

This discovery came not in the classroom, however, but as the result of my decision to become a counselor. During the course of that specialized training, I began to realize how I—and the whole educational system—have caused more hurt than help, more injury than instruction, more agony than aid. I realized for the first time that each student in every classroom is a unique individual, with hopes, dreams, problems, and needs which form the basis for his classroom behavior. (As a teacher I may have known this, but I was too wrapped up in textbooks, grades, and school rules to care.)

Through counseling I found that there was a whole human world inside that school which had never been visible to me before; in comparison, my English content became irrelevant. I had been preaching simile and metaphor to a girl whose father had been having sexual relations with her since the sixth grade. I was urging nouns and verbs on a boy who had a butcher knife hidden under his bed in wait for the right moment to kill his stepmother. I was assigning book reports to a sixteen-year-old common-law wife whose "husband" was stealing food for them at night and molesting small girls during the day. I was forcing *Julius Caesar* on a boy who believed that men from outer space were communicating with him and asking him to kill the President of the United States and anyone else in authority. These were the kids I was telling to spit out their gum, sit up straight in their seats, and practice introducing their parents to their friends properly.

The incongruity of it all was appalling.

Following my counseling training, I was again placed in an English class-room, only to find that, although I had changed, the educational system had not; now that I saw the possibilities and necessities for humanizing education, I found that rules and traditions bound me in. When I arranged my thirty-six desks in two semicircles rather than the traditional rows, the janitor complained that my room was too hard to sweep. When I used small group interaction, other teachers complained that my classes were too loud. When I suggested to the scheduling adviser that one of my students was enrolled in a course which he had already taken and passed (the boy had asked me what he should do about it), I was told to quit trying to be Jesus Christ in the classroom and to tell the boy that if he kept quiet in the course for the first semester he might get out the second semester. When a student came to me with a personal problem, I could rarely talk with him because teachers were constantly advised not to leave their classes unsupervised. As I began to be more and more student-aware, and less and less subject-aware, I found myself becoming more and more disillusioned by the little box in which I was supposed to fit, and less and less inclined to want to fit there. I found that humanizing education was not the game we were playing. So I became a teacher dropout.

The Present.

Now that I am outside the public school system rather than in it, I can more clearly see what is happening: the educational system seems designed to hinder rather than help a child fulfill his basic human needs. These needs, as listed by Abraham H. Maslow in *Motivation and Personality*, are:

1. *Physiological needs.* These are needs for air, food, water, and physical comfort, which must be met before the following needs can be satisfied.

2. *Safety needs.* Using children for an example, Maslow finds that they have a desire for freedom from fear and insecurity. Safety needs are needs to avoid harmful or painful incidents.

3. *Belongingness.* Needs to belong are the first of the higher-order needs. Maslow means that the human personality wants security. The human being wants to be somebody, even though in a small group.

4. *Love needs.* Man has always had and will always have the desire to love someone else and be loved in return.

5. *Self-esteem needs.* Man wants to feel that he is worthwhile, that he can master something of his own environment, that he has a competence and an independence and a freedom and a feeling of being recognized for some kind of endeavor.

6. *Self-actualization needs.* These are the highest needs, as Maslow considers them. They involve the needs for recognition and for aesthetic reality. Man has a strong desire and need to know and understand not only himself but the world about him.

If these are the basic needs that school children, as human beings, have, then the school should, in the course of its systemization, be attempting to fulfill them. A brief analysis will indicate that it is not.

First are the *physiological needs.* Although many cities have new, showy classroom facilities and buildings, many more do not, especially in small rural towns and inner cities. A dark, gloomy hall, a moldy room with stale bathroom smells, an unappetizing cafeteria tray or a can of pork and beans brought from home (or no lunch at all), a light bulb dangling from a frayed cord in the ceiling —is this the way the most affluent society in the world meets the physiological needs of its most precious human beings, the children?

Next are the *safety needs.* Do our children feel safe in our schools? This means freedom from fear, insecurity, harmful and painful incidents. How can they? Many of them live in mortal terror (little ones and big ones alike) of threatened or actual punishment with teacher's paddle, ruler, or rubber hose. They fear being shaken, slapped, scorned, ridiculed, lambasted, and ignored. They fear those inconsistent giants called teachers who can so mercilessly mete out punishment with the flick of the wrist or a slash of the tongue. It is no wonder that assaults on teachers increased 800 per cent between 1964 and 1968. The children have finally decided to show the teachers what it is like to feel a need for safety.

There is also the *belonging need.* Of course, our schools consider the belonging issue to be important—haven't we all heard teachers say, "He belongs in jail," or "She belongs in the slow group," or "I'm glad that one doesn't belong to me"? No one ever considers where the child *wants* to belong; no one helps him *feel* that he belongs. Instead, on their own bases, teachers issue out a kind of segregated belonging: "*You* belong with the rich, and *you* with the poor. *You* belong with the blacks, and *you* with the whites. *You* belong with the smart, and *you* with the dumb." In essence they are saying, "You belong where I put you and whether you like it or not, that's where you are going to stay." Since statistics show that more than one-third of all students drop out of the public schools before graduation, it is obvious that one place they feel they do *not* belong is in school.

Fourth are the *love needs.* This set of needs is truly ignored in the educational process. Who has ever heard of expressing, or feeling, love in the classroom? The formal, scientifically structured educational process seems aimed at avoiding admittance of such a need. Even when affection is displayed by students in the halls between classes, teachers—feeling that school is not the place for love—intervene.

Next are the *self-esteem needs*. These are needs that the schools seem especially adept at denying. This denial often takes the form of grading. The teacher, playing the game God in the Classroom, looks down on the efforts of the underlings below and passes a value judgment on them. He dares to say, "That is poor work—F work—even if you did do your best. You will just have to try harder." He takes an artificial yardstick and uses it to measure a human endeavor; he never gives self-esteem a chance. What the teacher is really doing is fulfilling his own self-esteem needs by playing Almighty with the Gradebook. Who does the school exist for, the teacher or the student?

The highest of all human needs is *self-actualization*. Well, here is the big one, the need that theoretically does not even reveal itself until the others have been met. Then why discuss it? Because somehow the teachers and the schools are confused. They think that this need, because it is the highest, should be dealt with first. They assume that all students have, or *should* have, an intense desire to know things, a need for abstract thoughts and aesthetic experiences. Therefore, they jam textbooks in students' faces and facts down students' throats. They disregard security, belonging, love, and self-esteem in their fanatic worship of knowledge, not realizing that the needs they are so casually tossing aside must be met first.

When are our schools going to place the basic human needs first and facts second? When are they going to help a child feel secure, loved, and important, instead of afraid, unwanted, unloved, and unnecessary? When is the *child* going to come first in education? How long before it is too late?

Suggested Reading

Adelstein, Michael E., and Jean G. Pival, eds. *Women's Liberation*. New York, St. Martin's Press, Inc., 1972.

Allport, Gordon W. *The Nature of Prejudice*. Reading, Mass., Addison-Wesley Publishing Co., Inc., 1954.

Banton, Michael. *Race Relations*. New York, Basic Books, Inc., 1967.

Beard, Mary R. *Woman as a Force in History*. New York, Collier Books, 1971.

Becker, Raymond. *The Other Face of Love*. New York, Grove Press, 1969.

Belliveau, Fred, and Lin Richter. *Understanding Human Sexual Inadequacy*. New York, Bantam Books, Inc., 1970.

**Suggested
Reading**
(continued)

Bird, Caroline. *Born Female*. Rev. ed. New York, Pocket Books, 1971.

Blalock, Hubert M. *Toward a Theory of Minority-Group Relations*. New York, G. P. Putnam's Sons, 1967.

Bosworth, Allan R. *America's Concentration Camps*. New York, W. W. Norton & Company, 1967.

Burma, John H. *Spanish-Speaking Groups in the United States*. Durham, N.C., Duke University Press, 1954.

———, ed. *Mexican-Americans in the United States: A Reader*. New York, Harper & Row, 1970.

Cahn, Edgar S. *Our Brother's Keeper: The Indian in White America*. Cleveland, World Publishing Company, 1969.

Clark, M. *Health in the Mexican-American Culture*. Berkeley, University of California Press, 1970.

Combs, Arthur W., ed. *Perceiving, Behaving, Becoming: New Focus for Education*. New York, Association for Supervision and Curriculum Development, 1962.

Cordasco, Francesco, and E. Bucohioni. *Puerto Rican Children in Mainland Schools*. Metuchen, N.J., Scarecrow Press, 1968.

Cory, Donald W. *The Lesbian in America*. New York, The Citadel Press, Inc., 1964.

Crary, Ryland. *Humanizing the School: Curriculum Development Theory*. New York, Alfred A. Knopf, Inc., 1969.

Debo, Angie. *A History of the Indians of the United States.* Norman, University of Oklahoma Press, 1970.

Deloria, Vine, Jr. *Custer Died for Your Sins: An Indian Manifesto*. New York, The Macmillan Company, 1969.

———. *We Talk, You Listen*. New York, The Macmillan Company, 1970.

Epstein, Charlotte. *Intergroup Relations for the Classroom Teacher*. New York, Houghton Mifflin Company, 1968.

Equal Educational Opportunity. Cambridge, Harvard University Press, 1969.

Farb, Peter. *Man's Rise to Civilization as Shown by the Indians of North America*. Englewood Cliffs, N.J., Prentice-Hall, Inc., 1964.

Feuer, Lewis S. *The Conflict of Generations: The Character and Significance of Student Movements*. New York, Basic Books, Inc., 1969.

Firestone, Shulamith. *The Dialectic of Sex: The Case for Feminist Revolution*. New York, William Morrow, 1970.

Gagan, John H., and William Simon, eds. *The Sexual Scene*. Chicago, Aldine Publishing Company, 1970.

Girdner, Audrie, and Anne Loftis. *The Great Betrayal: The Evacuation of the Japanese Americans During World War II*. New York, The Macmillan Company, 1969.

Glock, Charles, and Rodney Stark. *Christian Belief and Anti-Semitism*. New York, Harper & Row, 1966.

Goodman, Mary E. *Race Awareness in Young Children*. Rev. ed. New York, Collier, 1964.

Grebler, Leo, et al. *The Mexican-American People*. New York, The Free Press, 1970.

Hanna, Thomas. *Bodies in Revolt*. New York, Holt, Rinehart & Winston, Inc., 1970.

Hansen, G. C., *The Chinese in California*. Portland, Oreg., R. Abel Company, 1970.

Harris, Louis, and Bert H. Swanson. *Black-Jewish Relations in New York City*. New York, Praeger Publishers, 1970.

Heller, Celia S. *Mexican-American Youth: Forgotten Youth at the Crossroads*. New York, Random House, Inc., 1967.

Henderson, George, and Robert F. Bibens. *Teachers Should Care: Social Perspectives of Teaching*. New York, Harper & Row, 1970.

Hoffman, Martin. *The Gay World: Male Homosexuality and the Social Creation of Evil*. New York, Basic Books, Inc., 1968.

Holt, John. *How Children Fail*. New York, Dell Publishing Co., Inc., 1964.

Hosokawa, Bill. *Nisei: The Quiet Americans*. New York, W. W. Norton, 1969.

Hough, Henry W. *Development of Indian Resources*. Denver, Colo., World Press, 1967.

Howard, John R., ed. *Awakening Minorities: American Indians, Mexican-Americans, Puerto Ricans*. Chicago, Aldine Publishing Company, 1970.

Josephy, Alvin M., Jr. *The Indian Heritage of America*. New York, Alfred A. Knopf, Inc., 1968.

Jung, Carl G. *The Undiscovered Self*. Boston, Atlantic–Little, Brown, 1958.

Katz, Irwin, and Patricia Gurin, eds. *Race and the Social Sciences*. New York, Basic Books, Inc., 1969.

Kinsey, Alfred C., et al. *Sexual Behavior in the Human Female*. Philadelphia, W. B. Saunders Company, 1953.

Kitano, Harry L. *Japanese-Americans: The Evolution of a Subculture*. Englewood Cliffs, N.J., Prentice-Hall, Inc., 1969.

Kozol, Jonathan. *Death at an Early Age*. Boston, Houghton Mifflin Company, 1967.

Suggested Reading (continued)

Kramer, Judith R. *The American Minority Community.* New York, Thomas Y. Crowell Company, 1970.

Lamson, Peggy. *Few Are Chosen: American Women in Political Life Today.* Boston, Houghton Mifflin Company, 1968.

Lewis, Oscar. *La Vida: A Puerto Rican in the Culture of Poverty—San Juan and New York.* New York, Random House, Inc., 1966.

Marshall, Donald, and Robert Suggs, eds. *Human Sexual Behavior.* New York, Basic Books, Inc., 1971.

Millett, Kate. *Sexual Politics.* New York, Avon Books, 1971.

Momaday, N. Scott. *House Made of Dawn.* New York, Harper & Row, 1968.

Moore, Joan. *Mexican-Americans.* Englewood Cliffs, N.J., Prentice-Hall, Inc., 1970.

Morgan, Robin, ed. *Sisterhood Is Powerful: An Anthology of Writings from the Women's Liberation Movement.* New York, Random House, 1970.

Myrdal, Gunnar, et al. *An American Dilemma.* New York, Harper & Brothers, 1944.

Near, B. *Freedom to Live and Learn.* Philadelphia, Franklin Publishing Co., 1968.

Neill, A. S. *Freedom, Not License!* New York, Hart Publishing Co., Inc., 1966.

Noar, Gertrude. *Teaching and Learning the Democratic Way.* Englewood Cliffs, N.J., Prentice-Hall, Inc., 1963.

Orfield, Gary. *A Study of the Termination Policy.* Chicago, University of Chicago Press, 1966.

Pickney, Alphonso. *Black Americans.* Englewood Cliffs, N.J., Prentice-Hall, Inc., 1969.

Raab, Earl, and Seymour M. Lipset. *Prejudice and Society.* New York, Anti-Defamation League of B'nai B'rith, 1959.

Rogers, Carl. *Freedom to Learn: A View of What Education Might Become.* Columbus, Ohio, Charles E. Merrill Publishing Company, 1969.

———. *Person to Person: The Problem of Being Human.* New York, The Real People Press, 1967.

Rokeach, Milton. *The Open and Closed Mind.* New York, Basic Books, Inc., 1960.

Rose, Peter I. *The Subject Is Race: Traditional Ideologies and the Teaching of Race Relations.* New York, Oxford University Press, 1968.

Senior, Clarence. *The Puerto Ricans: Strangers—Then Neighbors.* Chicago, Quadrangle Books, 1965.

Seward, Georgene, and Robert Williamson. *Sex Roles in*

Changing Society. New York, Alfred A. Knopf, Inc., 1970.

Sexton, Patricia C. *Spanish Harlem: Anatomy of Poverty.* New York, Harper & Row, 1965.

Socarides, Charles W. *The Overt Homosexual.* New York, Grune and Stratton, 1968.

Steiner, Stan. *The New Indians.* Dell Publishing Company, 1968.

Sung, Betty L. *Mountain of Gold: The Story of the Chinese in America.* New York, The Macmillan Company, 1967.

United States Commission on Civil Rights. *Racism in America and How to Combat It.* Washington, D.C., U.S. Government Printing Office, 1970.

CHAPTER 8

Getting It Together

**The
Spiritual
Revolution**

Revolution in America is more than a probability; it is a reality. Most of the news stories focus on violent programs of change, while nonviolent programs receive much less coverage. Although less dramatic than violence-oriented programs, a spiritual revolution is sweeping across America.

Most religious people believe that the solutions to our social problems lie not in science but in God. Spiritual force rather than physical force, they believe, will change social institutions. In their view, if a revolutionary blows up a company building, his action does not change the "system." In fact, by destroying the building, the revolutionary has only inconvenienced the company. The executives simply find a new location in which to conduct their business. The part of the company the revolutionary should seek to change, then, is the people, not the buildings. If the company is bad, it is because its people are bad. The religious reformer tries to change the company by converting the executives to his commitment and behavior.

Many revolutionaries overlook the obvious: If America is a racist nation, it is because the American people are racists; if America is an immoral society, it is because the American people are immoral. A reformer impelled by religious faith seeks to change people.

Every true revolutionary dedicates his life to his cause, and love for his cause comes before anyone and anything else. This kind of devotion is hard for many Americans to understand, consumption-oriented as they are and conditioned to love things—cars, clothes, and money—more than people. Ob-

viously, the revolution that is centered in religious faith has many ramifications. In order to live up to his pledge, for example, the individual who truly commits himself to Christ must commit himself to accept and love other people. The love found in the Bible is neither sentimental nor passive, says the Christian. It is expressed in action. The true believer in the Christian ethic cannot love others and remain unconcerned about their welfare. Nor can he be uncommitted to social justice.

Angry nonwhite revolutionaries claim that there are too few true Christians among the whites. Pointing his finger inward in his book *Words of Revolution*, Tom Skinner spelled out the challenge to black Christians:

> You see, I know the other side of it. I used to run the streets of Harlem as a black revolutionary. And I used to rap down to the others in the community, "Brothers, we gotta get together, man. We gotta get together and do our black thing. We gotta come together and unite against Charlie because he's the enemy." But funny thing. Every guy whose head I busted, you know who he was? A black. Every store I raided, you know who owned it? A black. And yet I went around

saying, "We gotta get together." There is no way you can talk about getting together with each other until you become committed to each other.

Look at the political situation. We stand up in America and we say, "one nation under God." We're not one nation. We're not together. We have Democrats against Republicans, blacks and whites at each other's throats. We have Indians and white society now in a clash, minority groups being locked out of the system. And we stand up and claim with integrity that we are "one nation under God." We are not one nation and the closest thing to being "under God" is that we have His name on our money. That is all. We are still divided. And this division will keep any revolution of love from succeeding.[1]

Revolution is here. The alternatives are threefold: we can ignore our enemies, we can kill our enemies, or we can love our enemies. Love is the message not only of old religions but also of new psychologies. The question to ponder at this point is taken from a line of a Broadway play: "Which way, America?"

The Violent People

No society can exist without order. Violence is the result of the breakdown of social order. Social order is maintained—and violence is prevented—by the effective functioning of legal, political, and social institutions—especially the agencies of law enforcement. Individuals may form communities, but only through social institutions can they form nations. As a nation, communities solve their joint problems collectively and thereby become civilized. Though we are civilized in terms of institutions, it appears that we are not yet civilized in our interpersonal relations. As a nation we are afflicted by a kind of institutional paralysis, and we seem incapable of peacefully solving our rapidly growing national and international problems.

Through violence white Americans have kept nonwhite Americans from exercising their full citizenship rights. Nonwhite militants believe that nonwhite Americans have been patiently nonviolent for too long. Others, who reject violence as a means to freedom, do not believe that impatience per se will secure their rights. Nor do they believe that to injure or kill whites to gain their freedom will further the cause of human freedom. Nonwhites who assume that violence will not result in a counter-

---

[1] Tom Skinner, *Words of Revolution* (Grand Rapids, Zondervan, 1970), 55.

reaction of violence are naïve. On the other hand, however, whites who assume that continued segregation of and discrimination against non-whites will never be met with violence are equally naïve.

Even though ours is a violent history, most Americans are ignorant about violence.[2] We perpetuate childlike fantasies and smug assumptions that violence is bred by some unknown "bad guys" who will be destroyed by some unknown "good guys." Commissions are appointed, research is conducted, and books are written to reassure the public that justice will triumph. But the basic public attitude remains unchanged. Few people care enough to become actively involved in combating the conditions leading to violence.

There seems to be something fascinating about violence. The word "violence" has a menacing, disturbing quality. It implies something dreaded, powerful, destructive, or eruptive. It startles, frightens, and horrifies us. Yet violence is also exciting and dramatic. Reading about it and sometimes participating in it gives many people a tingling pleasure. On television screens there appear for our amusement scenes of fighting, beating, torturing, and killing. We are a Pow! Crash! Ugh! Bang! nation. We are even willing to write off the agony that is a part of war, the ultimate violence, as a cheap price to pay for securing "peace" throughout the world.

Much of the movie violence is portrayed semirealistically, even romantically. Jesse James, Billy the Kid, Al Capone, Bonnie and Clyde, Ma Barker, and other criminals are remembered, often with admiration. The superhero of the 1960's was James Bond, a machinelike man who was licensed to kill and destroy and who was even more violent, callous, and aggressive than old-style criminals. Heroes like Bond allow us to experience violence from the safe distance of our movie or television seats. The fake quality of this kind of violence gives the impression that being beaten, kicked, and cut, while unpleasant, is not really very painful or serious. Such physical treatment may incapacitate a weakling—but not our movie heroes. After being knocked down or shot, our heroes roll over, open their eyes, jump up, rub their chins, grin, and move on. This is one of the lessons children learn by watching movies.

Even sweet little old men and women peek at violent orgies when they get a chance. To accommodate them and others, entrepreneurs promote bloody sports spectacles. People pay large amounts to see their champions

2 James Campbell et al., *Law and Order Reconsidered* (New York, Bantam Books, Inc., 1970). A similar conclusion was reached in an unpublished paper, "Toward a Theory of Nonviolence in a Violent Nation," by Patricia Westbrook, graduate student in the University of Oklahoma, in 1971. Her paper formed the basis for this section.

of violence perform. Crowds come alive when a man is hit hard over the heart or head, when blood squirts out of his nose or eyes, when he wobbles under the attack, and his pursuer continues to smash at him with devastating impact; and they cheer when the loser falls. Athletes participating in these public spectacles are much like the ancient gladiators who risked their lives for the public that would cheer their victories.

We are becoming increasingly aware of our national characteristic of violence and to recognize it as a social problem. As our awareness of violence increases, so too do our responses. Once aware of the violence in our land, we tend to try to alter the facts to suit our definitions of the situation, responding as it were to our own fears. Some people maintain that we must meet force with force: an eye for an eye and a life for a life. The number of weapons purchased in this country for purposes of self-defense (that is, to have the power to kill or maim another human being) is, to say the least, frightening. At the national level the emergence of the United

"*I used to think it was wrong to coddle criminals,
but that was before I became a criminal.*"

States as a great power was accompanied by a growing commitment to violence as a technique for implementing international policy. But violence is not unique to our country; throughout the history of the Western nations violence has been a technique of those committed to social change and political control.

Children become acquainted with the uses of violence early in life. Many of their games and toys stimulate violence, rather than instilling in them the belief that it is immoral to injure another person or to take a human life. Such toys also teach children to use violence to suppress violence. Our penal system offers other illustrations of violence employed to suppress violence. At one time or another every concerned person—seeing policemen's drawn guns, soldiers firing on the enemy, hunters stalking the nation's wildlife—is shocked into the awareness that as a people we greatly value instruments made for the purpose of killing. The easy access that children, the mentally disturbed, and professional criminals have to the weapons of destruction is alarming. Yet scores of bills to establish gun controls have been defeated. Americans spend about two billion dollars a year on guns, and each year the federal government disposes of about 100,000 guns at bargain prices.

Today the pattern of violence appears to be changing. In 1967 there were 83 riots, in which 83 people were killed, and 2,000 were injured. Property damage—almost all of it in central cities—totaled $61 million. Since 1967 riots have been replaced by bombings, assaults on the police, and other random acts of violence. During the 15-month period ending in April, 1971, there were at least 4,330 bombings, 1,475 attempted bombings, and 35,129 threatened bombings in the United States.

What effective counter is there for violence? It will surely have to begin with motivating more people to seek an end to behavior that triggers violence. At the same time we must find ways to curtail individual acts of violence through education, medical treatment, counseling, and training. Such programs may be successful in most cases if they are undertaken in time. Our penal systems and courts of law do little to curtail violence. We are still using nineteenth-century methods in our prisons and early-twentieth-century codes of conduct in our courts. Basic human rights to dignity, fair trial, and rehabilitation are generally neglected. How, then, can we have law and order?

Law and Order

One of the most important issues in political campaigns of the past several years has been law and order. Federal, state, and local governments have appointed commissions to study problems attendant on maintaining order. Millions of words of copy have appeared in the press, and countless hours of rhetoric have been devoted to the subject. But crime rates continue to spiral upward. Public concern grows, but not public understanding.[3]

The 1970 annual report of the Federal Bureau of Investigation noted the continuing rise in the crime rate. In 1970 crime increased 11 per cent over 1969. During this period 5,568,200 major crimes were reported in the United States. Bank robberies increased 29 per cent, larceny 15 per cent, burglary 11 per cent, murder 8 per cent, aggravated assault 8 per cent, automobile theft 6 per cent, and rape 2 per cent. From 1960 to 1970 arrests of adults for violent crimes increased 67 per cent, while arrests of juveniles increased 167 per cent.

Robbery with guns increased from 99,000 in 1968 to 115,000 in 1969, aggravated assault by gun increased from 65,000 to 73,000, and murder by gun increased from 8,900 to 9,400 (equaling the number of Americans killed in combat in Vietnam that year).

Every year policemen are presented citations for outstanding achievement, often for capturing or killing dangerous criminals. To most policemen and to many civilians these citations and the brave deeds they symbolize are the sum total of law and order. But citations are an inadequate approach to this complex problem. Somehow we must make it unnecessary for people to break laws in order to survive.

The brunt of urban crime is borne by central-city property owners and residents. For example, the Small Business Chamber of Commerce in Harlem estimated that in 1970 the cost of crime in central Harlem was approximately $2 billion. This estimate included $1.8 billion as the cost of thefts to support the narcotics habit. Property loss not linked to narcotics was estimated at $12 million. The cost of crimes against persons, such as muggings and holdups, was estimated at $12 million. The cost of public law enforcement and criminal justice was excluded from these figures.

Alcoholism is also associated with crime. In the 1960's one-third of all homicides and one-half of all traffic deaths were linked to alcohol. In 1972 the National Institute on Alcohol and Alcoholism of the Department of Health, Education, and Welfare estimated that there are more than nine million alcoholics in America. The Institute concluded that alcohol is the nation's most abused—and socially accepted—drug. The life span of

[3] Erle Stanley Gardner, *Cops on Campus and Crime in the Street* (New York, William Morrow & Co., Inc., 1970).

alcoholics is shortened by ten to twelve years, their lost work time costs about $10 billion annually and the damage they cause to health, welfare, and property totals $5 billion a year.

While not as dangerous as heroin, marijuana is a much more controversial issue. Recent Gallup polls found that the percentage of adults (eighteen years of age and older) in the United States who use marijuana nearly tripled between October, 1969, and March, 1970. During this period marijuana use rose from 4 per cent to 11 per cent. Thus, in 1970, fifteen million people, according to the poll, had tried marijuana. The National Commission on Marijuana and Drug Abuse noted that in 1971 approximately twenty-four million Americans had tried marijuana.

The percentage of marijuana users is almost as high in the suburbs as in the central cities, but it is much lower in small towns and rural areas. Current use of marijuana is highest in the eighteen-to-twenty-nine age group; more men than women use the drug; and persons with a college background are much more likely to have used marijuana than those with less formal education.

In 1972 the National Commission on Marijuana and Drug Abuse recommended the elimination of all penalties for possession of small amounts of marijuana. This recommendation was based on the commission's conclusion that when it is used in small amounts and infrequently, marijuana is harmless and does not constitute a legal problem. Even so, the commission did not urge that marijuana be legalized. Critics of the commission's report compare marijuana with alcohol and demand its legalization. This, at best, is a weak argument, for a strong case could be built against letting alcohol remain legal. While the debate continues, hundreds of persons are arrested each year for possession of marijuana.

The concept of law and order as involving the preservation of the family, the prevention of cruelty by government regulations, and the restructuring of nonresponsive institutions such as public schools and welfare agencies is foreign to most Americans. Yet this aspect of law and order is tremendously important. Law and order must be accompanied by moral rightness. In October, 1971, the black and the white citizens of Hancock County, Georgia, surprised the people of surrounding counties by calling an end to their weapons race. In a rare mood of sanity, they decided not to pursue the weapon stock-piling that was likely to lead to several deaths. Perhaps other counties—and nations—will follow their example.

**The
Poor**

Despite our great national wealth, millions of American children grow up in circumstances which deny them the opportunity to achieve satisfying, productive lives. In this nation dedicated to freedom and equality, many of our citizens still struggle for survival on a day-to-day basis. The poor of the urban ghettos are the most brutalized and unprotected citizens of the nation. Without a doubt slums breed violent people, and, with our cities rotting at the core, a contagion of violence is spreading throughout them. Until the basic needs of the poor are met in a peaceful and orderly fashion and on a long-term basis, violence will continue.

In 1970 there were 25.5 million poverty-stricken persons in America, an increase of 1.2 million over 1969. More than 650,000 persons included in the increase lived in the suburbs—for the first time poverty grew at a faster rate in American suburbs than in the central cities. Most of the poor who live in the suburbs are "invisible"; they often live in neat, well-kept houses. Approximately 8.2 million (30 per cent) of the nation's poor live in the central cities, and 5.2 million (21 per cent) live in the metropolitan areas surrounding them.

Slightly more than one out of every ten Americans (12.6 per cent) had an annual income below the government-set poverty line (for example, the poverty line for a nonfarm family of four was $3,968). Many of the nation's poor are under fourteen years of age (34 per cent) or over sixty-five years of age (19 per cent), and these are the groups—the young and the old—whose basic needs for survival are being neglected. While many white Americans are trying to adjust to the psychological and economic problems associated with retirement from work, the average black man does not live long enough to collect his social security benefits.

The National Advisory Commission on Civil Disorders commented: "What white Americans have never fully understood—but what blacks can't forget—is that white society is deeply implicated in the ghetto. White institutions created it, white institutions maintain it, and white society condones it."[4] Now both white and black people must correct the inequalities found in the ghetto.

The poor of all colors have more legal problems than the rest of society. They cannot afford expensive legal counsel, bond, or retrials. The recent increase in efforts on their behalf, such as the store-front legal-aid

[4] *National Advisory Commission on Civil Disorders* (New York, Bantam Books, Inc., 1968), 2.

services, only emphasizes their unmet needs in our system of justice.[5] From birth to death the curse of poverty weighs heavily on the slum dweller, and the law gives little relief. The poor seldom have access to lawyers. Strategies to help the poor include abolishment of court costs and long-range reforms of laws and institutions that work unfairly against them. But long-range strategies are not enough. The poor need adequate legal redress for their grievances today. As the National Commission on the Causes and Prevention of Violence concluded, to be poor and denied justice is intolerable.

Poverty is not restricted to the big-city slums. It is a curse of the rural areas as well, particularly among migrant workers. Very much like the sweatshops of the 1930's, there is much abuse of child labor on farms

[5] Melvin M. Belli, *The Law Revolutions* (Hollywood, Sherbourne Press, 1968).

employing migrant workers. In 1970 a study by the American Friends Service Committee concluded that child-labor abuse is not only tolerated but encouraged in America. Though the employment of children as industrial laborers was outlawed in 1938, one-fourth of the farm workers in 1970 were under sixteen (some as young as six). Their pay ranged from 12 cents a crate for strawberries, to an average hourly wage of $1.12.

America's children need clearly defined legal rights and accessible legal procedures to enforce these human rights:

1. *The right to be well born.* Every child has the right to be born of a mother who has had adequate nutrition and prenatal care, who has been educated in the subjects of pregnancy and birth, and who has borne her child without the use of unnecessary drugs or procedures which may be dangerous to her or her child.

2. *The right to shelter.* Every child has the right to live in a home where he is protected from adverse environmental conditions and diseases, malnutrition, and injury to the spirit.

3. *The right to a humanistic education.* Every child has the right to be taught to respect himself and other people and to learn to be a productive member of his society.

4. *The right to liberty.* Every child has the right to be protected from abuse and given the same legal safeguards which the Constitution extends to adults.

Poverty affects all of society, not just the poor. The average citizen, the "Forgotten Man," is not poor enough to qualify for free legal service, and he is not wealthy enough to afford expensive legal counsel. To make matters worse, every day he read about proposals to increase taxes so as to provide more "free" assistance to the poor. Such proposals make him angry, and he is becoming angrier every year. In his anger and resentment he listens to racists, superpatriots, and demagogues.

Fortunately there are several organizations—including the National Urban League, the National Association for the Advancement of Colored People, the Society of Friends, and the Southern Christian Leadership Conference—committed to improving social conditions by nonviolent means. The efforts and achievements of the men and women who comprise these organizations offer much-needed encouragement during periods of pessimism.

**Social
Order**
Social order is not achieved or maintained without effort. We must consciously work at not destroying each other. Yet all around us we see men destroying men. Cavemen used clubs; modern men destroy with words. In many ways physical aggression is less brutalizing than verbal aggression. The modern casualties are walking dead; they are the socially and psychologically destroyed members of society.

As societies become more complex, the methods of maintaining social order also become more complex, impersonal, and structured. Indeed, when a society becomes highly complex, mobile, and pluralistic, the beneficiaries—and also the victims—of technological changes need more protection, not less. The influence of the traditional stabilizing institutions, such as the family and the church, have decreased as we have become more dependent on systems of law and government to maintain social order.

We have moved to a point where legal procedures and correctional institutions occupy a pre-eminent position in the preservation of social order. Whether for good or ill, we are committed to formal legal institutions as the primary agencies of social control. The "rule of law" and its corollary "respect for the law" reflect the idea that people should recognize the legitimacy of the law as a means of ordering and controlling the behavior of all people in a society. The incongruity of our commitment to legal order is that many people do not really want law-enforcement officials to follow "the letter of the law" when their own freedom is being restricted. They want officials to be lenient with them—to give them "arm-chair equity, or fireside justice"—but to prosecute with vigor people whom they do not know or like. There are two clear lessons to be learned from the maintenance of social order in America:

1. Social order requires that political and social institutions be able to improve themselves and respond more effectively to the legitimate complaints of minority groups within our society who are currently pressing their claims upon the larger public.

2. Social order in America demands a modern system of criminal justice which will effectively control deviant behavior in a fair and humane manner.

Reoccurring prison riots have caused many concerned citizens to support the following basic rights for prisoners:

1. The right to due process of law. Prisoners unable to afford lawyers should be provided free legal counsel.

2. The right to an education that will provide optimum intellectual stimulation and growth, and also vocational training for meaningful employment in the highest skill for which the prisoner is qualified.

3. The right to safety—freedom from assault and the fear of assault by fellow prisoners and guards.

4. The right to a decent place to live and healthful food.

5. The right to family visitation, including the right to conjugal visitation.

6. The right to uninhibited communication with family and friends.

7. The right to release at the earliest time.

8. The right to meaningful employment after release from prison.

Obviously, the securing of these rights will not prevent initial criminal acts, but they may greatly reduce prison riots and the rate of recidivism.

The fact that blacks and Spanish-speaking persons comprise more than 60 per cent of jail and prison inmates but less than 2 per cent of the employees of these institutions suggests additional areas of needed improvement.

In the past two decades many people have publicly supported the idea that civil disobedience and even violent acts in violation of existing laws are justified to achieve social or political goals. Cases in point include the white majority in the North and the South who resist enforcement of the public school rights of nonwhites. Other examples are the policemen who brutalized the demonstrators in Chicago during the Democratic convention in 1968. The same idea—that acts of disobedience to laws are justified if the social cause is moral—has been expressed by militant college students, blacks, and others pressing for social change. They cite the Boston Tea Party and other historical acts of civil disobedience as justification for their behavior. "Violence," they say, "is as American as apple pie."

It it is the latter acts—the illegal and violent activities of minority groups—that have been most perplexing and disturbing to the great majority of white Americans. They have prompted an intense interest in philosophical questions about man's obedience to the state. Business luncheons and suburban cocktail parties have come to sound like university seminars in philosophy. Middle Americans are preoccupied with the rightness or the wrongness of "what the kids and the blacks are doing." In fact, most Americans are experiencing a *conscience crisis*. The tactics of the minority-group demonstrators have encountered stiff opposition, but many white Americans sympathize with the goals sought by the angry demonstrators. "If I were black," some whites say, "I'd riot too."

To most whites, a radical black militant who bombs a college building or takes public officials as hostages or attacks a policeman is not an ordinary protestor—he is a *black* protestor. He is different. Social scientists say that he is acting out of a profound alienation from society; he believes that the existing social and political order in America is perpetuating his "colonial bondage" with an organized "imperialist force." Accepting the social scientific rhetoric, a growing number of blacks interpret their acts of violence as prerevolutionary acts to gain freedom, not as crimes. It is psychologically easier for groups to use violence against the police and other symbols of authority when they define their action as legitimate.

America's social problems, of which radical black militancy is but one aspect, are grave and deep. We are finally being forced, as a nation, to understand the awesome dimensions of these problems and what they have done to our people, both white and nonwhite. When enough of us realize that we must transcend our history and create new institutions, new customs, and new attitudes and lay to rest the old self-validating judgments of white supremacy and nonwhite inferiority—then we will achieve racial peace and justice.

Styles of Leadership

We learn our values, attitudes, and behavior from formal and informal social institutions. Whether institutional experiences are planned or just "happen," they become the basis on which we accept or reject people who are culturally different. For this reason, the quality of our interpersonal and intrapersonal activities significantly affects our readiness to live in a pluralistic society. With few exceptions, religious, educational, and business organizations bring together a great number and variety of cultural backgrounds. They also bring together a great number of human relations problems.

The ultimate goal of an organization's human relations program should be to help each member become aware of and achieve his optimum individual and social growth. This process includes freedom to be and to express oneself as long as one does not violate or infringe upon the rights of others. Specifically, a human relations program should teach all members of an organization that cultural and racial differences are not valid reasons for rejection. Individuals must be taught to live with and accept cultural differences.

Because we learn what we live, the major training emphasis in an organization should be upon living good human relations.[6] People should learn to live together. Learning about other people is not enough; we must also learn to live with them. For this reason interaction is the best medium for communicating appropriate behavior. Dynamic leadership is needed if we are to prevent intergroup and intragroup conflicts which reach destructive proportion.

Leadership is the art and exercise of influence to direct people in such a way as to obtain their confidence, respect, and cooperation. Administrators who practice good human relations are able to achieve the goals of their organization. There is a very appropriate saying in the military service: "One can command without being a leader, but the commander is more effective if he is also a good leader." Administrators must have

[6] Robert Tannenbaum and Sheldon A. Davis, "Values, Man, and Organizations," *Industrial Management Review*, Vol. 10 (Winter, 1959), 67–83.

interpersonal competence, the emotional ability to understand the effect of their own behavior and personality upon the behavior and personalities of others.[7]

Despite much breast-beating about democracy in work situations, most employees assume that autocratic control is necessary to get the work done. This assumption is not supported by scientific data. There is ample evidence to support the contention that democratic systems can result in more group output than autocratic control. Administrators who develop democratic work teams by allowing their subordinates to participate in group decisions usually have few production or morale problems. Unfortunately, most administrators have little understanding of group dynamics and are autocratic in leadership.

"Today, Melvin Mefwisse's house—tomorrow, the world!"

Artist: Herbert Goldberg. Copyright 1971 Saturday Review, Inc.

Autocratic leaders tend to be strict disciplinarians who believe in delegating very little decision-making responsibility to other members of the team. Some autocratic administrators are patronizing when they interact with their subordinates. They also make themselves the primary source of all standards of production (*"I* want you to . . .")*. Though autocratic leaders may get a fair amount of production from their groups, production is dependent on the presence of the leaders. There is, in short, a high degree of dependence on the leader for feedback and also for keeping the group intact. The autocratically controlled group is also characterized by intense competitiveness, lack of initiative in assuming responsibility, and buck-passing.

[7] See Robert Dubin, *Human Relations in Administration*, 3d ed. (Englewood Cliffs, N.J., Prentice-Hall, Inc., 1968).

Laissez-faire leaders project little confidence in their ability to lead others. They spend a great amount of time away from their subordinates, leaving too much responsibility with their subordinates and doing little to help the group arrive at decisions. Generally, laissez-faire groups have the lowest morale and productivity. Frustration, failure, and insecurity are greater in this group than in any other. Without active leadership there is no meaningful work goal around which to build a common group. If left unchecked, the frustrations growing out of the situation will lead to overt aggression, indifference, or disinterest. Ultimately, the group will reach the point where it will cease to function as a social unit.

Democratic leaders share the responsibility for planning and carrying out work activities with their subordinates. The democratic leader explains the "whys" of specific assignments, rules, and procedures. He seldom delivers praise or criticism in personal terms; instead, praise and criticism is stated in terms of work goals and results. With or without the presence of the leader the democratically led group displays high morale and achieves a high level of production.

Studies of leadership clearly illustrate that there is no single list of traits that characterize effective leaders. Among the attributes frequently cited are (1) the ability to speak and write fluently, (2) an inner drive to succeed, (3) the capacity to take responsibility and the initiative to seek it out, (4) the ability to get others to cooperate, (5) tact and courtesy, and (6) the ability to plan and organize the work of others. Seldom does a single leader possess all these traits.

The more effective leaders are able to lead their groups to *identify* with group goals and *motivate* them to reach those goals. Identification occurs when an individual adopts the values, interests, and behavior of his group, while motivation is the inspiration to perform his role. Members of groups achieve maximum proficiency only when they have been inspired to do so. A good sermon is frequently more effective than a threat.

The more effective leaders are aware of the fact that situations, individuals, and goals change constantly. They realize that most people like to do things that they do well and are reluctant to undertake activities in which they perform poorly or which are unfamiliar to them. A nonreligious person, for example, may not be against organized religion but simply unfamiliar with the rituals he must master to be a member of a religious denomination.

It is extremely important for both leaders and followers to remember that each individual is different and should not be placed in ethnic, sex, or color packages. Individuals differ in intellect, ambition, and response.

Each must be encouraged to develop to the limit of his capacities. But more than encouragement is needed, especially for members of minority groups. Opportunities must also be provided for all people to achieve in accordance with their aspirations. In terms of personality, group members tend to be one of the following:

1. The *hostile individual* resents authority. He must be dealt with firmly but fairly to confine his aggressiveness and channel his energies toward the organization's objectives. Of course, we sometimes mistakenly assume that the attitude of another person is hostile when in fact it is not. When in doubt, it is good to ask ("Are you angry about something?").

2. The *dependent individual* needs firm guidance. If unchecked, his dependence will cause him to flounder until the supervisor can tell him how to control his behavior. Few organizations are prepared to provide the amount of supervision that extremely dependent employees need.

3. The *cooperative individual* functions best when given an opportunity to participate fully in decision making. He can usually operate within a set policy and needs little guidance or control.

4. The *individualist*, or lone wolf, works best when left alone. However, the administrator should make sure that he is "on course" and not working at cross-purposes to the organization.

Every human being, regardless of his personality, responds in some manner to supervision. How he responds depends on the style of leadership. A man forced to do a job against his will is likely to become a problem worker. The nature of the task and its importance must be effectively communicated to those expected to carry it out. In-service training programs involving all members of a unit or team can improve work skills and individual attitudes.

The trend in administration is moving away from emphasis on achievement to emphasis on self-actualization, from self-control to self-expression, from independence to interdependence. In any kind of organization effective leaders understand the various personality types among their followers. They must be flexible in order to vary techniques and approaches as each situation demands. The rules may not be flexible, but those who administer them should be.

**Communi-
cation**

The key to most human relations problems is effective communication.[8] Effective communication is much more than sending messages back and forth. The receiver must absorb, understand, and, if necessary, heed the message. Effective communication is often disrupted. For example, many administrators refuse to listen to what long-haired, unkempt youth are saying. They "listen" with the eyes but not the ears and fail to hear important messages.

At all times we must be alert to the obstacles to good listening caused by prejudice against a speaker—prejudice against his jargon, his dress, or his ideology. It is also important to realize that the message being communicated may consist of more than facts. Many messages are distorted by the speaker's prejudices. A black separatist, for example, is not likely to send prointegration messages. Effective communications systems do not just happen; they must be created. Nor should quantity of communication automatically be equated with quality. Informal gatherings, staff meetings, and individual conferences are occasions when communications can be checked for accuracy. Whenever possible we should send messages that convey the thought, "I'm OK, you're OK." When there are so many positive things that we can say about people, it is an act of insensitivity to send only negative messages.

Many of us fail to hear the messages others are trying to communicate. More often than not we respond to a key word or phrase taken out of context. Listening is an art that few people—including administrators—learn to master. To be effective, listening must be an active process. That is, to be certain that he understands what the speaker is trying to communicate, the listener must interact with him. For example, the listener can summarize what he believes was communicated ("Am I correct in assuming that you meant . . .?").

Studies indicate that the effective listener does not try to memorize every word or accept every concept the speaker communicates but listens for the main ideas of the message. He also pays attention to nonverbal communication—facial expressions and gestures. It takes a great deal of courage to listen effectively. When we effectively listen to others, we run the risk of being changed by their arguments. Thus some people say, "Don't confuse me with facts." Many inadequately trained group members would rather misinterpret instructions than risk understanding them and

---

[8] Frances E. X. Dance (ed.), *Human Communication Theory* (New York, Holt, Rinehart & Winston, Inc., 1967).

be unable to carry them out. Nothing ventured, nothing failed. Instead of learning contradictory and psychologically disturbing facts, we spend much of our time filtering out messages that are counter to our own attitudes.

If we can stop hating and fighting each other long enough to communicate our hopes, aspirations, and frustrations, we may be able to come together as a united people. We have learned much, but we have much more to learn before we live up to our challenge as a democracy. Tomorrow may be the beginning of an era of *humane* relations.

Suggested Reading

Abrahamsen, David. *Our Violent Society*. New York, Funk & Wagnalls, 1970.

Abt, Clark. *Serious Games*. New York. The Viking Press, Inc., 1970.

Adams, Loyce. *Managerial Psychology: Human Behavior in Business and Industry*. North Quincy, Mass., Christopher Publishing House, 1965.

Arendt, Hannah. *On Violence*. New York, Harcourt, Brace & World, 1970.

Armstrong, G. *Protest: Man Against Society*. New York, Bantam Books, Inc., 1969.

Banard, Chester I. *Dilemmas of Leadership in the Democratic Process*. Princeton, Princeton University Extension Fund, 1939.

Bayton, James A. *Tension in the Cities: Three Programs for Survival*. New York, Clinton, 1969.

Beckhard, Richard. *How to Plan Workshops and Conferences*. New York, Association Press, 1956.

Belli, Melvin M. *The Law Revolutions*. Hollywood, Sherbourne Press, 1968.

Berkowitz, Leonard. *Aggression: A Social Psychological Analysis*. New York, McGraw-Hill Book Company, 1962.

Bienen, Henry. *Violence and Social Change*. Chicago, University of Chicago Press, 1968.

Blumberg, A. S., ed. *Law and Order: The Scales of Justice*. Chicago, Aldine Publishing Co., 1970.

Bondurant, Joan V. *Conquest of Violence: The Gandhian Philosophy Conflict*. Berkeley, University of California Press, 1970.

Buss, A. H. *The Psychology of Aggression*. New York, John Wiley & Sons, Inc., 1961.

Callwood, June. *Love, Hate, Fear, Anger, and the Other Lively Emotions.* Garden City, N.Y., Doubleday & Company, Inc., 1964.

Campbell, James S., et al. *Law and Order Reconsidered: A Staff Report to the National Commission on the Causes and Prevention of Violence.* New York, Bantam Books, Inc., 1970.

Dance, Frank E. X., ed. *Human Communication Theory.* New York, Holt, Rinehart & Winston, 1967.

Davies, James C., ed. *Why Men Revolt—and Why.* New York, The Free Press, 1971.

Davis, Keith. *Human Relations at Work: The Dynamics of Organizational Behavior.* 3d ed. New York, McGraw-Hill Book Company, 1967.

Dellinger, David, ed. *Revolutionary Non-Violence.* Garden City, N.Y., Doubleday & Company, Inc., 1971.

Dowling, William F., and Leonard R. Sayles. *How Managers Motivate: The Imperatives of Supervision.* New York, McGraw-Hill Book Company, 1971.

Endleman, Shalom. *Violence in the Streets.* Chicago, Quadrangle Books, Inc., 1968.

Etzioni, Amitai. *Modern Organizations.* Englewood Cliffs, N.J., Prentice-Hall, 1964.

Fordyce, Jack K., and Raymond Weil. *Managing with People: A Manager's Handbook of Organization Development Methods.* Reading, Mass., Addison-Wesley Publishing Co., Inc., 1971.

Gardner, Erle Stanley. *Cops on Campus and Crime in the Street.* New York, William Morrow & Co., Inc., 1970.

Gawthrop, Louis C. *Bureaucratic Behavior in the Executive Branch.* New York, The Free Press, 1969.

Goldwin, R. A., ed. *On Civil Disobedience.* Chicago, Rand McNally & Company, 1969.

Golembiewski, R. T. *Men, Management, and Morality: Toward a New Organizational Ethic.* New York, McGraw-Hill Book Company, 1965.

Graham, Hugh D., and Ted R. Gurr. *The History of Violence in America: Historical and Comparative Perspectives.* New York, Bantam Books, Inc., 1969.

Gurr, Ted R. *Why Men Rebel.* Princeton, Princeton University Press, 1970.

Heady, Ferrel. *Public Administration: A Comparative Perspective.* Englewood Cliffs, N.J., Prentice-Hall, Inc., 1966.

Hower, Ralph, and Charles D. Orth. *Managers and Scientists: Some Human Problems in Industrial Research*

Suggested Reading (continued)

Organizations. Cambridge, Mass., Harvard University Press, 1963.

Jones, Howard M. *Violence and Reason.* Kingsport, Tenn., Kingsport Press, 1969.

Kane, Frank, *Voices of Dissent: Positive Good or Disruptive Evil?* Englewood Cliffs, N.J., Prentice-Hall, Inc., 1971.

Kornbluth, Jesse. *Notes from the New Underground: An Anthology.* New York, The Viking Press, Inc., 1968.

Kunen, James S. *The Strawberry Statement: Notes of a College Revolutionary.* New York, Random House, Inc., 1969.

Leiden, Carl, and Karl M. Schmitt, eds. *The Politics of Violence: Revolution in the Modern World.* Englewood Cliffs, N.J., Prentice-Hall, Inc., 1968.

Lewin, Kurt. *Resolving Social Conflict.* New York, Harper & Row, 1948.

Libarle, Marc, and Tom Seligson, eds. *The High School Revolutionaries.* New York, Random House, Inc., 1970.

Likert, Rensis. *The Human Organization: Its Management and Value.* New York, McGraw-Hill Book Company, 1967.

Lipsky, Michael, ed. *Law and Order: Police Encounters.* New Brunswick, N.J., Transaction Books, 1970.

Lorenz, Konrad. *On Aggression.* New York, Bantam Books, Inc., 1963.

McGregor, Douglas. *The Human Side of Enterprise.* New York, McGraw-Hill Book Company, 1960.

Maslow, Abraham H. *Eupsychian Management: A Journal.* Homewood, Ill., Richard D. Irwin, Inc., 1965.

Menninger, Karl. *The Crime of Punishment.* New York, The Viking Press, Inc., 1966.

Merrihue, Willard V. *Managing by Communication.* New York, McGraw-Hill Book Company, 1960.

National Advisory Commission on Civil Disorders. New York, Bantam Books, Inc., 1968.

Nigro, Felix A. *Modern Public Administration.* 2d ed. New York, Harper & Row, 1970.

Powell, Elwin H. *The Design of Discord.* New York, Oxford University Press, 1971.

Rossi, Peter H., ed. *Ghetto Revolts.* Chicago, Aldine Publishing Co., 1970.

Sartain, Aaron Q., and A. W. Baker, *The Supervisor and His Job.* New York, McGraw-Hill Book Company, 1965.

Schein, Edgar H., and Warren Bennis. *Personal and Organizational Change Through Group Methods: The Laboratory Approach.* New York, John Wiley & Sons, Inc., 1965.

Segal, Ronald. *The Americans: A Conflict of Creed and Reality.* New York, The Viking Press, Inc., 1969.

Sherif, Muzafer. *Intergroup Relations and Leadership.* New York, John Wiley & Sons, Inc., 1962.

Simon, Herbert A. *Administrative Behavior: Study of Decision-Making Process in Administrative Organization.* 2d ed. New York, The Free Press, 1965.

Skinner, Tom. *Worlds of Revolution.* Grand Rapids, Mich., Zondervan Publishing House, 1970.

Storr, Anthony. *Human Aggression.* New York, Bantam Books, Inc., 1968.

Strouse, Jean. *Up Against the Law: The Legal Rights of People Under 21.* New York, The New American Library, Inc., 1971.

Summers, Marvin, and Thomas Barth, eds. *Law and Order in a Democratic Society.* Columbus, Ohio, Charles E. Merrill Publishing Company, 1970.

Taylor, Jack W. *How to Select and Develop Leaders.* New York, McGraw-Hill Book Company, 1962.

Weber, Max. *The Theory of Social and Economic Organization.* Trans. by A. M. Henderson and T. Parsons. Glencoe, Ill., The Free Press, 1947.

Zaleznik, Abraham. *Human Dilemmas of Leadership.* New York, Harper & Row, 1966.

CHAPTER 9

How to Succeed by Trying

Principles of Problem-Solving

In this chapter we will discuss several ways to prevent or abate the problems summarized in earlier chapters. The primary focus is on people, not on systems.

The dynamics of problem-solving are threefold:

1. The facts that constitute the problem must be understood. Most problems are very complicated because the facts consist of objective realities and the resultant subjective interpretations.

2. The facts must be thought through. For the best resolution, the facts must be probed into, reorganized, and turned over in our minds so that we can grasp as much of the total picture as possible.

3. A decision must be made that will resolve the problem. In most cases, this decision involves a change in attitude and behavior.

Stated another way, the three operations of problem-solving are fact-finding, analysis of facts, and implementation of conclusions. To achieve greater effectiveness, the persons affected must be involved fully in the efforts to solve their problems. It is possible for one of the persons involved to define the problem and prescribe the solutions; when this happens, however, the self-responsibility of the other participants is weakened. If this unilateral process is repeated several times, self-responsibility of the group is destroyed. It is always better if individuals who face a particular problem are actively involved in its diagnosis and resolution. The following principles are crucial to problem-solving.

A problem can be solved only if the necessary resources are available. An individual may want to understand people of other cultures but be unable to do so because he does not have adequate resources, such as reading materials or access to those who can supply the needed information. Most Americans are unable to learn about people of other cultures because of inadequate resources. As in any puzzle, in human relations situations we cannot see the whole picture if pieces are missing. The result is a lack of cultural sensitivity.

Cultural sensitivity is the ability to identify and empathize with the feelings, values, and behavior of others. Today more than ever we need culturally sensitive people. Unless we can see others as they see themselves, dispel fears of cultural differences, and communicate across cultural lines, our communities will become battlefields where all of us will lose. People in leadership positions who are unable to put themselves in the shoes of others should not be surprised if their subordinates are also unable to do so. Members of a majority group may have difficulty imagining what it is like to be a member of a minority group, but much of the difficulty can be overcome when they realize that at some time or other everyone is in a "minority" situation.

Improved human relations are dependent on the ability to think rationally and objectively. Most people are not only unable to analyze their attitudes and how they come about but also cannot understand the role their feelings play in the human relations process. Objective introspection is not a common process for most people. Rather than trying to isolate facts, we are prone to overgeneralize, to draw conclusions from a few un-

related and dramatic incidents. After all, it takes less time and effort to place persons we do not know in a stereotyped category. Obviously, assumptions derived in this manner lead to faulty generalizations when applied to individual members of a group; they lead to racism when applied to a racial group.

Most people need to learn how to explore new and contradictory ideas and facts. It takes much training to be able to see common points in views which on the surface appear contradictory. For example, political activists of the far left and the far right often fail to realize that they share a common goal—a better nation. They differ on means, not ends. Cultural pluralism adds to the confusion surrounding such views. The greater the cultural distance, the more likely it is that ideas and facts will be misread. Still, an understanding of basic psychological and sociological principles can provide an excellent basis for problem-solving. It is also important to note that the need to develop skills in resolving human relations problems is not limited to members of majority groups. Minorities, too, are active parties in human relations problems and must also learn to explore new and contradictory ideas and facts.

Group leaders may themselves cause problems. The ability of group leaders to achieve and maintain objectivity is the key to the entire problem-solving activity. If a leader is immobilized by his own inner world of hate, he will find it impossible to perceive clearly the feelings and needs of his followers. The challenge to the leader is awesome: he must empathize, but not to such an extent that he loses his objectivity. Control of external conflict requires putting aside feelings that may be a vital part of our personality.

The group leader must consciously focus on problems and solutions.

Courtesy of Oklahoman & Times © 1963 United Feature Syndicate, Inc.

Even when members resist efforts to abate problems, the leader must behave in such a way as to communicate: "If you disagree with my appraisal of the situation, what do you suggest?" Give and take of ideas are important because facts alone are relatively ineffective in altering prejudices that have deep emotional roots. Furthermore, the subjective aspects of each situation

183

may be more important to the conflicting parties than the objective realities. Because the subjective aspects include accounts and events seen and felt by the participants, all participants must be allowed and even, if necessary, encouraged to express their feelings. This activity—laying the issues on the table for all to see—is the best means of arriving at appropriate solutions.

Many people do not know how they feel about a particular individual, group, or issue until they have communicated their feelings to someone else. Many of us may be vaguely aware of internal discomforts but totally unaware of their full implications. Providing an opportunity for people to tell how they feel is usually the first step in isolating negative feelings. Some adults communicate internal discomforts as children do, by striking, laughing at, or ignoring others. The more useful approach is to talk about negative feelings to place them in proper perspective. Allowing all participants to "tell it like it is" is a valuable first step in resolving problems. Talking should be related to some end, however; it should have some purpose beyond relating unpleasant feelings. If solutions are not sought, talking will serve only to frustrate people further.

A distinction should be made between *thinking about* a problem and *thinking through* a problem. In the first instance little more than free association of ideas takes place. In the second instance more purposeful events occur: A problem is acknowledged, its implications are examined, and solutions are suggested. Thinking through a problem is physically as well as mentally stimulating; the heart beats faster, and perspiration breaks out. The whole person gets caught up in thinking through a problem.

People who think through problems are more patient with others who are also trying to do so. The person who says, "If you really wanted to, you would change your behavior," is insensitive to the pain and complexities involved in altering established behavior:

> During the life of a typical innovation or change-enterprise, perceived resistance moves through a cycle. In the *early stage*, when only a few pioneer thinkers take the reform seriously, resistance appears massive and undifferentiated. "Everyone" knows better: "no one in his right mind" could advocate the change. Proponents are labeled crackpots and visionaries. In the *second stage*, when the movement for change has begun to grow, the forces pro and con become identifiable. The opposition can be defined by its position in the social system, and its power can be appraised. Direct conflict and a showdown mark the *third stage*, as resistance becomes mobilized to crush the upstart

proposal. Enthusiastic supporters of a new idea have frequently underestimated the strength of their opponents. Those who see a favored change as good and needed find it hard to believe the lengths to which opposition will go to squelch that innovation. . . . The *fourth stage*, after the decisive battles, finds supporters of the change in power. The persisting resistance is, at this stage, seen as a stubborn, hide-bound, cantankerous nuisance. For a time, the danger of a counter-swing of the pendulum remains real. . . . Strategy in this fourth stage demands wisdom in dealing, not only with the overt opponents, but with the still dissonant elements within the majority which appears, on the whole, to have accepted the innovation. . . . In a *fifth stage*, the old adversaries are as few, and as alienated, as were the advocates in the first stage.[1]

Individuals who want to change may not know how or may feel threatened by the thought of changing. Some people become obsessed with the fear that they will be publicly embarrassed trying to behave differently. If they do not extend themselves, they rationalize, there can be no failure. They believe, then, that if nothing is attempted, nothing fails. What they fail to understand is that the inability to try can be construed as a failure in itself. There is no denying the vulnerability inherent in trying something new. When we really expose ourselves in this way, we are psychologically naked, an exposure few of us tolerate well. In addition, we are dependent on others to clothe us, to help us find solutions. Thus the man who commits suicide may have been too proud to ask for help but too desperate to go on living without it.

It is imperative that we focus on problems that we can be instrumental in resolving. To do so is to make the most efficient and effective use of our energies. Many of the problems of a specific community can be solved only by those who live there. The man who is angry because his house is going to be torn down to make room for a highway is not likely to feel happy about the situation until it changes, and those external to the situation cannot resolve it. It is important, therefore, that leaders of organizations take an active role in seeking solutions to their organizational problems. Finally, the more successful human relations programs are comprehensive. They hinge on neither a single approach nor an isolated activity, such as posting equal-opportunity statements.

[1] Goodwin Watson, "Resistance to Change," in Goodwin Watson (ed.), *Concepts for Social Change* (New York, National Education Association, 1967), 11–12.

Constructive Behavior

By now it should be clear that it is behavior—not color, social class, or language—that is the crucial aspect of human interaction. Hostile nonwhites are often provoked to aggressive acts by the discriminatory acts of whites. And, of course, nonwhites provoke white hostility by negative behavior. The foremost error committed by supervisors and teachers is to assume that "the other people" have different social and psychological needs.

Each person, regardless of color, should be treated with fairness and respect. Even though it may be difficult to interact fairly with people from a culturally different background, it is important that we try. A student, subordinate, peer, or supervisor who is treated with respect and dignity is likely to reciprocate in a similar manner. Most people learn best by example. Children who hate are likely to have been recipients of hate, and those who love are likely to have been recipients of love. Indeed, we learn what we live.[2]

It is extremely important that individuals in authority positions consciously seek to minimize unfair treatment and to maximize fair treatment within their spheres of influence. Showing favoritism to some individuals while constantly punishing others will indicate to onlookers our order of preferences. For example, when black employees observe a black supervisor continuously rejecting and downgrading white employees, they imagine that in order to be accepted by the black supervisor they too must reject the white employees. Thus the supervisor causes his black subordinates to reject their white peers. He is also responsible for causing bickering and even open hostility in the work situation.

If he wishes to work effectively with nonwhites, a white supervisor must convey the fact that he is truly concerned about and interested in them. The supervisor who tries to maintain an attitude of fairness to all and those whose behavior demonstrates this attitude usually finds his nonwhite subordinates, peers, and supervisors cooperative and friendly. Most people welcome an opportunity to interact with others whose behavior communicates acceptance. But acceptance is a two-way street built on trust and honest communication.

There are many techniques for improving levels of trust. Supervisors who strive to be fair with all subordinates are able to achieve remarkable results. Effective white managers who supervise both white and nonwhite

2 Lee Nichols, *Breakthrough on the Color Front* (New York, Random House, Inc., 1954).

subordinates conclude that there is no major difference between them. They do not automatically equate the behavior patterns of the disadvantaged with those of nonwhites. Not all nonwhites are disadvantaged, nor are all whites advantaged. Too few people grasp this fact.

When we realize that no group has a monopoly on humanness, we also discover that we are capable of successfully interacting in most groups, regardless of their racial or social composition. Equally important, we discover that, instead of living in a setting charged with fear and suspicion, we have people-centered organizations that are smoothly functioning units. Some organizations seek this kind of interaction through in-service training.

Weekend Laboratories and In-Service Training
Few objective evaluations have been made of institutes, workshops, and other efforts designed to bring about change in attitudes and behavior. Cursory studies indicate that, while such training programs can produce an initial high level of enthusiasm, most participants are unable to bring about significant changes in long-established behavior when they return to their jobs. Even the highly touted sensitivity training sessions have little effect when participants return to the job.

Lately human relations professionals have been coming to grips with the following issues of training: (1) the relevance of group learning to on-the-job effectiveness, (2) the nature and quality of follow-up sessions that focus on learning transference to "back-home" situations, (3) the fact that most training programs are not designed to create group learning for a total work group, and (4) the lack of reinforcement of group learning within an individual's work environment.

Chris Argyris offered the following suggestions to trainers in institutes which involve unrelated individuals:

> Creating learning that is transferable is extremely difficult, because of the variety of back-home situations from which the members come. One way to cope with this situation is to enlist the help of the members. Let them describe the major characteristics of the back-home situations that give them the most difficulty. Experience suggests that people are willing to do so and that differences do exist. Thus, executives tend to focus on superior-subordinate relationships, while ministers are helping people in resolving personal and usually

moral dilemmas. In enlisting the aid of the members, the faculty are helped to generate transferable learning. . . . Many participants of "stranger" laboratories are described by informants in back-home situations as better listeners—more patient, more accurate perceivers of reality. All these skills can be used without openly violating the traditional pyramidal values which demand the suppression of much of what the individuals learn (in the laboratory) to bring out in the open and attempt to solve.[3]

Ideally, training designed to increase organization effectiveness should begin with the top executives. Unfortunately, most training is conducted for middle managers. And, certainly, as many members of an organization as possible should receive well-designed training. Finally, periodic follow-up sessions can be extremely beneficial. It is important to note that the "back-home" work group can be used as a medium for change.

The Group as a Medium of Change

Dorwin Cartwright, Ronald Lippitt, Leon Festinger, and others have documented the importance of the group in influencing or impeding efforts to change the behavior of its members. Specifically, the group can be a *medium of change* or become the *target of change*. Because the commitments of the group are often indistinguishable from those of its members, the group can also be-

[3] Chris Argyris, "On the Future of Laboratory Education," *Journal of Applied Behavioral Science*, Vol. 3 (1967), 162–63.

come the *agent of change*. Following are some of the principles operative when groups are involved in the change process:

1. If the group is to be used effectively as a medium of change, the targets of the change and those exerting influence to change must have a strong sense of belonging to the group.

2. The more important or attractive the group is to its members, the greater its influence will be on its members.

3. Attitudes, values, and behavior identified with the function of the group are more vulnerable to group pressure than unrelated attitudes, values, and behavior.

4. The higher the status of a member of the group, the greater the influence he can exert.

5. Behavior which would cause members of a group to deviate from group norms will encounter strong resistance.

6. Strong pressure for changes in the group is more likely to culminate in behavioral changes if members of the group see the need for the changes.

7. Information relating to the need for change should be shared by all persons in the group who are to be affected by the change.

8. Changes in one part of a group tend to produce strain in other related parts and can be reduced only by eliminating the change or by readjusting the other parts to function smoothly with the changes.[4]

It is much easier to describe negative attitudes and behavior than to change them. Three techniques are commonly used to change attitudes and behaviors: offer new information, threaten punishment, or promise a reward. None of these techniques works well in situations requiring a modification of strong ego-defensive attitudes. When attitudes are based on defense of ego, additional techniques are required, such as removal of the threat, the opportunity for ventilation of feelings, and assistance in understanding the reasons for the individual's attitudes.

Attitudinal and behavior change is more likely to occur when there is free expression within the group without fear of reprisal and when the

[4] Daniel Katz, "The Functional Approach to the Study of Attitudes," *Public Opinion Quarterly*, Vol. 24 (Summer, 1960), 165–204.

group members are allowed full participation in important group decisions. The formal lecture method alone has practically no influence on attitudes. Teachers and supervisors can change attitudes by uncritically accepting questions and ideas and by helping others develop sophisticated skills of inquiry—stating, refining, and testing hypotheses. To do so teachers must orient their techniques to their students' or subordinates' backgrounds, needs, and abilities. The superior human relations environment has many components, including the following:

1. It accepts each individual as he is and encourages accepting behavior on the part of each group member toward every other member.

2. It leads each member to an understanding of the reasons why different people live as they do.

3. It fosters interaction among representatives of different groups by granting each representative equal status.

4. It makes it possible for each group member to achieve but not at the expense of others.

Attempts to bring about attitudinal and behavioral changes can and often do result in strong resistance to those changes. Alvin Zander has outlined a number of reasons for this resistance:

1. *Resistance can be expected if the nature of the change is not clear to the people who are going to be influenced by the change. . . .* There is some evidence to support the hypothesis that those persons who dislike their jobs will mostly dislike ambiguity in a proposed change. They want to know exactly what they must do in order to be sure to avoid the unpleasant aspect of their job. . . .

2. *Different people will see different meanings in the proposed change. . . .* We tend to see in our world the things that we expect to see. Complete information can just as readily be distorted as incomplete information, especially so if the workers have found discomfort and threats in their past work situations.

3. *Resistance can be expected when those influenced are caught in a jam between strong forces pushing them to make the change and strong forces deterring them against making the change. . . .*

4. *Resistance can be expected to the degree that the persons influenced by the change have pressure put upon them to make it, and will be decreased to the degree that these same persons are able to have some "say" in the nature or direction of the change. . . .*

    5. *Resistance may be expected if the change is made on personal grounds rather than impersonal requirements or sanctions.* . . . Many administrators can expect trouble in establishing a change if it is requested in terms of what "I think is necessary" rather than making the request in light of "our objective." . . .

    6. *Resistance may be expected if change ignores the already established institutions in the group.* Every work situation develops certain customs in doing the work or in the relations among the workers. The administrator who ignores institutionalized patterns of work and abruptly attempts to create a new state of affairs which demands that these customs be abolished without further consideration will surely run into resistance.[5]

Resistance to change is minimized to the degree that the change agent helps individuals understand the need for the change and gives them an opportunity to do so.

It cannot be said too often that good human relations center around treating every individual as an individual, respecting his "self-hood" and being willing to change if our behavior is wrong. The first step in resolving interpersonal conflicts is to understand the other person's point of view. To do so, we must allow him the freedom to participate in decisions which affect his welfare. As noted earlier, most human relations problems proceed from lack of information, lack of human relations skills, and decisions that are inadequate to resolve the given problem.

Most human relations problems can be resolved by

1. Following regulations and exercising proper jurisdiction
2. Getting all the facts
3. Correctly analyzing the facts
4. Involving all persons in the deliberations
5. Assigning responsibility for action
6. Follow up to see that action is carried out

The process of getting the facts involves both verbal and nonverbal communication. *How* something is said is just as important as *what* is said. *What is not said* is also important. Good human relations involves learning to listen. Many organizational problems have been quickly and effectively solved by individuals who decided to listen before rendering a decision.

---

[5] Alfred Zander, "Resistance to Change—Its Analysis and Prevention," *Advanced Management*, Vol. 15 (January, 1950), 10.

Quick mouths, like quick gun draws, may beat others but miss the mark. Along with responsibility there must be accountability. The undemocratic nature of prejudices about race, sex, color, and religion is the foremost reason for us to get on with the task of living together and providing all citizens with equal opportunities. When this happens, America will reflect an old slave poem:

> *We ain't what we ought to be.*
> *We ain't what we gonna be.*
> *We ain't what we wanta be.*
> *But, thank God,*
> *We ain't what we was.*[6]

Feedback for Problem-Solving

Essential to any problem-solving effort is a provision for *feedback*, a sharing of honest feelings. Problem-oriented feedback allows feelings to be expressed as directly and as clearly as possible. Often it is accomplished by such simple statements as, "I am angry," or, "I feel hostile." Ideally, these feelings are related as much as possible to the factors believed to have caused them. Thus more definitive feedback would be: "I am angry because I was not promoted, and I believe I am better qualified than the people who were promoted." This technique is based on the assumption that feelings *do* exist and should not be considered irrelevant or disruptive of a smoothly functioning organization. Those who would dismiss feelings as irrelevant would deny the humanity of man.

Most people prefer to express their real feelings. But when they believe that nothing will be done to solve their problems or that they will be penalized for expressing their views, they are likely to conceal their real feelings. Only when they are convinced that their opinions are to be given a fair hearing will most people be honest in expressing them.

An open, honest forum is not an automatic guarantee that the information gained will result in problem-solving. There are several options open to the recipient of the new information:

1. He can fail to hear or see the new information, or he can misunderstand it so that he perceives it to fit his existing values.

[6] Quoted in Charles Y. Glock and Ellen Siegelman, *Prejudice U.S.A.* (New York, Frederick A. Praeger, Inc., 1969), 194.

2. He can hear or see the information accurately but deny its validity so as to maintain intact the integrity of his existing values.

3. He can shift his existing opinions and beliefs toward the position of the new information and attempt to accommodate both in his value system.

4. He can abandon his previous value position and shift his beliefs and opinions to a point centering on the new information.

5. He can downgrade or abandon his previous opinions and beliefs, minimize or deny the importance of the new information and withdraw from involvement in the issue as a whole.

It is possible for a leader to increase the ability of his group to solve problems by concentrating on *quality* and *acceptance* in the feedback process. Quality refers to the objective aspect of a decision; in other words, how does the decision square with the known facts? *Acceptance* refers to the degree to which the people who must carry out a decision accept it; that is, how do they feel about the decision? Because high quality and high acceptance are both needed for effective decisions, group discussion must deal with both facts and feelings.

As noted earlier, success in problem-solving requires that efforts be directed toward overcoming *surmountable* obstacles. The first order of business is to agree on the problem. It is not unusual for people to disagree about the solutions only to discover later that they never agreed about the problem. While the problem is being defined, it is important that the group leader avoid becoming impatient with individuals who interrupt the thinking processes of others. Nor should he allow himself or others to force through their solutions when the discussion appears to get bogged down with problems instead of solutions.

Disagreements can lead either to more hostility or to problem-solving. At the outset innovators are usually perceived as deviants by other members of the group. When one person disagrees with another, the group leader must create a climate in which neither party feels that he is being attacked. When supervisors and subordinates are involved, there is a tendency for subordinates not to disagree with the boss. It is imperative that subordinates feel free to disagree, though no one should be encouraged to disagree simply for the sake of being negative.

Nor should we assume that the majority opinion is always the best solution. People who agree with others in order to conform may be well liked, but they may also be poor problem-solvers. It is to be expected that a group will resist a new idea that is so contrary to established group norms that its implementation would alter the basic structure of the group. At this point the discussion leader must guard against a premature dismissal of the idea. Sometimes a suggestion that at first seems farfetched or even laughable points the way to the best solution. It is occasionally difficult to distinguish between creative ideas and foolish ones. Both may represent a departure from the status quo; both may be unique to the group. The discussion leader can often squelch unfair criticism by asking for alternative solutions. An idea may not seem so bizarre after it has been turned upside down, backward, and placed right side up again. Indeed, we may even shake loose a better solution.

At all times the "idea-getting" process should be separated from the "idea-evaluating" process. Idea-getting requires a willingness to dream, to break away from past experience. Idea-evaluating is the practical side of problem-solving. It involves testing and comparing solutions in terms of what is known and estimating the probability of success. In some instances still another group may be needed to evaluate the effectiveness of solutions.

Establishing Rapport Concern for their minority status causes some group members to view every member of a majority group with deep suspicion. Many Mexican-Americans, for example, are constantly on their guard around "Anglos." The rise in nationalism among racial minorities has increased their feelings of prejudice against Caucasians (and their representatives in minority groups). Extreme cases of nationalism result in the belief that only a person from one's own minority group should supervise his work. This attitude overlooks the fact that *quality is colorless and without ethnic or social-class identity*.

The challenge to the administrator is to demonstrate that competence and empathy are not unique to members of a particular group. For example, a competent white administrator can be as black as any of the black employees in his organization. Blackness is more than a condition of the skin; it is thinking black, behaving black, and accepting black. Just as blacks grudgingly admit that some white people have "soul," whites will acknowledge that some black people have "culture." Skin color may be a help or a hindrance in establishing rapport.

The first step in establishing rapport with an individual is to help him to relax. To do so, the leader of the conference must be relaxed. If the discussion leader is worried about being verbally or physically attacked, he will be uncomfortable. Generally, subordinates are also anxious about their initial contact with the discussion leader; they may wonder about his "agenda" (his hidden goals). For most minority-group participants, the presence of majority-group participants produces feelings of great discomfort. They bring their community-related anxieties with them. If there is hate at home, they bring it to work.

During these periods of stress, organizational problems or conversations related to them may produce panic among the minority-group participants. Effective leaders know when to slow the pace and talk about nonthreatening subjects. A few minutes of "small talk" can often reduce the stress. Warm, informal, down-to-earth behavior—a smile or a handshake—that communicates acceptance is a prerequisite to establishing rapport. Even so, the most gregarious people do not always succeed in establishing rapport.

Some culturally disadvantaged people approach the culturally advantaged in ways that are outright defensive—they use profane language and behave indiscreetly. Such defense mechanisms do not necessarily reflect faulty personalities, however. Protection of the ego is normal; disproportionate uses of defense simply indicates a lack of security. Culturally disadvantaged people seek to maintain their psychological balance in several ways—by rationalization, reaction formations, overcompensation, and projection. Individuals who imagine that they are viewed as outsiders develop rigid, persistent, and chronic ego-protection devices. Prolonged feelings of rejection result in behavior inappropriate to reality. An excellent example of this condition is the Japanese-American postal inspector who imagined that all the white postal inspectors disliked him. To protect himself, he withdrew from all voluntary contact with them. Finally, a concerned white postal inspector asked him: "Why don't you like me?" He answered: "Because you don't like me. You talk and joke with the white guys but you never talk and joke with me."

Issues centering on race or color often cause administrators and their subordinates to overreact. In such instances it is difficult to sort out fact from fiction, objectivity from subjectivity—but it must be done. The development of excessive ego defenses by members of a group is especially disturbing to those who are unaware that they have done something to elicit such behavior. Most administrators want their subordinates to like them, but their behavior is anything but conciliatory. As an angry female employee observed, "They don't even know my name or that I exist." A smile or a nod—a friendly acceptance of the person—may prevent a labor-management dispute.

A member of an organization who understands the other members, wins their confidence, and perceives alternatives for meeting their needs is able to help them become effective members of the group. This kind of leader does not run from people; instead he runs to them and is received with enthusiasm. Group members who are preoccupied with sorting out colors, races, and social classes are not likely to treat all members fairly. They cannot communicate to rejected members that they care, because they do not. Members of organizations who care about others behave as though they are color-blind, realizing that they are interacting with *people*, not colors.

Most people join organizations wanting to be accepted. To be cared about by the various members of the organization is a sign of social worth. To be cared about by individual members whom they like and respect is to become someone very special. People who feel a need to move *away* from others are frightened, and those who move *against* members of the organization are angry. Neither the frightened nor the angry feel secure with leaders who indicate that they do not care about them.

Equal Opportunities in Employment

Minority-group business, once described as the hope of the ghetto, is a national failure. Businesses owned by members of minority groups took in less than 1 per cent of the total United States business receipts in 1969. Minority business receipts totaled $10.6 billion, compared with more than $1.6 trillion for all businesses. Equally significant is the fact that most of the minority-group businesses are small retail shops and service firms without paid employees.

197

In 1969 one-half of the 321,958 minority businesses were owned by blacks, Spanish-Americans owned 100,212 businesses, and 58,673 were owned by American Indians, Oriental Americans, and other minorities. The financially most important black businesses were 6,380 gas stations and automobile dealerships, which had receipts totaling $631 million. The financially most important Spanish-American businesses were 6,378 food stores, which had receipts totaling $373 million. Food stores were also the financially most important businesses for American Indians, Orientals, and other minorities, with receipts of $682 million in 1969.

It would be wrong to imply that there has been no progress. During the fiscal year 1971 the United States Office of Minority Business Enterprise began operations with a $4 million federal appropriation, and a projected budget of $60 million for the 1972 fiscal year. In addition, government grants, loans, and guarantees to minority entrepreneurs totaled $434 million in 1970, as compared with less than $200 million in 1969. During the same period government purchases from minority-owned enterprises increased from $8.2 million to $77.8 million. However, the gap between white and nonwhite businesses remains almost the same: minority groups make up 17 per cent of the population but control less than 5 per cent of the total business enterprises.

In 1971 members of minorities began to make more entry into corporate management. Blacks, for example, were elected to the boards of such companies as the Chase Manhattan Bank and the General Motors Corporation. During the same period, however, the Association for Integration of Management reported that black college graduates were still underemployed and working mainly in staff positions related to the sale of products to blacks. The progress of the other minorities was similar to that of blacks. There is much room for improvement.

Equality of treatment and opportunity has been the official policy of some organizations for many years. In their standards of recruitment, training, and group relations, government agencies have been more effective as equal-opportunity employers than the private business sector. But even in governmental agencies there is room for improvement. Most equal-opportunity employers are merely paper compliers; their behavior is anything but exemplary of equality in action.

The policy of equal employment opportunity (EEO) is applied without regard to sex, race, creed, color, or national origin. An important first step toward equality of opportunity is the recognition that many influential members of organizations do harbor prejudices and that they do not put these prejudices aside when they are on the job. Unless administrators carefully monitor on-the-job activities, prejudices will be manifested in official and semiofficial actions.

Administrators must not assume that it is adequate merely to issue memoranda and directives setting forth the policy of equal opportunity. They must find out for themselves whether their subordinates are accorded equal treatment. The following are several effective methods by which an administrator can make certain that his organization understands the policy of equal opportunity:

1. Discuss the policy in staff conferences.
2. Discuss the policy in informal talks with subordinates.
3. Issue periodic statements of the policy in newsletters or memoranda.
4. Explain the policy during the orientation of new employees.

Resolving cases involving discrimination always involves value judgments. Administrators should, however, try to abate discriminatory practices in such a way as to cause those doing the discriminating to alter their behavior. Transferring the individual being discriminated against does not solve the problem; it merely leaves the discriminator free to repeat the act. *Good human relations cannot be delegated—they begin and end with each of us.*

In 1971 the Xerox Corporation began a $500,000-a-year social service leave program. Under the program employees are granted up to twelve months' leave of absence at full salary to participate in a social program of their choosing. With the exception of work in partisan politics, which is not permitted, Xerox employees are free to focus on such problems as drug addiction, civil rights, literacy, and penal reform. During the same year the International Business Machine Corporation (IBM) started a faculty loan program. IBM scientists, engineers, and business-management specialists are given full-year salaried leaves to teach in southern black colleges. Other companies are also beginning to use their human resources to help solve domestic problems. But to date the total number of such companies is small.

Despite such innovations, we have yet to develop a national commitment to human relations to match our power to destroy a world. We will survive not through power alone but through a deep sensitivity to the needs and wants of others. Humaneness must become a part of the American moral fiber and must find expression in America's social institutions. The alternative is expressed in the old adage: "They have sown the wind, and they shall reap the whirlwind."

Suggested Reading

Argyris, Chris. *Executive Leadership.* New York, Harper & Row, 1953.

————. *Integrating the Individual and the Organization.* New York, John Wiley and Sons, Inc., 1964.

Barnlund, Dean, and Franklyn Haiman. *The Dynamics of Discussion.* Boston, Houghton Mifflin Company, 1960.

Beckhard, Richard, ed., *Conferences for Learning, Planning, and Action.* Washington, D.C., National Training Laboratories, National Education Association, 1962.

Bennis, Warren, et al. *The Planning of Change: Readings in the Applied Behavioral Sciences.* New York, Holt, Rinehart & Winston, Inc., 1961.

Borgardus, Emory S. *Leaders and Leadership.* New York, Appleton-Century-Crofts, 1934.

Brehm, Jack W., and Arthur R. Cohen. *Explorations in Cognitive Dissonance.* New York, John Wiley & Sons, Inc., 1962.

Brown, James A. C. *The Social Psychology of Industry.* Baltimore, Penguin Books, 1954.

Cartwright, Dorwin, and Alvin Zander, eds. *Group Dynamics.* Evanston, Ill., Row, Peterson & Company, 1953.

Crowne, Douglas P., and Davis Marlow. *The Approval Motive: Studies in Evaluative Dependence.* New York, John Wiley & Sons, Inc., 1964.

Gordon, T. *Group-Centered Leadership.* Boston, Houghton Mifflin Company, 1955.

Gorman, A. H. *The Leader in the Group.* New York, Teachers College, Columbia University, 1963.

Hage, Jerald, and Michael Aiken. *Social Change in Complex Organizations.* New York, Random House, Inc., 1970.

Jung, Carl G. *The Undisclosed Self.* Boston, Atlantic–Little, Brown, 1958.

Karrass, Chester L. *The Negotiating Game.* New York, The World Publishing Company, 1970.

Katz, R. L. *Empathy.* New York, The Free Press, 1963.

Lindgren, Henry C. *How to Live with Yourself and Like It.* Greenwich, Conn., Fawcett Publications, Inc., 1953.

Lippitt, Ronald, et al. *The Dynamics of Planned Change: A Comparative Study of Principles and Techniques.* New York, Harcourt, Brace & World, Inc., 1958.

Luft, Joseph. *Group Processes: An Introduction to Group Dynamics.* Palo Alto, Calif., National Press Books, 1970.

McClelland, David C., et al. *The Achievement Motive.* New York, Appleton-Century-Crofts, 1953.

McGregor, Douglas. *Leadership and Motivation.* Cambridge, Mass., Massachusetts Institute of Technology Press, 1969.

Maier, Norman R. F. *Problem-Solving Discussion and Conferences.* New York, McGraw-Hill Book Company, 1964.

Marini, F., ed. *Toward a New Public Administration.* San Francisco, Chandler Publishing Company, 1971.

Mills, C. R., ed. *Selections from Human Relations Training News.* Washington, D.C., National Education Association, 1969.

Maslow, Abraham H. *Motivation and Personality.* New York, Harper & Row, 1954.

Otto, Herbert A. *A Guide to Developing Your Potential.* New York, Wilshire Book Co., 1970.

Suggested Reading (continued)

Schein, Edgar H., and Warren G. Bennis. *Personal Organizational Change Through Group Methods*. New York, John Wiley & Sons, Inc., 1965.

Stogdill, Ralph M. *Individual Behavior and Group Achievement*. New York, Oxford University Press, 1959.

Walker, Kenneth. *Diagnosis of Man*. New Orleans, Pelican Publishing House, 1962.

Walton, Richard E. *Interpersonal Peacemaking: Confrontations and Third Party Consultation*. Reading, Mass., Addison-Wesley Publishing Company, Inc., 1970.

Watson, Goodwin, ed. *Concepts for Social Change*. Washington, D.C., National Training Laboratories, National Education Association, 1967.

Whyte, William F. *The Organization Man*. New York, Simon and Schuster, 1956.

Worchel, Philip, and Donn Dyrne. *Symposium on Personality Change*. New York, John Wiley & Sons, Inc., 1964.

*"We don't have a retirement plan. We don't think the
country will last that long."*

CHAPTER 10

Tomorrow and Tomorrow

The closer we get to the year 2000, the more our thoughts turn to the future. Some writers believe that we are moving irreversibly toward the antiseptic societies of *1984* and *Brave New World*. Others foresee chaos and an uninhabitable planet. The future will be what we make it—no more, no less.

The Year 2000

No one can deny that we are changing our environment with fantastic rapidity. The implications of these changes defy even the best scholars. Only one thing seems certain: wherever we are going, we are going with great speed. In the last century we have increased our speeds of communication by a factor of 10^7, our speeds of travel by 10^2, our speeds of data handling by 10^6, our energy resources by 10^3, our power of weapons by 10^6, and our ability to control diseases by 10^2.

We are a nation of *mobicentric* people. Our lives are centered on motion—arriving, doing, and becoming. One out of every five Americans changes his residence every year. The implication is clear: To adjust to this new form of existence, we have to learn to develop relationships quickly. Along with mobility comes the challenge to find a few people with whom we can be intimate.[1]

There are four basic sources in our society for change: technology, diffusion, structural developments, and the relationship of the United States to the rest of the world. The basic technological changes are likely to grow out of new biomedical engineer-

[1] Eugene Jennings, "Mobicentric Man," *Psychology Today*, Vol. 4 (July, 1970), 35–36, 70–72.

ing, the computer, and weather control. Diffusion of goods and privileges in society can do much to equalize health, education, and welfare opportunities for all people. Structural developments—especially in politics, education, and industry—are already moving us into a postindustrial society. Finally, our relationship to the rest of the world will determine whether we will even have a world in the year 2000.

The newness of our scientific breakthroughs is seen in the following statistics:

1. Approximately 90 per cent of all scientific achievements have been made in the twentieth century.

2. The gross national product of goods and services in the technologically advanced nations of the world is doubling every decade and a half.

3. Until the mid-nineteenth century, the speed of transportation never exceeded twenty miles per hour. Today rockets carry astronauts at more than twenty thousand miles per hour, and the speed of some airplanes exceeds the speed of sound.

4. The number of scientific journals and articles is doubling every fifteen years, with a current output in excess of twenty million pages per year.

In their book *The Year 2000*, Herman Kahn and Anthony Wiener identified what they call "the basic long-term manifold trend."[2] They warn that, as we gain technological power over the world and become more affluent, alienation—cynicism, emotional distance, and hostility—rather than contentment will characterize our lives. The most important contribution of "futurologists" is that they attempt to bring some order into the chaos of predictions about the future. However, the major flaw in most such studies is that they plan in such detail that they close future options. They leave nothing for future generations to control. It seems wiser to allow for realistic options that can be exercised by future generations.

Moving further into the future is not likely to be without negative consequences. However, these consequences need not be as negative as some futurologists imagine. Our world is becoming a global culture, but this fact alone is neither good nor bad. By providing an extended range of common experiences through the facility of transmission-shared symbols and attitudes, the societies of the world are becoming more similar in norms and behavior. But it seems unlikely that a single political ideology will

---

[2] Herman Kahn and Anthony Wiener, *The Year 2000* (New York, The Macmillan Company, 1967).

emerge. If the world is to survive, it will require prodigious talents and also considerable skills in human relations. Specifically, the quality of life in the future will depend on how those who control technology today use their power.

"And how are we feeling this morning? Reply when you hear a beep."

The Communications Future

Seventy-five per cent of the world's population lives in a narrow strip of land from thirty-three to fifty-three degrees north latitudes, or between the southern boundary of the United States to Labrador in North America, from the Mediterranean to the Baltic in Europe, and through the North Temperate Zone in China and Russia. Ninety per cent of the world's industry also lies in that narrow strip on the northern half of the globe (most of it in North America and Western Europe). It is also the region in which most of the news is gathered and reported.[3]

The extent of monopolization of news gathering and reporting is vividly illustrated in the United States. Some writers predict that we are entering an era in which more than 95 per cent of the daily newspapers in the United States will have no local competition, where only national news-gathering organizations will supply virtually everything broadcast over radio and television stations, and where a handful of news executives will determine what the American audience will be allowed to know about the world in which they live.

As we look to the future, it is tempting to write a piece of science fiction in which the only news we receive is controlled by "Big Brother." On the contrary, I believe that we are moving into an era in which the profits generated by the major news organizations will be recycled into more public service programs, thus providing a wider range of viewpoints. We do not lack the *capacity* for presenting more and better balanced news. Today's technology makes possible more than forty television channels, but only 1 per cent of the cable systems in the United States are operating in more than twelve channels.

Other hopes for better communication come from the technology of the book.[4] It is now possible to print six books on a single three-by-five-inch card. *The New York Times* is perfecting the first fully automated system for the retrieval of general information. This data bank will store all news and editorial matter from the *Times*, as well as selected materials from more than sixty other newspapers and periodicals. Additional data banks are being planned by other organizations. Nor should we overlook the cassette video player. Soon millions of people will be able to "listen" to their favorite books. The problem is not equipment and methodology but

[3] Richard L. Tobin, "The Coming Age of News Monopoly," *Saturday Review*, October 10, 1970.

[4] John Tabbel, "Libraries in Miniature: A New Era Begins," *Saturday Review*, January 9, 1971.

a re-evaluation of the aims and standards of communication in our post-modern world.

The Value of Work in the Future

Governments have lagged behind big business in speculating about the future. In modern large-scale industry, where the market is dominated by a few firms, the name of the game is survival, and cutthroat competition is the means used to gain the edge over another company, generally by dreaming up new products. On the other hand, in government, where politicians live from election to election, the pressures are against innovations which offer long-term advantages. There are few votes to be gained by improving living conditions for people not yet born. Even so, both business and government are finding themselves affected by the "social fallout" resulting from changes in our concept of work.

In *The Future of the Future* John McHale describes an impending crisis surrounding the work ethic.[5] Work as previously defined is no longer a viable concept for the future. It has lost its relation to the compulsive work ethic, the principles of rationality and efficiency, and the equation of time with money. We can no longer relate job happiness to income or work efficiency. Work has become a means to consumer goods but seldom to personal happiness.

Furthermore, evolving patterns of prolonged education, extended vacations, greater fringe benefits, and earlier retirement are indicators that we no longer live in a work culture. Traditional notions of the virtues of hard work and self-profit are giving way to new values related to mass leisure. With mass leisure may also come political frustration. Free to become more involved in community life, the citizen of the future may feel "less free" because of the possible detachment from those controlling the technetronic age. If people receive fewer personally satisfying experiences, mental illness may increase. Today about one person in ten is affected by mental illness. Will the new leisure ethic bring us personal happiness or cause us greater mental anguish?

The concept of democracy in management centers on such values as freedom of expression, equality, and respect for the individual.[6] Along with increased personal freedom and consciousness of individuality have

---

[5] John McHale, *The Future of the Future* (New York, George Braziller, Inc., 1969).

[6] Margaret Mead, "The Challenge of Automation to Education for Human Values," in William W. Brickman and Stanley Lehrer (eds.), *Automation, Education, and Values* (New York, Thomas Y. Crowell Company, 1969), 70.

come interpersonal conflicts that must be controlled if we are to avoid national chaos.

As difficult as it is, forecasting is necessary. In short, we cannot refuse to make judgments about the future if we are to act rationally to improve the human condition. We will either control the social processes set in motion by our fabulous technology or become passive and be controlled by technology.

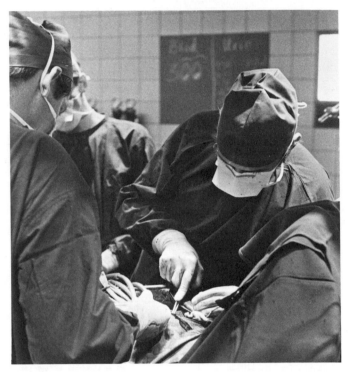

Medical Science and the Future

Modern man is on the threshold of duplicating and altering life processes. Of the one hundred million species of plants and animals that have inhabited the earth, 98 per cent are extinct. If man can succeed in his scientific endeavors, he may avoid joining the 98 per cent unable to meet evolutionary challenges.

In 1953, James Watson and Francis Crick, two Cambridge biologists, discovered what they call "the secret of life"—deoxyribonucleic acid (DNA). Scientists now believe that DNA is the master molecule of life. Watson and Crick accomplished a feat comparable to the splitting of the atom; they ushered in the beginning of molecular biology. In 1967, Arthur

Kornberg synthesized in a test tube a single strand of DNA that eventually duplicated itself.

Recently R. Michael Davidson described the "evolution revolution." He attributed this revolution to Hermann Muller, the winner of the Nobel Prize in physiology and medicine in 1946. Muller's program for genetic betterment, "germinal choice," thrust us into the first phase of a world in which men and women may practice sex only for pleasure and repopulate the species by artificial insemination. Davidson believes that this will not only improve the quality of man but also give the barren woman the experience of childbirth (today one-fourth of all fetuses fail to reach an age at which they can survive outside the womb).[7]

Through artificial insemination and the techniques of egg implantation, one of man's most sacred institutions, motherhood, will be usurped by science. In addition, the traditional concept of a family consisting of a husband, wife, and children may not be functional in societies in the future. Today approximately twenty-five thousand women whose husbands are either sterile or have genetic flaws are inseminated each year. Of this number nearly ten thousand women give birth to children conceived in this manner. The psychological and social adjustments that will be required are anxiety-producing, to say the least. But it does not end there. The "baby factory" of Aldous Huxley's *Brave New World* is already in the beginning stages. Researchers at several university medical centers are developing placental simulators and artificial wombs. Scientists are now beginning to wonder whether society will be able to cope with test-tube babies.

We may be near the day when man will be able to delete undesirable genes, insert others, and mechanically or chemically transform still others. Thus we may be able to predetermine the physical, mental, and even the racial characteristics of the individual. The geneticist, Joshua Lederberg, who won a Nobel Prize in 1958, has recently predicted that genetic surgery will become a reality within two decades if an aggressive research program is sustained. Imagine what will happen if we are able to reproduce complete individuals identical to living ones. *Cloning*, as this process is called, has awesome implications. Fanatics and madmen, as well as humanitarians and saints, can be duplicated. It may even be possible for an individual to be in two different places at the same time, producing double trouble or double happiness.

Man may also be able to solve the mystery of the brain's ten billion nerve cells. While the human brain can comprehend as many as fifty pieces

7 R. Michael Davidson, "And Now: The Evolution Revolution," *Avant-Garde*, January–February, 1969.

of visual information at once, it cannot file away more than ten of them per second for later reference. What will happen when we improve the brain's ability to store many times its present capacity for information?

The City of the Future

The city of the year 2000 has the potential for excellence in engineering, architecture, and city planning. Athelstan Spilhaus described the city of tomorrow in glowing terms.[8] He envisioned it as a total experiment in the social sciences, human ecology, environmental biology, and environmental engineering. Preventive medicine, comprehensive education, artistic endeavors, and true human rights may characterize the city of the future.

Small pneumatically or electrically driven pods with propulsion in the track would comprise Spilhaus' mass transportation system. There would be no air-burning machines within the city limits. The main public utilities would be in underground tunnels; interconnecting utility tunnels would double as multiplex or traffic tunnels and utility trenches for the transport of heavy freight, for telephone lines, for power and gas lines, for water and sewer mains, and for the rapid transit of emergency vehicles. Above all else, the ideal city of the future would be designed and built so that it could change easily.

One of the most pressing problems in the future cities will be to learn to relate to ourselves and to others in terms of what is sometimes called the "human condition." Man has not solved this problem in the past and is not solving it in the present; it will be solved in the future—if it is solved at all. Alvin Toffler's book *Future Shock* is filled with examples of problems created by change.[9] We are becoming a throwaway culture, developing new things and throwing them away at a faster-than-ever pace. Each year more consumer goods are produced for short-term purposes. Our search for newness is seen in our constantly changing vocabularies. Words are dropping out of usage and being replaced at rates three times faster than during the 1920's. We have become urban nomads moving from place to place in search of the illusive "better life." Even the concept of a permanent community may become extinct because of the constant movement of persons from city to city.

[8] Athelstan Spilhaus, "The Experimental City," *Daedalus*, Vol. 96 (Fall, 1967), 80–81.
[9] Alvin Toffler, *Future Shock* (New York, Random House, Inc., 1970).

"*I'm here, Mom. Outdoors.*"

Planning for the Future

To a great extent man has already altered himself and his environment. We can only guess at the human lives that will be lost from radioactive fallout, chemical contamination, and other assaults on the environment. Improved medical care does not merely assure survival; it assures the survival and reproduction of genetically caused mental and physical defects. Geneticist Theodore Dobzhansky succinctly expressed the ethical dilemma: "If we enable the weak and the deformed to live and to propagate their kind, we face the prospect of a genetic twilight. But if we let them die or suffer when we can save or help them, we suffer certainty of a moral twilight."[10] Clearly, some difficult decisions must be made about who shall survive.

It is one of the ironies of our time that, while there have been many cataclysmic social and physical changes, one of mankind's most pressing problems remains to be solved: the utilization of our positive capabilities. In the words of a once-popular song, "We're on our way to somewhere." The question is, Where? The unwillingness of either social scientists or natural scientists to assume responsibility for planning the future has been described by Andrew Shonfield:

> When social scientists and natural scientists meet to discuss the future, one is struck by the way each group adopts towards the other a mock-humble accusatory tone, the accusation being that the other's role is the decisive one. . . . The social scientists say: "If you would only tell us clearly the kind of technological changes we can expect, we could begin to analyze how society is likely to change." To which the natural scientists answer: "Never mind about us; all we need are some marching orders. Given enough time, modern technology has an almost limitless capacity to invent—so long as society decides that a sufficient volume of resources is to be put at the disposal of any particular program. So you tell us what is wanted by society: that is going to be the decisive factor in shaping the future."[11]

The necessity for social scientists and natural scientists to become involved in planning social changes is evident. It seems certain that the misfit between traditional patterns of social relationships and social control on the one hand and technology and industrialization on the other will not disappear if we simply pretend that it does not exist. The need for planned

---

[10] "Health Care: Supply, Demand & Politics," *Time*, Vol. 98 (June, 1971), 86–94.

[11] Andrew Shonfield, "Thinking About the Future," *Encounter*, Vol. 32 (February, 1969), 15–26.

social changes is inherent in the conditions of industrial cultures. However, the best guarantee of democratic social planning (social engineering) is a methodology of planned change which unites the principles of democracy with the skills of group dynamics.

In democratic social planning each person is treated as an end, and social arrangements are judged by their effects on persons influenced by them. For this to happen, organizations must foster an atmosphere which permits each person to make unique contributions to organizational improvement. Even more so than today, citizens of tomorrow will need to learn the skills of contributing to collective thinking, and their leaders will need to master the skills of eliciting effective individual contributions to group thinking. The engineering of change must be collaborative and educational, involving effective communication across lines of prestige and power.

Implicit in the statements above is the belief that social engineers must leave the persons and groups with whom they are working better able to solve future problems. Furthermore, engineering for change must be task-oriented: there must be a choice of goals, decisions made about the means to achieve the goals, and persons identified who can implement the changes recommended. John Platt has suggested six areas in which social engineers must work:

1. *Peace-keeping mechanisms and feedback stabilization.* Our various nuclear treaties are a beginning. But how about a technical group that sits down and thinks about the whole range of possible and impossible stabilization and peace keeping mechanisms? Stabilization feedback-design might be a complex modern counterpart of the "checks and balances" used in designing the constitutional structure of the United States 200 years ago. With our new knowledge today about feedback, group behavior, and game theory, it ought to be possible to design more complex and even more successful structures. . . .

2. *Biotechnology.* Humanity must feed and care for the children who are already in the world, even while we try to level off the further population explosion that makes this so difficult. Some novel proposals, such as food from coal, or genetic copying of champion animals, or still simpler contraceptive methods, could possibly have large-scale effects on human welfare within 10 to 15 years. New chemical, statistical, and management methods for measuring and maintaining the ecological balance could be of very great importance.

3. *Game theory.* . . . zero-sum-game theory has not been too academic to be used for national strategy and policy analysis. Unfor-

tunately, in zero-sum-game, what I win, you lose, and what you win, I lose. This may be the way poker works, but it is not the way the world works. We are collectively in a non-zero-sum-game in which we all lose together in nuclear holocaust or race conflict or economic nationalism, or all win together in survival and prosperity. Some of the many variations of non-zero-sum-game theory, applied to group conflict and cooperation, might show us profitable new approaches to replace our sterile and dangerous confrontation strategies.

4. *Psychological and social theories.* Many teams are needed to explore in detail and in practice how the peaceful new ideas of behavior theory and the new ideas of responsible living might be used to improve family life or community and management structures. New ideas of information handling and management theory need to be turned into practical recipes for reducing the daily frustrations of small businesses, schools, hospitals, churches, and town meetings. New economic inventions are needed, such as urban development corporations. A deeper systems analysis is needed to see if there is not some practical way to separate full employment from inflation. Inflation pinches the poor, increases labor-management disputes, and multiplies all domestic conflicts and our sense of despair.

5. *Social indicators.* We need social indicators, like the cost-of-living index, for measuring a thousand social goods and evils. Good indicators can have great "multiplier effects" in helping to maximize our welfare and minimize our ills. Engineers and physical scientists working with social scientists might come up with ingenious new methods for measuring many of these important but elusive parameters.

6. *Channels of effectiveness.* Detailed case studies of the reasons for success or failure of various social inventions could also have a large multiplier effect. Handbooks showing what channels or methods are now most effective for different small-scale and large-scale social problems would be of immense value.[12]

Highway and street planning offers a clear illustration of the need for better social planning. In less than one hundred years since the invention of the steam engine, the average rate of airspeed that man can maintain continuously has increased to approximately 25,000 miles per hour. Some scientists believe that airspeeds of 670 million miles per hour are within our physical limits. The irony is that flying in the sky is safer than walking or driving on our streets.

12 John Platt, "What We Must Do," *Science*, Vol. 166 (November 28, 1969), 1115–21.

In the next fifty years the population of the United States will increase to 350 to 390 million people. These estimates suggest upwards of 158 million additional cars in urban America. If these predictions come true, there will be almost as many cars as people. Grass will have been converted to parking space, bedrooms to parking ramps, and children to parking lot attendants.

As cars proliferate, freedom of movement will be limited. Without adequate planning, optimum freedom—the ability to go where we desire, when we desire, in our own vehicles, by the route we choose—will have to be limited to prevent the collapse of urban circulation. If this happens, who will determine the priority for traveling?

A final thought about congestion: Highways beget motor vehicles, and motor vehicles beget highways. The more highways we build, the more people buy cars and make use of the "extra" space. Planners, in turn, predicting more vehicles, are frantically trying to build additional highways. When will it stop? Equally important, can we stop this vicious circle of congestion?

Using the Social Sciences

Five social sciences form a foundation for understanding today's problems and planning the future: (1) political science, (2) economics, (3) sociology, (4) social psychology, and (5) cultural anthropology. Aristotle, the author of *Politics*, is most frequently called the "father of political science." Economics, once called "political economy," gained academic prominence in the work of Adam Smith in the late eighteenth century. Sociology began to receive national attention in the nineteenth century with the writings of Emile Durkheim, Leonard T. Hobhouse, and Franklin H. Giddings. A little later, social psychology gained momentum from the work of William James. Even though cultural anthropology was an outgrowth of Lewis Henry Morgan's analysis of the family systems of the Seneca Indians, the science did not become prominent until after the turn of the century.

In nontechnical terms, *social science* can be defined as the application of the scientific method to the study of human relations. A skeptic may ask: What do we know about human relations that is dependable? The chaos resulting from nonsocial-scientific common-sense approaches suggests that we had better seek other approaches to planning group activities. When a race riot erupts or a depression strikes or college students picket buildings, administrators responsible for resolving these problems seldom seek wild generalizations but instead look for tested, reliable social-science observations and alternatives.

There is considerably more social-scientific knowledge available than has been put to use. At least three conditions are required in order to solve the major problems of human relations with some hope that they will stay solved:

1. More people must become involved in the scientific study of individuals, groups, and societies.

2. Greater understanding is needed of what constitutes the scientific method, as well as a greater willingness to utilize it.

3. A political structure is needed in which scientific knowledge about man in society is applied for the benefit of the masses.

From the outset, in America the social sciences have been jealously divided into tight disciplines with little interchange of ideas. As a result, the social sciences have cut man into many pieces, and seldom do the pieces fit together for students studying them. Gradually this situation is changing. With the social-scientific teamwork developed during World War II as a model, scattered interdisciplinary research projects are emerging. At least one writer predicts that before long the separate disciplines will merge into a single broad discipline, perhaps to be called the "science of man."[13] This prediction, however, presupposes an overriding incentive for the social sciences to merge. To date, this incentive has been absent. Even more distressing is the fact that few social scientists are actively seeking solutions to current human relations problems.

In the introduction to his classic study *The Conditions of Economic Progress*, Colin Clark bade farewell to his academic colleagues in London. Even though he liked all of them personally, he was disappointed by their preference for the theoretical rather than the scientific approach to economic problems. He believed that not one in a hundred, including those who were most eager to proclaim the scientific nature of economics, really understood what constitutes the scientific approach, which he defined as:

1. The careful systemization of all observed facts.
2. The framing of hypotheses from the facts.

[13] Stuart Chase, *The Proper Study of Mankind* (New York, Harper & Row, 1948).

3. The prediction of fresh conclusions on the bases of these hypotheses, and

4. Testing the conclusions against further observed facts.

It was ironic, Clark commented, to see stacks of books dedicated to solving exceptionally complex economic problems by the use of logic and argument but containing hardly a reference to social reality.[14]

In many universities the social sciences continue to be highly intellectual, bookish, and remote from community issues. The "best" students are those who deal brilliantly with abstract logic and can correctly manipulate formulas. Most professors still sequester themselves in libraries writing critiques of the books of others, and their students still sit in hard chairs, writing term papers about the theories of scholars who lived hundreds of years ago. But as the science of man advances, it is becoming clear that the more relevant social scientists are interacting with and studying people, not isolating themselves in libraries. It is hoped that the day is coming when social scientists will become more deeply involved in social change.

But until the human relations millennium comes to pass, most social science students continue to be trained to argue and to cite authority, but not to handle concrete community situations. They are much like the man who took a correspondence course in aviation: He knew all about airplanes but could not fly. Many social scientists feel comfortable with theories but very uncomfortable with people. In his experiments at the Hawthorne plant Elton Mayo demonstrated that social-scientific conclusions can be drawn through clinical as well as laboratory methods. In fact, many of Mayo's students went on to use the techniques he taught them at the Harvard School of Business to solve labor-management problems in factories and offices all over the country. Today, other universities are following Mayo's lead and teaching social skills which can be used to meet specific community problems.

The social sciences are probably the only sciences in which most of the leaders of half a century ago would still find themselves very much at home. The social sciences have undergone very little substantive change. The social science texts of the 1970's still contain much theory that was "relevant" in the 1920's. This lack of progress is baffling, since theories about human societies were formulated by the Greeks and other ancient philosophers long before the physical world was systematically investigated

14 Colin Clark, *The Conditions of Economic Progress* (New York, The Macmillan Company, 1940).

by natural scientists. Despite this early start, the study of human relations in most universities is still full of ancient guesses. It has now become apparent that the major task of the social scientist is to sweep out the traces of dead ideologies, keep the verified conclusions, and test the viable hypotheses.

In both social sciences and natural sciences many untested hypotheses that have great social implications remain unchallenged. Fortunately, this lack of inquiry is not as prevalent today as it was in Victorian days, when narrow-minded men tried to silence Thomas Huxley for describing evolution. But we are not as open to inquiry as were the Greeks 2,500 years ago: Their iconoclastic culture permitted them to doubt everything and to investigate anything. The hope for the future lies in questioning current practices.

Despite failures, lags, and difficulties, the scientific study of man is essential to our survival. The argument that man is too unpredictable to be studied objectively is dead. A body of genuine social-scientific knowledge has been created, and it is growing. Many Americans now concede that social scientists can answer the problems of society better than any dictator, better than any council of elders, and better than intuition or common sense. Each year many men and women are devoting their lives and talents to advance the social sciences.

It is not necessary to learn all about man and his behavior in order to improve living conditions. No one in the natural sciences has yet been able to tell what life is or what light is. But they know enough to direct some of the processes of life and light—enough to eradicate plague and to light cities. Paraphrasing Ralph Linton, I have an even grander vision for the social scientist: He will press on, sustained by the belief that somewhere in this vast territory called the universe there lies hidden the knowledge which will prepare man for his greatest victory, the conquest of himself.[15]

Prescription or Description?

Many social scientists engaging in action research have been overtly or covertly accused by their colleagues of becoming intellectual prostitutes or "socialists and not scientists." It seems to take a rare breed of social scientist to remain in academe and engage in action research but not become a marginal man. The increasing complexity of urban living, coupled with improved research methodology, makes the social scientist a much-

[15] Quoted in Chase, *The Proper Study of Mankind*, 46.

needed partner in social intervention aimed at extending the good life to all people.

The schism between pure and applied science need not be as antithetical as many writers propose. At one extreme of the imagined schismatic continuum are the social scientists who ardently advocate that the definition and application of prescriptive values are within their purview. At the other end are those who unequivocally maintain that such an application is beyond their roles as scientists. The former is an *applied-science* position, and the latter is a *pure-science* position.

A closer look at the extreme positions discloses a basic disagreement regarding the defined presence or absence of values in science. Many of those who argue that social scientists should use their scientific findings to solve community problems also argue that value judgments are inevitable in both social and physical sciences. Conversely, many of those who argue against such an application do so because they believe that social scientists, like natural scientists, should conduct their scientific activities without making value judgments. In *A Time To Speak*, Herbert Kelman compared the two views:

> The social scientist today—and particularly the practitioner and investigator of behavior change—finds himself in a situation that has many parallels to that of the nuclear physicist. The knowledge about the control and manipulation of human behavior that he is producing or applying is beset with enormous ethical ambiguities, and he must accept responsibility for its social consequences. Even the pure researcher cannot withdraw into the comforting assurance that knowledge is ethically neutral. While this is true as far as it goes, he must concern himself with the question of how this knowledge is *likely* to be used, given the particular historical context of the society in which it is produced. Nor can the practitioner find ultimate comfort in the assurance that he is helping others and doing good. For, not only is the goodness of doing good in itself a matter of ethical ambiguity but he also confronts the question of the wider social context in which a given action is taken. The production of change may meet the momentary needs of the client—whether it be an individual, an organization, or a company—yet its long-range consequences and its effects on other units of the system of which this client is a part may be less clearly constructive.[16]

[16] Herbert C. Kelman, *A Time to Speak: On Human Values and Social Research* (San Francisco, Jossey-Bass, Inc., 1968), 13.

In the past many social scientists have naïvely assumed that their research would aid mankind through diffusion in governmental programs. It is now evident that special-interest groups can use research findings to design and implement programs that are not in keeping with the researcher's beliefs and goals. This is happening while social scientists are accelerating their efforts to duplicate pure science models.

The pure-science model is of limited value to social scientists. Time and time again social scientists in general and sociologists in particular have ruled out the probability of achieving the quantitative precision of the physical sciences. In addition, recent flights into outer space have greatly altered some of our "precise" axioms of the physical sciences. To onlookers the quest for perfection in methodology seems to be a stalling tactic, designed to delay the full plunge into the cold, uncertain seas of human relations.

How strange it is that those who conduct the most definitive studies of the detrimental aspects of cultural differences, deprivations, and so forth have the least to say about their abatement. Their attitude is to some extent analogous to a physician who has thoroughly researched a rare disease but hesitates to suggest methods to cure it. His role, he reasons, is merely to observe the disease; others must decide how best to prevent or treat it.

Emile Benoit-Smullyan concluded that what initially seems to be an insurmountable schism need not be if both pure and applied social scientists become involved in human decisions as does a medical doctor:

> A doctor may tell a diabetic patient that he ought to take insulin, but the science of medicine says no more than that, in the case of diabetics, the use of insulin will have effect A: the omission of insulin will have effect B. The diabetic cannot know whether he ought to take insulin without appealing to a general value, namely, that of health: Only if he wants to be healthy ought he use the appropriate means.[17]

If social scientists take their cue from the science of medicine, then it becomes plausible that they can and should engage in human relations program planning and implementation. The role of the social scientist becomes that of providing decision makers with a series of alternatives based upon the best possible guesses. This is not to say that social scientists should be equally concerned with determining which community programs are

17 Emile Benoit-Smullyan, "Value Judgments and the Social Scientists," *Journal of Philosophy*, Vol. 42 (April, 1945), 179.

"good" and which are "bad." Decisions of this nature are more properly left to human relations officials, school-board administrators, and others committed to rendering such judgments. Instead, using the methods of science, social scientists can assist others in understanding the dynamics of human interaction and possible alternatives for resolving community problems. However, we should pay attention to Daniel Moynihan's warning:

> Advocates of social change, especially to the degree that they base their advocacy on normative grounds, are naturally disposed to be impatient, to ask that remedies be as immediate as possible. So long as social science was asked to certify chiefly that normative grounds for change were justifiable, its task was relatively simple. But once it is asked to *implement*—forthwith—the normative imperative, it is up against a serious dilemma. Even the most rapid social change, as seen from the perspective of history, comes very slowly indeed from the point of view of the individual demanding it. But to say that nothing is done overnight is to be accused of supporting those who want nothing done ever. However, to assert the contrary is to debase the science by distorting the evidence. There are few who will accept the former condition and more than a few—certainly more than enough—who will submit to the humiliation of the latter.[18]

It is easier for a scientist to criticize an existing community practice than to analyze it objectively and then, if necessary, offer practical alternatives for improvement. It is even more difficult for him to criticize his stated alternatives; such criticism is psychologically disconcerting—it highlights the gaps between social theory and social practice and, moreover, reminds him of his own inadequacies. Even so, social researchers can assist social practitioners in their efforts to build a sturdy bridge between today and tomorrow.

Ethical Concerns of the Future	In the growing concern about the future of man traditional beliefs are being questioned, including the notions that (1) scientific progress is automatically good, (2) what is medically beneficial for one man is necessarily good for society, and (3) scientists know how to improve humanity.

18 Daniel P. Moynihan, "Eliteland," *Psychology Today*, Vol. 4 (September, 1970), 35–37, 66–70.

In 1969 the Institute of Society, Ethics and the Life Sciences was organized in New York to study the ethical questions involved in the areas of population control, genetic engineering, death and dying, and behavior control. A similar organization, the Institute of Religion, was organized in Houston, Texas. Its purpose is to explore the ethical problems that arise out of medicine and medical research, including heart transplants. Smaller institutes with similar purposes include the Center for Human Values in the Health Sciences, in San Francisco, and the Institute for Theological Encounter with Science and Technology, in St. Louis. All these groups have interdisciplinary teams consisting of representatives of the humanities, theology, and the social and physical sciences.

The range of questions which these groups discuss is broad: Does an individual have a right to his uniqueness? Does a dying person have the right to ask not to be treated? Where do the rights of society come in when physicians, funds, and hospital beds needed for terminal patients are in short supply? Should criminals be forced to accept rehabilitation that would involve direct electrical or chemical stimulation of their brains or even brain surgery? What would be the societal effects of using a drug that raised the general level of intelligence of all citizens?

Implicit in the questions being discussed is the assumption that change for the sake of change is not a commendable goal. Those changes which seem to promote a more humane society are the ones we should support. Indeed, the problems of tomorrow are likely to be closely related to our solutions of today's problems. Tomorrow will reflect today's commitments to human relations. A racist nation will pass racism on to future generations unless steps are taken to alter traditional patterns of segregation and discrimination.

In 1971, at the convention of the American Psychological Association, Kenneth B. Clark proposed the creation of new drugs that could routinely be given to persons, especially leaders holding great power, to subdue hostility and aggression and allow more humane and intelligent behavior to emerge. The full implications of Clark's proposal could and should be the subject of an association of behavioral and neuropsychological scientists. Among the many questions inherent in the proposal is whether science can enhance man's empathy and kindness without destroying his creative, evaluative, and selective capacities.

An equally challenging question grew out of a 1972 report of the Federal Commission on Population Growth and the American Future. The majority of the commission members concluded that women should be free to determine their own fertility and that the matter of abortion should be left to the conscience of the individual concerned, in consultation with her physician. Dissenting, Commissioner Paul B. Cornley stated that "such moralistic monism, simplistic as it is, at bottom fails to consider the freedom of the unborn child to live." Do the following data presented by the majority report minimize Cornley's argument?

1. According to a 1970 national fertility study conducted by the Office of Population Research of Princeton University, between 1966 and 1970 there were 2.65 million births that never would have occurred if the couples had had fertility controls.

2. If blacks could have the number of children they want and no more, their fertility rate would probably be similar to that of whites.

3. In more than two-thirds of the states abortion is a crime except to preserve the life of the mother.

4. Medically safe abortions have always been available to wealthy women.

5. It is estimated that from 200,000 to 1,200,000 illegal abortions are performed each year in the United States.

In summary, do the various prohibitions against abortion stand as an obstacle to the exercise of individual freedom—the freedom of women to make difficult moral choices based on their personal values, the freedom of women to control their own fertility, and the freedom from the burden of unwanted childbearing?

Bringing children into the world gives rise to a wide range of questions, especially those which focus on their human rights. At the other end of the life spectrum is old age. Currently there are twenty million Americans who are sixty-five years of age and older—one-tenth of our population. With birth rates declining and life expectancy increasing, the aged will constitute an even larger proportion of the United States population in the year 2000. Will the senior citizens of tomorrow be like those of today, plagued by ill-health and social financial insecurity? The aged are mainly unwanted; they are pushed aside, thrown away, and often stranded in socially sterile environments built especially for "old folks." What must our society become so that old age as we know it will be non-existent?

Between youth and old age lies what is sometimes referred to as the "most productive years." This is the time when our energies are likely to be devoted to preventing or abating the problems of hunger, disease, pollution, population, war, and ethnic strife. We have tried in limited ways to solve these problems, and we have failed. If we are to succeed, more than hope and love will be needed. We will need affirmative action on a national scale. The major domestic problem is black-white relations. What can be done to help black and white citizens live together voluntarily when they are still unwilling to sit next to each other on buses, trains, and airplanes? Will the ethnic groups of the future be taught or conditioned peacefully to go to school together, live in the same neighborhoods, and work together on the same jobs? Or will we become the Separate States of America?

Ideally we will reshape our physical and social sciences to improve the quality of our human relationships. But more than this is needed. The physical and social sciences must combine with the other disciplines, especially the humanities, to create a humane world. If the special abilities of human beings are the creation, transmission, understanding, reordering, and re-creation of symbols, then we should be able to improve greatly our definitions of life and their cultural, biological, and ethical realities. Indeed, freedom and equality, along with their implicit rights and responsibilities, can become our primary reason for being.

Each year, more young people doubt the ability of their adult models to be humane persons. Perhaps adults are ceasing to be significant models for youth, who are rebelling because they have discovered that adults have lied to them. They are learning that money, clothes, cars, houses, and education are *not*, as many adults would lead them to believe, more important than people. They discover that the concept of race is a myth, existing only in the imagination of the classifiers. They learn that knowledge is not limited to those over thirty, and that love need not be restricted to those within the family.

When young people stop reaching out to adults for facts and instead start reaching for understanding, they find most adults woefully inadequate. I am not speaking of a generation gap but of an empathy gap—and empathy is not a function of age.

For these and many other reasons our young people are not so much *angry at us* as they are *sorry for us*. They are sorry that we have forgotten the impatience of youth. They are sorry that we are no longer committed to sweeping social changes. And they are sorry that we have forgotten how to laugh *at* ourselves and *with* other people. A four-year-old girl got to the essence of it when she asked, "Daddy, does it hurt to be an adult?"

"Yes, my love," her father answered. "It hurts very much at times. But I pray that you will live in freedom and happiness." That, I believe, is a necessary beginning for all our tomorrows.

Suggested Reading

Alberts, David S. *A Plan for Measuring the Performance of Social Programs.* New York, Praeger Publishers, 1970.

Alinsky, Saul D. *Reveille for Radicals.* Chicago, University of Chicago Press, 1946.

Barton, Richard F. *A Primer on Simulation and Gaming.* Englewood Cliffs, N.J., Prentice-Hall, Inc., 1970.

Becker, Ernest. *The Lost Science of Man.* New York, George Braziller, Inc., 1971.

Benne, Kenneth D., et al. *Group Development and Social Action.* New York, Anti-Defamation League of B'nai B'rith, 1950.

Suggested Reading (continued)

Bennis, Warren G., et al., eds. *The Planning of Change: Readings in Applied Behavioral Sciences.* New York, Holt, Rinehart & Winston, Inc., 1962.

Bugental, J. *Challenges of Humanistic Psychology.* New York, McGraw-Hill Book Company, 1967.

Carleton, William. *Technology and Humanism.* Nashville, Tenn., Vanderbilt University Press, 1970.

Clarke, Arthur C. *Profiles of the Future.* New York, Bantam Books, Inc., 1960.

Commoner, Barry. *Science and Survival.* New York, The Viking Press, Inc., 1966.

Dobzhansky, Theodosius. *Mankind Evolving: The Evolution of the Human Species.* New York, Bantam Books, Inc., 1962.

Dubin, Robert. *Theory Building.* New York, The Free Press, 1969.

Editors of *Fortune. The Environment: A National Mission for the Seventies.* New York, Perennial Library, 1969.

Editors of *Ramparts. Eco-Catastrophe.* San Francisco, Canfield Press, 1970.

Ewald, William R., ed. *Environment and Change: The Next Fifty Years.* Bloomington, Indiana University Press, 1968.

Fellin, Philip, T. Tripodi, and H. J. Meyers, eds. *Exemplars of Social Research.* Itasca, Ill., F. E. Peacock Publishers, Inc., 1969.

Fletcher, Joseph. *Situation Ethics: The New Morality.* Philadelphia, The Westminister Press, 1966.

Forcese, Dennis P., and Stephen Richer, eds. *Stages of Social Research: Contemporary Perspectives.* Englewood Cliffs, N.J., Prentice-Hall, Inc., 1970.

Frieden, Bernard, J., and Robert Morris, eds. *Urban Planning and Social Policy.* New York, Basic Books, Inc., 1968.

Fromm, Erich. *The Revolution of Hope: Toward a Humanized Technology.* New York, Bantam Books, Inc., 1968.

Fuller, Richard. *Utopia or Oblivion: The Prospects for Humanity.* New York, Bantam Books, Inc., 1969.

Gardner, John W. *No Easy Victories.* New York, Harper & Row, 1968.

———. *Self-Renewal: The Individual and the Innovative Society.* New York, Harper & Row, 1964.

Garre, W. J. *Basic Anxiety: A New Psychological Concept.* New York, Philosophical Library, Inc., 1962.

Heidt, Sarajane, and Amitai Etzioni. *Societal Guidance: A New Approach to Social Problems.* New York, Thomas Y. Crowell Company, 1969.

Helfrich, H. W., ed. *Agenda for Survival: The Environmental Crisis.* New Haven, Yale University Press, 1970.

Horowitz, Irving, ed. *The Use and Abuse of Social Science.* New York, E. P. Dutton & Company, Inc., 1971.

Isaac, Stephen, and William B. Michael. *Handbook in Research and Evaluation.* San Diego, Robert R. Knapp, 1971.

Kahn, Herman, and Anthony Wiener. *The Year 2000.* New York, The Macmillan Company, 1967.

Kahn, Theodore C. *An Introduction to Hominology: Study of the Whole Man.* Springfield, Ill., Charles C. Thomas, 1969.

Kelman, Herbert C. *A Time to Speak: On Human Values and Social Research.* San Francisco, Jossey-Bass, Inc., 1968.

King, Clarence. *Working with People in Community Action.* New York, Association Press, 1965.

Kress, Paul. *Social Science and the Idea of Process.* Urbana, University of Illinois Press, 1971.

Kurtz, Paul. *Moral Problems in Contemporary Society: Essays in Humanistic Ethics.* Englewood Cliffs, N.J., Prentice-Hall, Inc., 1969.

McCurdy, Harold C. *Personality and Science: A Search for Self-Awareness.* Princeton, C. Van Nostrand, 1965.

McHale, John. *The Future of the Future.* New York, George Braziller, Inc., 1969.

Maltz, Maxwell. *Psycho-Cybernetics.* Englewood Cliffs, N.J., Prentice-Hall, Inc., 1960.

Maslow, Abraham H. *Toward a Psychology of Being.* Princeton, C. Van Nostrand, 1962.

Mead, Margaret, ed. *Cultural Patterns and Technical Change.* New York, The New American Library, Inc., 1955.

Michael, D. N., ed. *The Future Society.* Chicago, Aldine Publishing Company, 1970.

Miller, Delbert C. *Handbook of Research Design and Social Measurement.* 2d ed. New York, David McKay Company, Inc., 1970.

Mills, C. Wright. *The Sociological Imagination.* New York, Oxford University Press, 1959.

Osborn, Ronald E. *Humanism and Moral Theory.* Buffalo, N.Y., Prometheus Books, 1969.

President's Science Advisory Committee. *Strengthening Behavioral Sciences.* Washington, D.C., U.S. Government Printing Office, 1962.

Suggested Reading (continued)

Ranney, David. *Planning and Policies in the Metropolis.* Columbus, Ohio, Charles E. Merrill Publishing Company, 1969.

Reich, Charles A. *The Greening of America.* New York, Random House, Inc., 1970.

Royce, Joseph R. *Encapsulated Man.* Princeton, C. Van Nostrand, 1964.

Schmandt, Henry J., and Warner Bloomberg, Jr., eds. *The Quality of Urban Life.* Beverly Hills, Calif., Sage Publications, Inc., 1969.

Schooler, Dean, Jr., *Science, Scientists and Public Policy.* New York, The Free Press, 1971.

Selltiz, Claire, et al., eds. *Research Methods in Social Relations.* Rev. ed. New York, Holt, Rinehart, & Winston, Inc., 1962.

Sherif, Muzafer, and Carolyn Sherif. *Interdisciplinary Relationships in the Social Sciences.* Chicago, Aldine Publishing Company, 1969.

Skinner, B. F. *Science and Human Behavior.* New York, The Free Press, 1953.

———. *Walden Two.* New York, The Macmillan Company, 1962.

Slater, P. E. *Microcosm: Structural, Psychological and Religious Evaluation in Groups.* New York, John Wiley & Sons, Inc., 1966.

Theobald, Robert. *An Alternative Future for America, II.* Chicago, The Swallow Press, Inc., 1970.

Thompson, James, and Donald Houten. *The Behavioral Sciences: An Interpretation.* Reading, Mass., Addison-Wesley Publishing Co., Inc., 1970.

Tillich, Paul. *The New Being.* New York, Charles Scribner's Sons, 1955.

Toffler, Alvin. *Future Shock.* New York, Random House, Inc., 1970.

White, Leslie A. *The Science of Culture: A Study of Man and Civilization.* New York, Farrar, Straus, Inc., 1949.

Winter, Gibson. *Elements for a Social Ethic: Scientific Perspectives on Social Process.* New York, The Macmillan Company, 1966.

Glossary of
Human Relations Terms

The wide variety of approaches to solving human relations problems is partly reflected in the terminology of the various helping professions. While not a complete list, the following glossary is a basic foundation upon which an adequate understanding of professional human relations activities can be built. Several of the books listed at the end of Chapter 1 discuss these terms in greater detail.

Body-Movement Session

A session of activities which seek to mobilize energy through breathing and vigorous movement of the legs and the arms. Also called *bio-energetic analysis*.

Creative Activity Group

A group which uses art, drama, dance, and music to help participants express themselves and become more open and creative.

Encounter Group

A group which promotes personal growth, using the interpersonal inter-actions within the group as the primary learning vehicle. Encounter groups use various techniques, including psychodrama, structural exercises, and Gestalt therapy. Each participant is encouraged to take responsibility for what is happening to him in the group. Questions are discouraged because they are believed to be statements that participants make without taking responsibility for them. The primary focus is on feelings rather than on thoughts or ideas. *Feedback*, leveling by letting the other person know how you feel, either positively or negatively, and *confrontation*, dealing with individual behavior which you dislike, are the necessary components of an *encounter*. Generalizations are avoided, and all communications are encouraged to be stated in the first person—not as "we" or "people." Finally, participants in encounter groups are encouraged to translate as much verbal information as possible into physical movement; that is, they are encouraged to act out their feelings.

Gestalt Group

An encounter group which emphasizes a Gestalt therapeutic approach where an expert aids one individual in focusing on himself.

Gestalt Therapy

A psychological treatment process which assumes that what is most important to the group participants will emerge in the "here and now." Participants try to get in touch with their habits by analyzing and acting out their dreams, fantasies, and gestures.

Human Relations Training Laboratory

A planned activity which seeks to build on and enhance the *T-group* experience. The word *laboratory* identifies it as a T-group experience. The laboratory may include theory sessions, demonstrations, simulation games, films, verbal and nonverbal exercises, sensory awareness, creative activity, or body-movement sessions.

Instrumental Lab

A planned program which uses pencil-and-paper questionnaires to obtain data about group interaction and performance and then presents these data to the group for their use. The Blake Grid and the Reddin 3-D Grid are the two instruments most commonly utilized.

Kinesics (Body Language)

The scientific study of nonverbal communication for the purpose of breaking through defenses. Kinesics also includes a study of personal zones of space.

Marathon

A continuous group which may run from a few hours to a few days. The focus is usually on encounter or therapeutic experiences.

Meditation

A highly individual method used to teach people how to find the quiet zone at the center of their existence. The purpose of meditation is to allow an individual to break through consciousness and intellect and get in touch with his inner self.

Mini, or Micro, Lab

A short-term experience of a few minutes or a few hours. Used as a warm-up experience, the mini lab attempts to present a cross section of typical laboratory experiences.

Organizational Development Group

A group with the primary aim of improving leadership skill. Most OD groups use T-group techniques.

Psychodrama

One of the oldest and most widely used human relations techniques, psychodrama involves spontaneity and role playing. Group members reconstruct a situation and play the persons who were involved in incidents in their own lives or racial encounters in which they were not involved.

Sensitivity Training

A popular term for *T-group*. Technically, sensitivity training involves paying more attention to personal and interpersonal awareness than does the T-group. In practice, however, sensitivity groups may be T-groups or encounter groups.

Sensory Awareness Groups, Body Awareness Groups, Body Movement Groups

Groups which emphasize physical awareness and expression through movement, spontaneous dance, and other activities.

Sensory Awakening

Primarily a nonverbal method of unfreezing oneself to gain deeper awareness of one's body nature and energy. The primary techniques involve experiences centering on touching, tasting, seeing, and smelling.

Structural Experiences

Preplanned activities, such as games, exercises, and demonstrations, which have a specific structure. Usually these experiences are used to create more data for a group to look at.

T-Group

Any group whose primary learning activity is the exploration and analysis by the participants of their own experiences as a group (*T* stands for "training"). Participants are encouraged to *tune in, turn on,* and *talk up about how they are feeling at the moment.* The group is the medium through which learning occurs. T-groups place primary emphasis on the *process* of the group, particularly as it applies to organizational development and pattern.

T-Group Component

A large-group (fifty to five hundred) experience which emphasizes *trust, openness, realization,* and *interdependence (TORI).* Spontaneous happenings are the primary focus of each subgroup. TORI seeks to provide an experience of growing for each person; an experience of being a free member of a creative and growing group; an opportunity to try out new theories, behavior, and feelings; and an opportunity to take full responsibility for behavior.

Task-oriented Group

A group which focuses on the task of the group as opposed to T-groups, which focus on content of the interpersonal interaction.

Team Building Group

A group employing T-group or encounter techniques to develop more cohesive and effective working teams in organizations.

Transactional Analysis

A method of examining social intercourse and systematizing the information by using words which have the same meanings for all participants in the interaction. An analysis of the "games people play" is a central aspect of transactional analysis.

Sources of Illustrations

Dedication page: Author's collection.

Page xii: New Detroit, Inc., Detroit, Mich.

Page 1: Photo by Bill Anderson. Globe Photos, Inc., New York, N.Y.

Page 2: Globe Photos, Inc., New York, N.Y.

Page 11: Photo by Bill Anderson. Globe Photos, Inc., New York, N.Y.

Page 21–22: Photo by Leonard Lessin. Globe Photos, Inc., New York, N.Y.

Page 28: New Detroit, Inc., Detroit, Mich.

Page 36: Newsweek, copyright © 1968 by Newsweek, Inc.

Page 41: By Charles Barsotti. Copyright Newsday, Inc. Reprint with permission Los Angeles Times Syndicate.

Page 42: Tom Blevins, *Norman Transcript*, Norman, Okla.

Page 55: Ann Kelly Wood, Norman, Okla.

Page 61: By J. B. Handelsman. Reproduced by special permission of PLAYBOY magazine; copyright © 1971 by Playboy.

Page 62: Don Burk, Norman, Okla.

Page 64: New Detroit, Inc., Detroit, Mich.

Page 76: New Detroit, Inc., Detroit, Mich.

Page 78: Photo by Lloyd Greenberg. Globe Photos, Inc., New York, N.Y.

Page 85: Author's collection.

Page 86: New Detroit, Inc., Detroit, Mich.

Page 90: New Detroit, Inc., Detroit, Mich.

Page 99–100: Photo by Clark Sumida and Bob Harvey. Globe Photos, Inc., New York, N.Y.

Page 107: Artist: Henry Martin. Copyright 1971 Saturday Review, Inc.

Page 108: David C. Campbell, Norman, Okla.

Page 117: Ted Wise, American Photique, Norman, Okla.

Page 121–22: New Detroit, Inc., Detroit, Mich.

Page 136: By Donald Reilly. Reproduced by special permission of PLAYBOY magazine; copyright © 1971 by Playboy.

Page 138: Photo by David Blatchley. Globe Photos, Inc., New York, N.Y.

Page 141: Photo by John Cameola. Globe Photos, Inc., New York, N.Y.

Page 143: Photo by Bill Anderson. Globe Photos, Inc., New York, N.Y.

Page 153: Tom Blevins, *Norman Transcript*, Norman, Okla.

Page 154: Tom Blevins, *Norman Transcript*, Norman, Okla.

Page 156: Tom Blevins, *Norman Transcript*, Norman, Okla.

Page 159: Globe Photos, Inc., New York, N.Y.

Page 160: Drawing by J. B. Handelsman; © 1971 The New Yorker Magazine, Inc.

TO LIVE IN FREEDOM

Page 165: *Civil Rights Digest*.

Page 168–69: Don Burk, Norman, Okla.

Page 172: Artist: Herbert Goldberg. Copyright 1971 Saturday Review, Inc.

Page 180: Oklahomans for Indian Opportunity, Norman.

Page 182–83: Courtesy of Oklahoman & Times © 1963 United Feature Syndicate, Inc.

Page 188: Don Burk, Norman, Okla.

Page 196: Oklahomans for Indian Opportunity, Norman.

Page 197: *Civil Rights Digest*.

Page 198: Don Burk, Norman, Okla.

Page 203: By John Dempsey. Reproduced by special permission of PLAYBOY magazine; copyright © 1971 by Playboy.

Page 204: Photo by Bill Anderson. Globe Photos, Inc., New York, N.Y.

Page 207: Drawing by Donald Reilly; © 1971 The New Yorker Magazine, Inc.

Page 210: Globe Photos, Inc., New York, N.Y.

Page 213: Drawing by Edward Frascino; © 1971 The New Yorker Magazine, Inc.

Page 224: Globe Photos, Inc., New York, N.Y.

Page 231: Photo by Andrew Schneider. Globe Photos, Inc., New York, N.Y.

Index

Giddings, Franklin H.: 217
Gonzáles, Rodolfo ("Corky"): 133
Graham, Billy: 114
Gregory, Dick: 80
Group dynamics: 4, 11–13, 115, 183
Groups, social: roles in, 48; membership in, 49–50; social interaction forms of, 50–53; and ecological factors, 53–54
Growth-experience laboratories: 11
Guardians, the (New York City and Pittsburgh): 127
Guth, William: 8

Harvard School of Business: 218
Hatcher, Richard G.: 77
Hate: 103–108, 186
Hawthorne researches: 4
Hayakawa, Samuel I.: 134
Henson, Matthew: 75
Hitler, Adolf: 113, 116
Hobhouse, Leonard T.: 217
Homans, George: 4
Homosexual liberation movement: 135–36, 142; and Gay People, 140–41
Hopi Indians: 130
House Made of Dawn: 130
Housing: 96, 125, 127–28
Hughes, Langston: 67, 69
Humanness, characteristics of: 46–48
Human relations: 3, 53, 63, 90, 102, 109, 124–25, 182, 190–91, 200, 207, 217–19; in business, 4–11; training in, 11–15; specialists in, 15–18, 187; goals, shortcomings of, 29–33; and "Humpty Dumpty" allegory, 43–46; main goal of, 57–58; in education, 145–49; leadership styles in, 171–74; and communication, 175–76, 191
Hunt, Robert: 24
Hunts Point Multi-Service Center (New York City): 128
Huxley, Aldous: 211
Huxley, Thomas: 220

Indians, American: 25, 26, 28, 30, 32, 34, 78, 128, 133, 145, 157, 198; disadvantaged, 129–32; and English language, 130; and militancy, 131
Indian Water Rights Office: 131
Inouye, Daniel: 134
In-service training: 187–88
Institute of Religion: 224
Institute of Society, Ethnics and the Life Sciences: 224
Institute for Theological Encounter with Science and Technology: 224
Integration: 70, 111

International Business Machines Corporation: 200

Jackson, Jesse: 79–80
James, Jesse: 158
James, William: 217
Japanese-Americans: 27, 34, 134–35
Jews: 24–27, 34, 101, 104–105
Jones, LeRoi: 77
Journal of Humanistic Psychology: 18
Journal of Intergroup Relations: 18
Julius Caesar (William Shakespeare): 113–14

Kachongeva, Dan: 130
Kahn, Herman: 206
Kelman, Herbert: 221
Kennedy, John: 29
Kennedy, Robert: 29
King, Martin Luther, Jr.: 29, 70, 79–80, 82
Konwitz, Milton R.: 81
Kornberg, Arthur: 210-11
Ku Klux Klan: 71

Langston, John M.: 75
Law and order: 161–63, 167–71
Leadership: 6; in management, 8–10; in civil rights, 78–82; in problem-solving, 183–85; in planning the future, 214–17
Lederberg, Joshua: 211
Lee, Tsung Dao: 134
Lewin, Kurt: 4, 5, 12, 115
Lewis, Joe: 89
Lincoln, Abraham: 33
Linton, Ralph: 220
Lippitt, Ronald: 12, 17, 188

McGregor, Douglas: 10
McHale, John: 209
Machiavelli, Niccolò: 112–13, 116
McKissick, Floyd: 80
Malcolm X: 80, 82
Maoism: 34
March on Washington, 1940: 69–70
Marijuana: *see* drug abuse
Marxism: 34
Maslow, Abraham H.: 8, 147
Massachusetts State Legislature: 67
Matzeliger, Jan: 75
Mayo, Elton: 4, 219
Mead, George Herbert: 16, 56
Mein Kampf: 113
Meredith, James: 80
Mescalero Apache Indians: 130
Mexican-American Legal Defense and Educational Fund: 133
Mexican-Americans: 30, 32, 34, 78, 128, 145; disadvantaged, 132–33; leaders of, 133